AUSTRALIAN
WRITERS

Debra Adelaide was born in Sydney, Australia, where she has lived for most of her life. After completing two degrees majoring in English Literature at the University of Sydney, she began researching Australian women's literature focusing on the lesser-known authors. She is currently editing a collection of critical essays on Australian women's writing.

PANDORA

AUSTRALIAN LITERARY HERITAGE

Series Editor: Dale Spender
Consultant: Elizabeth Webby

Other books in this series:

Australian Women Writers: The Contemporary Scene
by Pam Gilbert

There are a number of outstanding contemporary Australian women writers about whom relatively little is known. This book fills that gap with a comprehensive discussion of the work of Helen Garner, Kate Grenville, Elizabeth Jolley, Barbara Hanrahan, Robin Klein, Thea Astley, Jessica Anderson, Jean Bedford, Olga Masters and Antigone Kefala.

Writing a New World: Two Centuries of Australian Women Writers
by Dale Spender

A lively, provocative overview of the history of the literary scene and the position of women writers in Australia which shows that any image of the country as a cultural desert was not based on the achievements of Barbara Baynton, Ada Cambridge, Dymphna Cusack, Eleanor Dark, Katharine Susannah Pritchard, Christina Stead and many other Australian women who have enjoyed tremendous international success.

Pandora Press is reprinting a selection of nineteenth- and twentieth-century novels written by Australian women. The first in the series are:

A Marked Man: Some Episodes in His Life (1890) by Ada Cambridge
Introduced by Debra Adelaide

An Australian Girl (1890) by Catherine Martin
Introduced by Elizabeth Webby

The Incredible Journey (1923) by Catherine Martin
Introduced by Margaret Allen

The Bond of Wedlock (1887) by Rosa Praed
Introduced by Lynne Spender

Outlaw and Lawmaker (1894) by Rosa Praed
Introduced by Dale Spender

Lady Bridget in the Never-Never Land (1915) by Rosa Praed
Introduced by Pam Gilbert

Uncle Piper of Piper's Hill (1889) by Tasma
Introduced by Margaret Harris

AUSTRALIAN WOMEN WRITERS:
A bibliographic guide

DEBRA ADELAIDE

PANDORA
London Sydney Wellington

First published in paperback by Pandora Press, an imprint of the trade division of Unwin Hyman Limited, in 1988

Set in 10 on 11pt Ehrhardt
by Input Typesetting Ltd, London

Unwin Hyman Limited
15–17 Broadwick Street
London W1V 1FP

Allen & Unwin Australia Pty Ltd
8 Napier Street, North Sydney, NSW 2060, Australia

Allen & Unwin New Zealand Pty Ltd with the Port Nicholson Press
60 Cambridge Terrace, Wellington, New Zealand

ISBN 0–86358–148–X(h/b)
ISBN 0–86358–149–8(p/b)

British Library Cataloguing in Publication Data
Adelaide, Debra
Australian women writers: a bibliographic guide.
1. English literature. Australian women writers. Bibliographies
I. Title
016.8209'9287

Library of Congress Cataloging in Publication Data also available

Contents

Acknowledgments

A book such as this does not exist without the work of all who have previously researched and published on Australian literature, and I offer an acknowledgment to all. Apart from the published sources quoted in the Introduction, I would also like to acknowledge the following: the Australian Literature Resource and Research Centre in the English Department of the University of Sydney; the English Department of the Australian Defence Force Academy, Canberra; the *Australian Dictionary of Biography* Index and Biographical Register at the Australian National University, Canberra; the staff of the Victorian State Library, Melbourne, and of the ABC Archives, Sydney.

Those to whom I owe special thanks are: Elizabeth Webby, who has been so generous with her time and advice and who so patiently corrected a difficult manuscript; Dale Spender, who has offered encouragement from the start; Joy Hooton, whose suggestions were of great assistance; and the late Barry Andrews, whose enthusiasm will be as greatly remembered as it is missed. I am also grateful to Elizabeth Lawson, Pamela Gilbert, Margaret Allen, Jani Haenke, Rodney Lumer, Janet O'Connor and Ray Koppe of the ASA, who have all supplied information, located authors, or been otherwise helpful, and to my husband Terence who has been a constant support.

Mostly, however, I am indebted to the authors themselves, especially those who generously supplied information beyond my requests, who responded promptly to my queries, and whose kind and encouraging letters I will always treasure. This book is dedicated to all of them.

Introduction

This book aims to preserve a part of our literary heritage. Its purpose is to restore from the past those Australian women writers who have fallen into neglect and to provide a reference for contemporary women writers in the hopes of overcoming the same possibility.

This book is not an attempt to argue for the validity of women's writing. That argument, thankfully, is now over. But it is an attempt to foster critical awareness of our women writers – something, regrettably, still in its infancy – by offering a directory for reading and study upon a wide range of women writers.

As every researcher of Australian literature knows, numerous forgotten literary treasures lie neglected on library shelves. Having fallen out of print, they remain unread and so are excluded from critical discussion. My reading for this project included many such books which had frequently also enjoyed success and attracted praise in their time. Even as recently as the last decade, books appeared which were claimed as landmarks in Australian fiction, in women's writing, but which are now neither in print nor easily available and whose authors seem to have vanished into obscurity.

In compiling this book I have tried to ensure that history is not repeated by the loss of many of our women writers again, for loss it must be when books become unobtainable and authors forgotten. I do not want readers in twenty years' time to wonder who Helen Garner was and what other books she wrote apart from that one which had something to do with monkeys. Of course, this notion seems ridiculously fanciful at the moment. Helen Garner and other contemporaries, such as Kate Grenville or Elizabeth Jolley, are well-known literary figures. They receive attention in the press, in journals; they receive awards. But in terms of historical precedent, their disappearance is more than a possibility.

During my research for this book I came across many writers who had won awards, whose work had received considerable critical acclaim and had gone into several editions but who are unread now. If their names are not forgotten, many of their works are. Books by some of our best-known women writers – Eleanor Dark, Dymphna Cusack, Kylie Tennant, Miles Franklin – are still out of print despite availability of and attention to their other, well-known works. The present favourable climate for the publication of women's fiction (poetry and drama to a far lesser extent) should not fool us into disregarding the lessons of the past. While compiling this book I have been mindful of the need to restore to the records the women writers who have contributed so richly to our literary heritage.

When I first began researching Australian women writers (before I even had the idea for this book) I found myself creating lists of writers and their works since no reference work contained all the information I needed. Of course, the earlier writers are to be found in Miller and Macartney's bibliography of Australian literature (see below) and this still remains the most comprehensive listing of its kind up until 1950. However, when my interest extended well into this century the gaps became wider. Finding information upon well-known writers such as Christina Stead or Katharine Susannah Prichard is not difficult. Critical books and even articles often cite fairly complete lists of works and in the cases of some authors separate bibliographies are available. And, importantly, they are well-represented in our libraries. But finding information upon that great number of women writers not elevated into the literary canon is most difficult (in some cases it has been almost impossible).

Many of the existing reference books do not provide complete bibliographies (of course, not all of them aim to do so). Others might have comprehensive lists of primary works, but none of critical; and the reverse even applies in some instances. Biographical information may be found in some, but lacking elsewhere, while other shortcomings can be found. The massive *Australian Dictionary of Biography*, for instance, is limited by its restriction to deceased persons. And while the few existing bibliographies have made valuable contributions to the study of Australian literature, none is up-to-date and none provides anything approaching a reasonable or representative coverage of women writers.

When I began this research the excellent *Oxford Companion to Australian Literature* (1985) had not been published. While it has now filled many gaps, it does not include many contemporary writers and also does not provide the full bibliographical information that has been the major part of my research.

Research for this book was undertaken in two different ways. With deceased or very elderly authors it was based upon the resources of the

Mitchell Library catalogue and collection (the best collection of Australian literature in the world) and those of the National Library of Australia. Many secondary sources have also been used, the most important being the invaluable *Australian Literature, A Bibliography to 1938, Extended to 1950*, by E. Morris Miller and Frederick Macartney (1956). I have also referred to: *Women in Australia: An Annotated Guide to Records*, by Kay Daniels, et al. (1977), the *Australian Dictionary of Biography*, *Contemporary Authors* (current), the *Who's Who of Australian Women* (1982) plus bibliographies of individual authors and general historical and critical books on Australian literature.

Contemporary authors were mostly written to directly. I included an answer sheet indicating the kind of information I wanted, but left a great deal up to the author herself. Where possible I have used the words or phrasing of the author in her entry, especially if she had commented upon her own work.

Entries for better-known authors have been kept brief, with only selective lists of critical material where it has been possible to direct the reader to full bibliographical studies (such as Shirley Walker's on Judith Wright). Lesser-known authors have been presented in as much detail as possible. Naturally, this has proved better in theory than in practice, and there appear great discrepancies in the length of the biographical paragraphs. This was not determined by prior judgments as to a writer's importance, merely by the amount of information available.

Of course one is only as good as one's sources (and I soon learnt that the primary source – the author – is invariably the most unreliable). Every effort has been made to check facts, although since it has not been possible to sight all books listed, accuracy cannot be guaranteed. Similarly, birth and death dates could not be chased interminably through registries of births, deaths and marriages, particularly since many of these authors were born overseas. Where they could not be obtained through my own network, I have omitted them or added a question mark. The birth dates of a couple of contemporary authors have been deliberately omitted.

When an author did not reply I compiled her entry from library catalogues, book jackets, interviews, reviews and so on. In doing so I assumed that these authors didn't disapprove of my project and were not averse to being included. Ruth Park, it should be noted at this point, does not appear at her own request. I also hope to have done justice to those authors whose addresses I could not locate and those who could not be contacted at all.

I have attempted to cover as many writers as I could, though for various reasons have not included merely a name and list of works. Where no information could be found on a writer (if, for instance, she might be listed in Miller and Macartney but not even her books could be located) I have omitted that author rather than merely reproduce information from elsewhere. (Many writers who for reasons of space could not be included here will appear in an expanded version of this book to be submitted as part of my doctoral thesis at the University of Sydney.)

'Australian women writers' is a wide-sweeping term. While this is primarily a guide to novelists, poets, dramatists and so on, I have also included many non-fiction writers, especially those who have contributed significantly to the history of women in Australia: Germaine Greer, Miriam Dixson, Drusilla Modjeska, Anne Summers, and others not so well known – historians, biographers, travel writers and journalists. The criteria for inclusion were flexible, although at some stage a line simply had to be drawn if only to bring the work to completion. Unlike other reference books of this type I did not stop at any particular date, since one of my aims was always to offer material as up-to-date as possible. The lines I drew depended upon the publications of the authors. An author had to have a work published in book form before I considered including her, and in many cases more than one book. Again, however, such guidelines were stretched to include writers with one outstanding publication: Robyn Davidson, Annie Baxter, Jan McKemmish, for example.

While this tends to stress the importance of publication in book form, I do not wish to undervalue the contributions of journals and the like to Australian literature. Indeed many prolific authors, particularly poets, are lucky to get one collection published (many have none) though they are widely represented in magazines, periodicals, newspapers and anthologies. The task of annotating all the short stories, poems, or articles published in journals and periodicals was beyond the scope of this work. I have included a category which indicates the range of an author's publications by mentioning other places in which her work appears.

On the subject of favouring publication in book form, while I have listed novels published in serial form, I have not done so for those later also published in book form. Thus Catherine Helen Spence's *Gathered In* listed as being published by Sydney University Press, 1977, rather than in the *Adelaide Observer*, 1881–1882; Ada Cambridge's *A Marked Man* by Heinemann, 1890, rather than as *A Black Sheep* in the *Age*, 1888–1889. Elizabeth Morrison in *Books, Libraries and Readers* (Monash University, 1985) has made some essential challenges to bibliographical (mal)practices such as the elevation of the book over the serial form of a novel. I acknowledge that my 'bibliographical revisionism' is compromised, but necessarily so. One of the objects of this book is to make accessible information forgotten or buried about women's literature. Therefore I have listed the book form. It is far easier to locate and read a novel in its book than its serial form (especially when newspapers and magazines are nowadays mostly available only on microfilm).

Further on the subject of accessibility, authors have been listed under their actual rather than their assumed names, even where it is still customary to refer to them by their pseudonyms, for example 'Henry Handel Richardson' or 'Criena Rohan'. I have only diverged from this where it has been entirely impractical, such as in the case of collaborative pseudonyms.

To have done this is unorthodox (it may even be presumptuous) but firstly, it adheres to the feminist principles under which I originally began this project. It is a generalisation that is true all the same that women usually published under pseudonyms to conceal their identities from the fear of criticism or discrimination in all its forms. If we are serious about the recovery of women's history and literature we will not shirk from challenging existing conventions. Secondly, it has at least the virtue of consistency; all the catalogues and references I consulted shift from actual to assumed name with no apparent method. Thirdly, it is in keeping with the tendency, after a period of time, to refer to writers by their real names; 'Tasma', for example, is being increasingly forsaken in favour of Jessie Couvreur. There is sufficient cross-referencing to avoid confusion; readers will assuredly have no trouble in finding 'Henry Handel Richardson' or 'Criena Rohan'.

A few notes on the format of each entry: each author's name and dates are followed by biographical details or some comment upon their work. Then follows a list of works arranged in categories of fiction, poetry, drama and non-fiction by date of publication. For each title the place, publisher and date of the original edition is given, except where untraceable. Subsequent editions have only been noted in extraordinary cases, and this usually in the preceding paragraph. Where a book was published simultaneously by different publishers in more than one country I have only noted its Australian or English appearance to avoid cramming the lists with unnecessary detail. The 'OTHER' category includes less important works, books the author may have edited, or books that for some reason do not fit into the above categories, plus a list of other books, journals, newspapers, etc., where the author's work also appears. This is followed by (where applicable) a list of the manuscript holdings in the major Australian libraries. Under 'SEE ALSO' is given selected secondary material including journal articles, biographies, bibliographies, chapters from books and individual studies of the author. Despite the selectiveness applying to well-researched authors, very often the brevity in this category is a fair reflection of the amount of critical material available upon that author. The same few books and journals are also constantly cited; this is due to the extremely limited discussion of women writers in our critical literature.

Playwrights have posed a unique problem since so many plays appear in performance yet remain unpublished (Oriel Gray is a prime example). I have tried to overcome this by listing in the 'DRAMA' category all the plays wherever they have been published, then including underneath plays that have been performed and (where possible) when and where.

Finally, there is in particular a small handful of books which would be generally useful to the reader or student of Australian women writers. They have all been mentioned in this book at various places, but it might be helpful to list them here as well:

Candida Baker, *Yacker* and *Yacker 2* (Pan/Picador, 1986, 1987)
Flora Eldershaw (ed.), *The Peaceful Army* (Sydney, 1938)
Jennifer Ellison, *Rooms of their Own* (Penguin, 1986)
Carole Ferrier (ed.), *Gender, Politics and Fiction* (UQP, 1985)
Lucy Frost, *No Place for a Nervous Lady* (McPhee Gribble/Penguin, 1984)
Drusilla Modjeska, *Exiles at Home, Australian Women Writers 1925–1945* (Sirius, 1981)
Shirley Walker (ed.), *Who is She? Images of Woman in Australian Fiction* (UQP, 1983)

Abbreviations

ABC	Australian Broadcasting Commission/Corporation
ABR	*Australian Book Review*
ACT	Australian Capital Territory
AIF	Australian Imperial Forces
AJA	Australian Journalists' Association
ALS	*Australian Literary Studies*
ANU	Australian National University
AO	Officer of the Order of Australia
A & R	Angus and Robertson
ASA	Australian Society of Authors
ASAL	Association for the Study of Australian Literature
AWGIE	Australian Writers' Guild award
BA	Bachelor of Arts
BBC	British Broadcasting Corporation
CAE	College of Advanced Education
CLF	Commonwealth Literary Fund
CPA	Communist Party of Australia
DBE	Dame Commander of the Order of the British Empire
FAW	Fellowship of Australian Writers
JRAHS	*Journal of the Royal Australian Historical Society*
MA	Master of Arts
MBE	Member of the Order of the British Empire
ML	Mitchell Library, State Library of NSW
MUP	Melbourne University Press
NL	National Library of Australia
NSW	New South Wales
OAM	Medal of the Order of Australia
OBE	Officer of the Order of the British Empire

OUP	Oxford University Press
PEN	Poets, Playwrights, Essayists, Editors, Novelists (International)
PhD	Doctor of Philosophy
PLC	Presbyterian Ladies' College
SA	South Australia
SPACLALS	South Pacific Association for Commonwealth Literature and Language Studies
SUP	Sydney University Press
UQP	University of Queensland Press
UN	United Nations
USA	United States of America
VAD	Voluntary Aid Detachment
WA	Western Australia
WAAAF	Women's Auxiliary Australian Air Force
WAIT	Western Australian Institute of Technology
WEL	Women's Electoral Lobby
WRANS	Women's Royal Australian Naval Force
WWI; WWII	World War One; World War Two

Bibliographic guide

A

Abdullah, Mena (1930–)
Short story writer. Born at Bundarra, NSW, of Indian origins. Grew up on a sheep property and was educated at Sydney Girls' High. Worked as an administrator for the CSIRO. Her stories are about Indian-Australian life, and are amongst the best of their kind.

FICTION *The Time of the Peacock* (with Ray Mathew), Sydney, A & R, 1965.
OTHER Contributed to *Coast to Coast* (1956, 1958, 1960, 1962) and to *Two Ways Meet* (ed. L. Rorabacher, 1963).
SEE ALSO T. S. Ryan in *Literary Criterion*, Vol. 6, No. 4 (1965).

Adams, Glenda (1939–)
Novelist, short story writer. Born in Sydney. Educated at the University of Sydney and later Columbia University, New York. Left Australia for New York 1964 to study and write. Has taught fiction writing at Columbia University, at Sarah Lawrence College, and at Brooklyn College. During returns to Australia has been writer-in-residence at the University of WA, Adelaide University and Macquarie University. Her stories have appeared in many journals both overseas and in Australia.

FICTION *Lies and Stories*, New York, Inwood Horizon, 1976; *The Hottest Night of the Century*, Sydney, A & R, 1979; *Games of the Strong*, Sydney, A & R, 1982; *Dancing on Coral*, New York, Viking, 1987.
OTHER Stories have also appeared in the following: *The Oxford Anthology of Australian Literature* (OUP, 1985), *Room to Move* (Redress/Unwin,

1985), *Quadrant: 25 Years* (Quadrant, 1982), and in the journals: *Meanjin*, *Quadrant*, the *Bulletin*, the *Transatlantic Review*, the *Village Voice* and the *Seattle Review*.

Adams, Nancy (1890–1968)
Historical writer, illustrator. Born in Melbourne; brought up in Melbourne and England, where she lived during WWI. Married a Melbourne wine merchant and was for many years a member of the social elite there. Was a great-granddaughter of pioneer Janet Templeton, who arranged and financed the introduction of the Saxon merino sheep into Australia; her first book gives an account of the history of the two families involved in the venture. Her autobiography is told in *Family Fresco*.

NON-FICTION *Saxon Sheep*, Melbourne, Cheshire, 1961; *Family Fresco*, Melbourne, Cheshire, 1966.

Adam-Smith, Patsy (1924–)
Historian. Born in the remote country bordering Victoria and SA and educated via correspondence school. Enlisted in the AIF 1941 as a nursing VAD. After the war became the first woman to be articled as a radio officer and worked on several Australian trading ships. Was an Adult Education Officer 1960–66 and in 1970 was appointed Manuscripts Field Officer for the State Library of Victoria. Since then has studied and worked in oral history in Australia, Ireland, England and the USA. Research in history, folklore and the preservation of national traditions has taken her to over 60 countries in the past 30 years. Her books cover a wide range of topics, but one of her deepest interests has always been the Australian railways. Has written some 300 feature articles for Australian and overseas journals. Since 1953 has given over 600 interviews on radio and since 1962 made over 400 television appearances. *The Anzacs* shared the *Age* Book of the Year Award 1978. In 1980 was awarded the OBE for services to literature and oral history.

NON-FICTION *Hear the Train Blow*, Sydney, Ure Smith, 1964; *Moonbird People*, Adelaide, Rigby, 1965; *There was a Ship*, Adelaide, Rigby, 1967; *Tiger Country*, Adelaide, Rigby, 1968; *Hobart Sketchbook*, Adelaide, Rigby, 1968; *The Rails Go Westward*, Melbourne, Macmillan, 1969; *Folklore of the Australian Railwaymen* (ed.), Melbourne, Macmillan, 1969; *No Tribesman*, Adelaide, Rigby, 1971; *Tasmania Sketchbook*, Adelaide, Rigby, 1971; *Port Arthur Sketchbook*, Adelaide, Rigby, 1971; *Across Australia by Indian Pacific*, Melbourne, Nelson, 1971; *The Barcoo Salute*, Adelaide, Rigby, 1973; *Launceston Sketchbook*, Adelaide, Rigby, 1973; *Romance of the Australian Railways*, Adelaide, Rigby, 1973; *The Desert Railway*, Adelaide, Rigby, 1974; *Neon Signs to the Mutes* (ed. with M. Dugan & J. S.

Hamilton), Melbourne, Reed, 1976; *The Anzacs*, Melbourne, Nelson, 1978; *Islands of Bass Strait*, Adelaide, Rigby, 1978; *Victorian and Edwardian Melbourne from Old Photographs*, Sydney, John Ferguson, 1979; *Outback Heroes*, Sydney, Mead & Beckett, 1981; *The Shearers*, Melbourne, Nelson, 1982; *When We Rode the Rails*, Sydney, Lansdowne, 1983; *Australian Women at War*, Melbourne, Nelson, 1984; *Seven Young Irishmen*, Melbourne, Nelson, 1985; *Heart of Exile*, Melbourne, Nelson, 1986.

'Ames, Jennifer' *See:* **Greig, Maysie**

Anderson, Ethel (1883–1958)
Poet, short story writer, essayist. Born in Leamington, England and brought to Australia as a girl. Educated at the Sydney Church of England Girls' Grammar School. Married to a British Army offier and spent time in India before returning to Australia 1926 where her husband was attached to a number of vice-regal positions. Contributed essays to both English and Australian journals, some of which were later included in her two collections. Considered herself to be mainly a poet, but is now best appreciated for her witty and ironic stories, in particular *At Parramatta* (reprinted by Penguin 1985), recently claimed as a precursor of the 'discontinuous narrative'.

POETRY *Squatter's Luck and Other Poems*, Melbourne, MUP, 1942; *Sunday at Yarralumla: A Symphony*, Sydney, A & R, 1947; *The Song of Hagar to the Patriarch Abraham*, Sydney, Edwards & Shaw, 1957.
FICTION *Indian Tales*, Sydney, Australasian Publ. Co., 1948; *At Parramatta*, Melbourne, Cheshire, 1956; *The Little Ghosts*, Sydney, A & R, 1959; *The Best of Ethel Anderson* (ed. J. D. Pringle), Sydney, A & R, 1973.
NON-FICTION *Adventures in Appleshire*, Sydney, A & R, 1944; *Timeless Garden*, Sydney, Australasian Publ. Co., 1945; *Joy of Youth: The Letters of Patrick Hore-Ruthven* (ed.), London, Peter Davies, 1950.
SEE ALSO B. Foott in *Australian Quarterly*, Vol. 32 No. 3 (1960), J.K. Ewers in *Creative Writing in Australia* (1962), J. D. Pringle in *Australian Essays* (A & R, 1971) and B. Jefferis in *Hemisphere*, Vol. 19, No. 4 (1975).

Anderson, Jessica
Novelist. Born in Queensland. Left school at 16 and studied at Brisbane Technical College Art School for one year. Has spent some time in London but lived mainly in Sydney. Began writing novels when 40 years old, but had previously written a number of plays and adaptations of novels for radio. From a politically active family, has been a member of the Australian Labor Party since 1976. In 1978 won the Miles Franklin and the Australian Natives' Association Literary Awards for *Tirra Lirra by the River;* in 1980 again won the Miles Franklin as well as the NSW Premier's Fiction Award for *The Impersonators*.

FICTION *An Ordinary Lunacy*, London, Macmillan, 1963; *The Last Man's Head*, London, Macmillan, 1970; *The Commandant*, London, Macmillan, 1975; *Tirra Lirra by the River*, London, Macmillan, 1978; *The Impersonators*, Melbourne, Macmillan, 1980; *Stories from the Warm Zone and Sydney Stories*, Melbourne, Penguin, 1987.
MANUSCRIPTS ML, Sydney: Jessica Anderson Papers ML MSS 3773 (Partly restricted).
SEE ALSO E. Barry in *Meridian*, Vol. 3, No. 1 (1984), R. D. Haynes in *ALS* (May, 1986), A. Sykes in *Southerly*, Vol. 26, No. 1 (1986) and C. Baker (interview) in *Yacker 2* (Pan/Picador, 1987).

'Anglo-Australian' *See:* **Hay, Agnes Grant**

Armstrong, Millicent (1888–?)
Playwright. Born in Sydney. Educated at the University of Sydney. Went to France to nurse during WWI where she began to write and produce plays. After the war was awarded a land grant under the Returned Soldiers' Settlement Scheme and worked as a farmer. The play *Drought* won the Rupert Brooke Award 1934, and *Fire* the *Daily Telegraph* Drama Competition 1923.

DRAMA *Drought*, in *Prize One-Act Plays*, London, Harrap, 1934; *At Dusk*, in *Best Australian One-Act Plays*, Sydney, A & R, 1937; *Thomas* and *Penny Dreadful*, in *Plays in One Act*, Sydney, Edwards & Shaw, 1958.
OTHER Unpublished plays include: *Fire* (1923), *Nina* (1936), *Windward* (1937) and *The Moon Sets* (1958). A profile, 'Miss Millicent Armstrong', appears in *Green Room* (Nov. 1924).

Asher, Helen (1927–)
Novelist. Born in Bytom, Germany (now Poland). Attended school until at the age of 16 was forced out to work under a Nazi scheme. Came to Australia in the 1950s with her husband and eventually settled in Sydney. Has worked in factories and hotels and only concentrated upon writing in the last few years. As an ethnic writer wanting to write in English, has undergone a long apprenticeship in the craft, and prefers novels to any other form of writing. Is presently working on the first volume of a trilogy.

FICTION *Tilly's Fortune*, Melbourne, Penguin, 1986.
OTHER Short stories have appeared in *The Tracks We Travel* (Australasian Book Society, 1976), *Cleo* and *Womenspeak* (as Helen Ulrich), and in *Room to Move* (Redress/Unwin, 1985).

Astley, Thea (1925–)
Novelist. Born in Brisbane and educated at the University of Queensland. Taught in primary and secondary schools until 1967 and spent the last 13 years of her teaching career at Macquarie University, Sydney, until 1980. Her work is rich in social comedy and wittily exposes the plight of the social misfit. Has received a number of awards, including the Miles Franklin Award (three times), the *Age* Book of the Year Award, the James Cook Australian Studies Award, and the Australian Literary Society's Gold Medal 1986. *A Descant for Gossips* was televised by the ABC 1983.

FICTION *Girl with a Monkey*, Sydney, A & R, 1958; *A Descant for Gossips*, Sydney, A & R, 1960; *The Well Dressed Explorer*, Sydney, A & R, 1962; *The Slow Natives*, Sydney, A & R, 1965; *A Boatload of Home Folk*, Sydney, A & R, 1968; *The Acolyte*, Sydney, A & R, 1972; *A Kindness Cup*, Melbourne, Nelson, 1974; *Hunting the Wild Pineapple*, Melbourne, Nelson, 1979; *An Item from the Late News*, St Lucia, UQP, 1982; *Beachmasters*, Melbourne, Penguin, 1985.
OTHER *Three Australian Writers* (Foundation for ALS Monograph No. 5, 1979).
MANUSCRIPTS ML, Sydney: Thea Astley Papers ML MS 4736 (1962–73).
SEE ALSO B. Matthews in *Southern Review*, Vol. 6, No. 2 (1973), K. Goldsworthy in *Meanjin*,Vol. 42, No. 4 (1983), E. Perkins in *Hecate*, Vol. 11, No. 1 (1985) and J. Ellison (interview) in *Rooms of their Own* (Penguin, 1986). For a full bibliography see C. Frost & R. Smith in *LiNQ*, Vol. 10, No. 4 (1982–83).

Aston, Tilly (1873–1947)
Poet, prose writer. Born Matilda Ann Aston in Carisbrook, Victoria; became totally blind at the age of 7. Attended a school for the blind, Melbourne, for 11 years followed by 1 year of university but was forced to leave due to the lack of Braille texts. Taught singing and piano before beginning to teach blind children in private. Was appointed head teacher, School for the Blind, Melbourne at the age of 39 and held the position for 13 years. Was active in various organisations for the education and advancement of the blind including the early Victorian Association of Braille Writers.

POETRY *Maiden Verses*, Melbourne, Massina, 1901; *The Austral Year*, Melbourne, R. Jolley, 191–?; *Singable Songs*, Melbourne, Robertson & Mullens, 1924; *Songs of Light*, Melbourne, Lothian, 1935; *The Inner Garden*, Melbourne, Hawthorn Press, 1940.
FICTION *The Woolinappers, or Some Tales of the By-ways of Methodism*, Melbourne, *Spectator*, 1905; *The Straight-Goer*, in the *Spectator*, from

Sept. 1908; *Gold from Old Diggings*, in the *Bendigo Advertiser*, from August 1937; *Old-Timers: Sketches and Word Pictures of the Old Pioneers*, Melbourne, Lothian, 1938.
OTHER *Memoirs of Tilly Aston, Australia's Blind Poet, Author and Philanthropist* (Hawthorn Press, 1946).
SEE ALSO G. A. Hunter in *All About Books* (August, 1936).

Atkinson, Louisa (1834–1872)
Novelist, botanist. Born Caroline Louisa Atkinson near Berrima, NSW, daughter of Charlotte Barton (q.v.), author of the first educational book for children written in Australia. Educated by her mother at home due to poor health; suffered all her life from a weak heart which was responsible for her early death. Was the first Australian-born woman novelist, naturalist and botanist, who also skilfully illustrated her own works. Regularly published articles and illustrations in the *Sydney Morning Herald* and the *Sydney Mail*. Married explorer James Snowdon Calvert 1870 and died 1872, three weeks after the birth of her daughter. Several species of native flora have been named in her honour.

FICTION *Gertrude the Emigrant: A Tale of Colonial Life by an Australian Lady*, Sydney, J. R. Clarke, 1857; *Cowanda, the Veteran's Grant: An Australian Story by the Author of Gertrude*, Sydney, J. R. Clarke, 1859; *Debatable Ground of the Carlillawara Claimants*, *Myra, Tom Hellicar's Children, Bush Home* and *Tessa's Resolve*, all serialised in the *Sydney Mail*, between 1861–1872.
OTHER Recent reprints or publications: *A Voice from the Country* (Mulini Press, 1978), *A Tribute: Louisa Atkinson of the Kurrajong* (Kurrajong Heights Garden Club, 1979), *Excursions from Berrima* (Mulini Press, 1980) and *Tom Hellicar's Children* (Mulini Press, 1980).
SEE ALSO M. Swann in *JRAHS*, Vol. 15 (1929), W. Birkett in *The Peaceful Army* (ed. F. Eldershaw, Sydney, 1938) and M. Franklin in *Laughter, Not for a Cage* (A & R, 1956).

Auchterlonie, Dorothy *See:* **Green, Dorothy**

'Australian, An' *See:* **Bunn, Anna Maria**

'Australie' *See:* **Manning, Emily**

B

Backhouse, Elizabeth (1917–)
Novelist, scriptwriter, playwright. Born in Northam, WA. After serving in the WAAAF during WWII, worked as a scriptwriter in England, returning to Australia 1951. Has written detective novels.

FICTION *In Our Hands*, Perth, Paterson's, 1942; *The Sky Has its Clouds*, Perth, Pitman, 1944; *Leaves in the Wind*, Perth, Pitman, 1946; *Day Will Break*, Perth, Pitman 1946; *Enone and Quentin* (children's) Perth, Pitman, 1946; *The Mists Came Down*, London, Hale, 1959;*The Web of Shadows*, London, Hale, 1960; *The Night Has Eyes*, London, Hale, 1961; *Death of a Clown*, London, Hale, 1962; *Death Climbs a Hill*, London, Hale, 1963.
OTHER Performed plays include *The Thin Line* (1968) and *Mirage* (1972). Has also written scenarios for ballet and television.

Baily, Elsie Marion
Novelist. Wrote two novels, the first concerning the problems of half-castes in the Australian outback, the second inspired by the Flying Doctor service.

FICTION *Outcast of Eden*, Sydney, Frank Johnson, 1933; *Pathways of the Sky*, Sydney, Macquarie Head Press, 1933.

Baker, Kate (1861–1952)
Critic, editor, biographer. Born in Ireland and brought to Victoria as a child. Taught in Victorian schools 1881–1913, and is best known for being friend, advisor and champion of writer Joseph Furphy whom she met in 1886. Arranged for the publication of many of his works and researched the material for the book on Furphy that was written by Miles Franklin. Was awarded the OBE 1937 for her efforts on behalf of Furphy and for services to literature generally.

NON-FICTION *The Poems of Joseph Furphy, Tom Collins*, Collected and Edited by Kate Baker, Melbourne, Lothian, 1916; *Joseph Furphy: The Legend of a Man and His Book* (with Miles Franklin), Sydney, A & R, 1944
MANUSCRIPTS ML, Sydney: Kate Baker Papers 1882–1953 MS2022 (full guide available). NL, Canberra: Papers (guide available).

Balderson, Margaret (1935–)
Children's author. Born in Concord, NSW. Worked as a librarian in Sydney before travelling to Greece, India, Israel and Norway. Later

settled at Shoalhaven Heads on the NSW coast. *When Jays Fly to Barbmo* won the Australian Children's Book Council Book of the Year Award 1968.

CHILDREN'S *When Jays Fly to Barbmo*, London, OUP, 1968; *A Dog Called George*, London, OUP, 1975; *Blue and Gold Day*, London, A & R, 1979.

Ballantyne, Gina (1916–)
Poet. Born in Adelaide. Wrote poetry identified with the Jindyworobak movement of the 1920s and 1930s, i.e. distinctively nationalistic. Won the C. J. Dennis Memorial Prize 1942.

POETRY *Phantom*, Adelaide, F. W. Preece, 1942; *Vision*, Sydney, C. J. Dennis Memorial Society, 1942; *Vagrant*, Adelaide, Rex Ingamells-Jindyworobak, 1943.
OTHER Also edited the *Jindyworobak Anthology* (1945.)

Bandler, Faith (1918–)
Writer, Aboriginal rights activist. Born in Murwillumbah, NSW, the daughter of a Pacific Islander brought to work in the Queensland canefields as a Kanaka by slave traders in the 1880s. Served for many years on the executive of the Federal Council for the Advancement of Aboriginals and Torres Strait Islanders. Was co-founder of the Aboriginal Australian Fellowship 1956 which fought discrimination against Aborigines. Was director of the referendum campaign 1967 which established equal citizenship rights for Aborigines under the Australian constitution. Her father's story is told in the novels *Wacvie* and *Marani in Australia;* the former won the Braille Book of the Year Award 1979. Declined an MBE 1976, but accepted the AO in 1984.

FICTION *Wacvie*, Adelaide, Rigby, 1977; *Marani in Australia* (with L. Fox), Adelaide, Rigby, 1980; *The Time was Ripe* (with L. Fox), Sydney, Alternative Co-operative Ltd, 1983; *Welou, My Brother*, Sydney, Wild & Woolley/Aboriginal Artists' Agency, 1984.

Bannister, Sallie
Novelist. Born in Sussex, England into a working-class family with political inclinations. Came to Australia as a girl and later became active in the Communist Party and committed to socialist and feminist causes. Wrote as a team with husband Frank Bannister under the name S. F. Bannister, although their work is largely attributed to her. Was foundation member of the Union of Australian Women and member of the Modern Writers' Club, Sydney.

FICTION *Tossed and Blown, A Story of a Rolling Stone*, Melbourne, Austra-

lasian Book Society, 1953; *God's Own Country*, Melbourne, Australasian Book Society, 1953.
OTHER A short story, 'Wanted – A Pensioner', appeared in *Realist Writer*, No. 8 (1962).

Barbalet, Margaret (1949–)
Novelist, historian. Born in Adelaide and brought up in Tasmania. Educated at various state schools in Tasmania and SA and at the University of Adelaide, graduating MA 1973. Has worked as lecturer in history, as a research officer in Adelaide, and for the public service. Has lived in various parts of Australia as well as in New Guinea. Presently lives in Canberra where she is continuing to write fiction.

FICTION *Blood in the Rain*, Melbourne, Penguin, 1986.
NON-FICTION *The Adelaide Children's Hospital 1876–1976*, Adelaide, Griffin Press, 1975; *Far From a Low Gutter Girl, The Forgotten World of State Wards 1887–1940*, Melbourne, OUP, 1982.
OTHER Contributed to *Preserving Historic Australia* (Rigby, 1978).

Barnard, Marjorie (1897–1987)
Novelist, historian. Born in Sydney; educated at the University of Sydney graduating 1918 with first class honours and the first University Medal for History. Was offered a scholarship to Oxford, but was forced to decline when her father refused permission for her to go. Worked as librarian at the Sydney Technical College, but resigned 1935 to become a full-time writer. Joined the FAW and became a friend of Nettie Palmer, Miles Franklin (qq.v.) Frank Dalby Davison and many other literary figures of her day. With Flora Eldershaw, whom she met at university, collaborated to write novels and historical works under the pseudonym 'M. Barnard Eldershaw' (q.v.). Continued to publish independently after the collaboration ended and returned to library work 1942–50. Contributed literary articles and reviews to *Meanjin* and *Southerly* 1940s– 1960s. Was awarded the AO 1981, the Patrick White Award 1983, the NSW Premier's Special Award 1984, and an honorary Doctor of Letters from the University of Sydney 1986. *The Persimmon Tree* was reprinted by Virago 1985.

FICTION *The Ivory Gate* (children's), Melbourne, Champion, 1920; *The Persimmon Tree and Other Stories*, Sydney, Clarendon, 1943.
NON-FICTION *Macquarie's World*, Sydney, Limited Editions, 1941; *Australian Outline: A Brief History of Australia*, Sydney, Ure Smith, 1943, *The Sydney Book*, Sydney, Ure Smith, 1947; *Australian Quarterly Index 1929–1953* (with others), Sydney, AIPS, 1953; *Sydney, the Story of a City*, Melbourne, MUP, 1956; *Australia's First Architect, Francis Greenway*, Melbourne, Longmans, 1961; *A History of Australia*, Sydney, A & R,

1962; *Lachlan Macquarie*, Melbourne, OUP, 1964; *Miles Franklin*, New York, Twayne, 1967.
MANUSCRIPTS ML, Sydney: Marjorie Barnard Literary Papers 1927–70 ML MS 457 & 2809 (uncatalogued).
SEE ALSO L. E. Rorabacher, *Marjorie Barnard and M. Barnard Eldershaw* (Twayne, 1973), D. Modjeska, *Exiles at Home* (Sirius, 1981), and C. Baker (interview) in *Yacker 2* (Pan/Picador, 1987) For a full bibliography see L. Brown in *Biblionews*, Vol. 43, No. 4 (1970).

Barton, Charlotte (1797–1862)
Children's author, educationalist. Born Charlotte Waring in London and came to Australia when 29 to take up a position as governess for Mrs King, daughter-in-law of Phillip King (Governor of NSW 1800–1806). Became engaged to James Atkinson on the voyage out and married in NSW, September 1827. Lived in Sutton Forest and had four children including Louisa Atkinson (q.v.); two months after her birth James died 1834 and Charlotte married Charles Barton two years later. His mental problems led to a separation soon after and she went to Sydney, then Kurrajong, for Louisa's health. Her book, published anonymously, was the first Australian book for children; written in question and answer form, it covers topics from Aborigines to shipwrecks and natural history.

NON-FICTION *A Mother's Offering to her Children*, by A Lady Long Resident in New South Wales, Sydney, Gazette, 1841.
SEE ALSO Marcie Muir, *Charlotte Barton: Australia's First Children's Author* (Wentworth Books, 1980).

Barton, Emily Mary (1817–1909)
Poet. Born Emily Darvall in England and came to Australia with her father 1839. Married Robert Johnstone Barton and settled on 'Boree Nyrang' station near Molong, NSW. Took up writing late in life, writing most of the poems from her second published volume after the age of 60; continued writing until her death at 91. Many of her poems won prizes in the *Illustrated Sydney News* where they first appeared. Was the grandmother of Andrew Barton 'Banjo' Paterson, born 1864.

POETRY *A Few of Grandmamma's Prizes for the Little Ones*, Sydney, Gibbs, Shallard, 1885; *Straws on the Stream*, Sydney, W. E. Smith, 1910.
OTHER Also published: *In Memoriam, Mrs George F. Wise*, (with others, Sydney, Sands, 1889?). Her shipboard diary on the voyage to Australia appeared as *The Diary of Miss Emily Darvall 1839–1840* (Campbelltown, Richardson, 1985). *Straws on the Stream* was reprinted 1986 (Dubbo, NSW, The Book Connection).

Bassett, Marnie (Lady Bassett) 1890–1980
Historian. Born in Melbourne and published a number of interesting historical books. Was foundation fellow of the Australian Academy of the Humanities. Received honorary doctorates from Monash (1968) and Melbourne (1974) Universities. Was an author for the *Australian Dictionary of Biography*.

NON-FICTION *The Governor's Lady: Mrs Phillip Gidley King*, London, OUP, 1940; *The Hentys, An Australian Colonial Tapestry*, London, OUP, 1954; *Realms and Islands, the World Voyage of Rose de Freycinet in the Corvette Uranie 1817–1820*, London, OUP, 1962; *Behind the Picture: HMAS Rattlesnake's Australia-New Guinea Cruise 1846–1850*, Melbourne, OUP, 1966; *Letters from New Guinea*, Melbourne, Hawthorne Press, 1969.
OTHER *A Company of Carols* (with M. Casey, R. Dobson and J. Lindsay, Melbourne, 1967).
MANUSCRIPTS NL, Canberra: Marnie Bassett Papers MS 2311. La Trobe Library, Melbourne: Lady Marnie Bassett Papers MS 8521/68.

Bates, Daisy (1863–1951)
Journalist, anthropologist, Aboriginal welfare worker. Born Daisy O'Dwyer in Tipperary, Ireland and sent to Australia 1884 for her health. Married twice (apparently bigamously) but left second husband Jack Bates 1894 to work in England as a journalist. Returned 1899 to WA and began working and studying in Aboriginal missions, compiling a native dictionary for the government. Lived almost entirely with the Aborigines, 1912–45, collecting and recording information regarding customs and legends. Published hundreds of newspaper and journal articles on the Aborigines and fought hard for reforms for their welfare. Provoked ambivalent responses to her work in her own time and later but was greatly regarded by the Aborigines themselves who named her 'Kabbarli' or 'wise woman'. Was awarded the CBE 1934; is the subject of several biographies and memoirs, an opera and a dance-drama.

NON-FICTION *The Passing of the Aborigines, A Lifetime Spent Amongst the Natives of Australia*, London, John Murray, 1938; *Tales Told to Kabbarli: Aboriginal Legends Collected by Daisy Bates*, Retold by B. Ker Wilson, Sydney, A & R, 1972; *The Native Tribes of Western Australia*, edited by Isobel White, Canberra, National Library of Australia, 1986.
MANUSCRIPTS State Archives of WA, Colonial Secretary's Office: Personal File. State Archives of SA: Letters 1937– 49. La Trobe Library, Melbourne: Correspondence & Papers 1918–46. NL, Canberra: Papers MS 365 (major collection, guide available). ML, Sydney: Correspondence 1910–42.

SEE ALSO E. Salter, *Daisy Bates, the Great White Queen of the Never-Never* (A & R, 1971).

Baxter, Annie Maria (1816–1905)
Diarist. Born in Devon, England and came to Australia aged 17 with her husband Andrew Baxter, a lieutenant sent to a regiment in Tasmania. An unhappy marriage and steadily deteriorating fortunes led to her keeping journals recording her life as an officer's and then settler's wife in Launceston, Sydney, Port Macquarie and many other parts of NSW and Victoria. The journals record Baxter's death 1855 and her second marriage to Robert Dawbin (also an unsuccessful one) extending to about 35 volumes in nearly as many years. *Memories of the Past* was based upon these volumes and is a lively and readable account of colonial life.

NON-FICTION *Memories of the Past, by a Lady in Australia*, Melbourne, W. H. Williams, 1873.
OTHER See Lucy Frost, *No Place for a Nervous Lady* (McPhee Gribble/Penguin, 1984).
MANUSCRIPTS Dixson Library, Sydney: Original volumes MS Q 181/2–3. La Trobe Library, Melbourne: Microfilm volumes 1834–67 MS 7648. NL, Canberra: Annie Maria Baxter Sketchbook MS 3276.

Baynton, Barbara (1857–1929)
Born Barbara Lawrence in Scone, NSW, into a fairly humble home, although she later misrepresented the facts of her early life after social advancement through her marriages. Married selector Alexander Frater 1880 and had three children, but divorced 1890 after his infidelity. Married Thomas Baynton 1890 and began to write, publishing her first story in the *Bulletin* 1896; after his death 1904 travelled between England and Australia, married for the third and last time to Lord Headley, and became known in later years for her interest in antiques and her socialising. Her literary output was minimal but outstanding; she was one of the first writers to challenge the bush ethos, representing the bush instead as a place of unmitigated cruelty and oppression, particularly for women.

FICTION *Bush Studies*, London, Duckworth, 1902; *Human Toll*, London, Duckworth, 1907.
OTHER *Bush Studies* was reprinted with two other stories as *Cobbers* (Duckworth, 1917).
MANUSCRIPTS NL, Canberra, Barbara Baynton (Lady Barbara Headley) Papers MS 3077 (small collection).
SEE ALSO T. Astley in *Three Australian Writers* (ALS Monograph No. 5, 1979), K. Iseman in *ALS*, Vol. 11, No. 1 (1983), L. Frost in *Who is She? Images of Woman in Australian Fiction* (ed. S. Walker, UQP, 1983) and

E. Webby in *Southerly*, Vol. 44, No. 4 (1984). For a full bibliography see S. Krimmer & A. Lawson in *The Portable Barbara Baynton* (A & R, 1980).

Bedford, Jean (1946–)
Novelist, short story writer. Born in Cambridge, England, but brought up in Victoria, Australia. Educated at Monash University and the University of Papua New Guinea, qualifying as a teacher. Also a journalist, for three years was literary editor of the *National Times*, and is now a literary consultant to the Australian Film Commission. Presently also works as a literary agent in Sydney. Received a NSW Writers' Fellowship 1983. *Sister Kate* is based on the story of the sister of bushranger folk hero, Ned Kelly.

FICTION *Country Girl Again*, Melbourne, Sisters, 1979; *Sister Kate*, Melbourne, Penguin, 1982; *Country Girl Again and Other Stories*, Melbourne, McPhee Gribble/Penguin, 1985; *Coloring-In, A Book of Ideologically Unsound Love Stories* (with Rose Creswell), Melbourne, McPhee Gribble/Penguin 1986, *Love Child*, Melbourne, Penguin, 1986.
OTHER Short stories have also appeared in *Nation Review* (1977), the *National Times* (1980) and *Meanjin* (1981).
SEE ALSO J. Ellison (interview) in *Rooms of their Own* (Penguin, 1986).

Bedford, Ruth (1882–1963)
Poet, playwright, children's author. Born in Sydney and worked as a freelance writer and journalist. Collaborated with poet Dorothea Mackellar (q.v.) in two works of fiction.

POETRY *Rhymes by Ruth*, Sydney, the author, 1893; *Sydney at Sunset and Other Verses*, Melbourne, Australasian Authors' Agency, 1911; *Rosycheeks and Goldenhead* (children's), London, Alston Rivers, 1913; *Fairies and Fancies* (children's), London, A. C. Black, 1929; *The Learner and Other Verses*, Sydney, A & R, 1931; *Hundreds and Thousands* (children's, Illust. Pixie O'Harris), Dymocks, Sydney, 1934; *Who's Who in Rhyme and Without Reason*, Sydney, Australasian Publishing Co., 1948.
FICTION *The Little Blue Devil* (with Dorothea Mackellar), London, Alston Rivers, 1912; *Two's Company* (with Dorothea Mackellar), London, Alston Rivers, 1914.
NON-FICTION *Think of Stephen, a Family Chronicle*, Sydney, A & R, 1954.
DRAMA *Fear: A Play in Blank Verse*, Sydney, the author, 1930.
OTHER Unpublished plays include: *At the Inn*, *The Girls from the Marsh Croft*, *Hide the Thimble*, *Murder Next Door*, *Pear's Soap* and *Postman's Knock*.

Bennet, Stefanie (1945–)
Poet. Born in Townsville, Queensland, and has had a variety of occupations including being a rock musician. Has published eleven books of

poetry and one novel, and been active over the years as an editor, in the field of publishing, and in the Poetry Society of Australia.

POETRY *Blackbirds of Superstition*, Brisbane, the author, 1972; *Shade*, 1973; *Madame Blackboots*, St Lucia, Makar, 1974; *Five Poets*, 1974; *Poems from the Paddy Wagon*, Townsville, Cochon, 1975; *Radio City 2AM* (with J. Burns and R. K. Fordham), Townsville, Cochon, 1976; *Tongues and Pinnacles*, Townsville, Cochon, 1976; *Fronts*, 1976; *The Medium*, 1976; *The Tenth Lady*, Townsville, Cochon; Sydney, Wild & Wooley, 1977; *One Plus Two*, 1977.
FICTION *Stefan*, Kedron, North Queensland CAE, 1978.

Bevan, Beatrice
Poet. Was a writer of sentimental verse and of patriotic occasional poetry celebrating national events. *The Unknown Warrior* was inspired by the monument to the same in Westminster Abbey. Sometimes published as Mrs Willet Bevan.

POETRY *Sketches in Verse*, Adelaide, W. K. Thomas, 1922; *Sketches in Verse and Prose*, Adelaide, W. K. Thomas, 1928; *The Unknown Warrior*, Sydney, Dey, 1941.
NON-FICTION *Adam Lindsay Gordon*, Sydney, Dey, 1938.

Bird, Carmel (1940–)
Novelist, short story writer. Born and educated in Tasmania. Also studied in France, Spain and the USA and has taught French and English in Melbourne. Is interested in the performance aspect of her work and that of others, and produced the cassette, *Dr God*. Lives and works in Victoria where she is an editor of *Syllable* magazine and a teacher of fiction writing.

FICTION *Births, Deaths and Marriages*, Victoria, the author, 1983; *Cherry Ripe*, Power Press, 1985; *The Woodpecker Toy Fact*, Melbourne, McPhee Gribble/Penguin, 1987.
OTHER Stories have also appeared in *Soft Lounges* (Fringe Anthology, 1984), *Strange Attractions* (Hale & Iremonger, 1985), *Room to Move* (Redress/Unwin, 1985), *Difference* (Waterloo Press, 1985), *Australian Short Stories No. 11* (Pascoe Publs. 1985) and *Transgressions* (Penguin, 1986).

Birkett, Winifred (1897–1966)
Novelist, poet. Born in Sydney and educated at the North Shore Church of England Girls' Grammar School. Published three novels and a collection of poetry before marrying late 1942. Her best work was *Earth's Quality* (also published overseas) which recounts the story of three generations of a pastoral family.

FICTION *Three Goats on a Bender*, Sydney, A & R, 1934; *Earth's Quality*, Sydney, A & R, 1935; *Portrait of Lucy*, London, Cassell, 1938.
POETRY *Edelweiss and Other Poems*, Sydney, Beacon Press, 1932.
OTHER Contributed the chapter, 'Some Pioneer Australian Women Writers' to *The Peaceful Army* (ed. F. Eldershaw, Sydney, 1938).

Birtles, Dora (1903–)
Poet, novelist, children's author. Born Dora Toll in Newcastle, NSW. Educated at the University of Sydney where she met and married Bert Birtles. Achieved recognition in the early 1930s when she undertook a voyage in the cutter *Gullmarn* from Newcastle to Singapore, a journey which formed the basis of her travel narrative, *North-West by North*. For five years travelled widely in Europe and Asia. With her husband and others was amongst the first Australians to live in and write about Greece prior to WWII. *Exiles in the Aegean*, about her time in Greece, is still a recommended text for modern Greek students. Was English correspondent for the *Newcastle Sun* 1932–4, and had a weekly series in the Sydney *Sunday Sun* during the war years. An unpublished satirical account of London, 'Lovely, Lousey London', was recommended for the S. H. Prior Memorial Prize 1945. *North-West by North* was reprinted by Virago 1985.

FICTION *Bonza the Bull*, Sydney, Shakespeare Head, 1944; *Pioneer Shack*, Sydney, Shakespeare Head, 1946; *The Overlanders*, Sydney, Shakespeare Head, 1946.
NON-FICTION *North-West by North: Journal of a Voyage*, London, Jonathan Cape, 1935; *Exiles in the Aegean* (with B. Birtles), Sydney, Gollancz, 1938; *Australia in Colour*, Sydney, Ure Smith, 1944.
OTHER Poems, articles and stories appeared in *Hermes* (1923), the *Sydney Morning Herald*, the *Newcastle Sun* (1932–34), the *London Evening Star* (1934) and the Sydney *Sun*. The short story, 'Prison', appeared in *Coast to Coast* (1944) and 'Three Days in the Averoff' in *Australian New Writing* (1946). Contributed a chapter (with B. Birtles) to *Australian Writers Speak* (A & R, 1942).

Bjelke-Petersen, Marie (1874–1969)
Novelist. Born in Denmark, educated in Copenhagen and London. Migrated with her family to Tasmania 1891. Became an instructor at her brother's Physical Culture School in Hobart, later teaching in schools before taking up writing. Contributed to various newspapers and magazines with short sketches and stories before achieving great success with her first novel. Her novels were particularly popular in England and the USA; several were translated into other lanugages. Was awarded the King's Jubilee Medal for fiction 1935.

FICTION *The Mysterious Stranger*, Hobart, J. Walch, 1913; *Before an Eastern Court*, Hobart, Monotone Printers, 1914; *Muffled Drums*, Hobart, Monotone Printers, 1914; *The Captive Singer*, London, Hodder & Stoughton, 1917; *Dusk: A Novel*, London, Hutchinson, 1921; *Jewelled Nights*, London, Hutchinson, 1923; *The Immortal Flame*, London, Hutchinson, 1926; *The Moon Minstrel*, London, Hutchinson, 1927; *Monsoon Music*, London, Hutchinson, 1930; *The Rainbow Lute*, London, Hutchinson, 1932; *The Silver Knight*, London, Hutchinson, 1934; *Jungle Night*, London, Hutchinson, 1937.

Blewett, Dorothy, 'Ann Praize'
Playwright, novelist. Born in Melborne and educated at the Methodist Ladies' College where she edited the school magazine. Published her first story 1928. Worked as a secretary, and was involved with International PEN. Her main interest in writing was seeing her own plays performed. *Quiet Night* won the WA Drama Festival Prize 1941, while *The First Joanna* won the Playwrights' Advisory Board competition 1947.

DRAMA *The First Joanna*, 1941; *Quiet Night: A Play in Three Acts*, Sydney, Australasian Publ. Co., 1944.
FICTION *Vision*, by Ann Praize, Melbourne, Lothian, 1931; *Pattern For a Scandal*, Sydney, Australasian Publ. Co., 1948.

Bloom, Norma (1924–)
Poet. Born in Melbourne and lived in England and New Zealand, and now in Hobart, Tasmania. Has written sensitive poems which illuminate the seemingly trivial aspects of love and life. Also writes for live theatre.

POETRY *The Larger View*, Hobart, Fullers Bookshop, 1972; *When I See You*, Hobart, Cat & Fiddle Press, 1978.
OTHER Plays produced include *Ruby* (Victoria, 1973).

'Boake, Capel' *See:* **Kerr, Doris Boake**

Boult, Jenny (1951–)
Poet. Born in England and came to Australia with her parents 1966. Has lived mainly in Perth, and taught for short terms in various schools, tertiary institutions and prisons. Has been writer-in-residence at a number of schools, conducting poetry workshops and seminars. Was winner of the Anne Elder Poetry Award 1981.

POETRY *The Hotel Anonymous*, Adelaide, Bent Enterprises, 1980; *Handbaggery*, Adelaide, Bent Enterprises, 1982; *The White Rose and the Bath*,

Adelaide, Friendly St., 1984; *Flight 39*, Melbourne, Abalone Press, 1986.
DRAMA *Can't Help Dreaming*, Melbourne, All Out Ensemble, 1981.
FICTION *'I' is a Versatile Character*, Melbourne, Words & Visions, 1986.
OTHER Edited *Broadview* (Association of Country & City Women Writers, 1979), *Pearls: Writing by South Australian Women* (with Kate Veitch, Women's Art Movement, 1980), and *After the Rage* (with Tess Brady, Tutu Press, 1983). Poems have appeared in many journals and papers including *Poet's Choice, Compass*, *Meanjin, Westerly, Overland*, the *Bulletin*, the *Canberra Times, LiNQ, Hecate, Scarlet Woman*, etc, and in over 60 anthologies.

Brand, Mona (1915–)
Poet, playwright, non-fiction writer. Born in Sydney and educated at North Sydney Girls' High. Has worked as an advertising copywriter and as a research officer in Industrial Welfare. Now retired, is a freelance writer and married to writer Len Fox. Lived in Europe 1948–54 and in Hanoi 1956–7, where she taught English. Her plays from 1948 onwards were produced mainly at Sydney's New Theatre. Won first prize in the NSW Arts Council Drama Festival 1968 for *Our 'Dear' Relations* (in *Here Under Heaven*, 1969). Other awards include the James Picot Memorial Prize for poetry, the Moomba Festival Prize 1972 for a children's film script, and the Noosa Arts Theatre Prize 1985.

POETRY *Wheel and Bobbin*, Sydney, Deaton & Spence, 1938; *Silver Singing*, Melbourne, Regent Press, 1940; *Lass in Love*, Melbourne, Cloister Press, 1946; *Daughters of Vietnam, Hanoi,* Foreign Languages Publ. House, 1958.
DRAMA *Two Plays about Malaya*, London, Lawrence & Wishart, 1954; *Mona Brand: Plays*, Moscow, Foreign Languages Publ. House, 1965; *Here Under Heaven (Three Plays)*, Sydney, Wentworth Press, 1969; *Flying Saucery: Three Plays for Young People*, Sydney, Alternative Publ. Co-op. Ltd, 1981; *Here Comes Kisch!*, Melbourne, Yackandandah Playscripts, 1983.
NON-FICTION *How Our Country is Governed*, Melbourne, Nelson, 1976; *The Chinese*, Melbourne, Nelson, 1978; *Transport*, Melbourne, Nelson, 1979; *Australia*, Sydney, Ure Smith, 1979.
OTHER Plays performed include: *First Aid* (1940), *Out of Commission* (1955), *Hold the Line* (1960), *Come All Ye Valiant Miners* (1965), *On Stage Vietnam* (1967), *Going, Going, Gone* (1968), *And a Happy New Year* (1976) and *The Pirates of Pal Mal* (1977).
SEE ALSO W. Stone in *ALS*, Vol. 6 (1973) and for a checklist of works see C. Tilley in *ALS*, Vol. 10 (1981).

'Brent of Bin-Bin' *See:* **Franklin, Miles**

Brett, Doris (1950–)
Poet. Born and lives in Melbourne. Educated at the University of Melbourne graduating MA honours in clinical psychology. Her collection, *The Truth About Unicorns*, won both the Anne Elder Award from the FAW and the ASAL Mary Gilmore Award for the best first book of poetry published in 1984. Apart from writing poetry, has also taught breadmaking, is married with a daughter, and practises as a clinical psychologist.

POETRY *The Truth About Unicorns*, Brisbane, Jacaranda Wiley, 1984.
OTHER Also published *Doris Brett's Australian Bread Book* (Pitman, 1984) and a children's psychology book, *Annie Stories* (McPhee Gribble/ Penguin, 1986). Poems have appeared in several magazines including *Poetry Australia, Island, Luna*, the *Age* and *Overland.*

Bridges, Hilda (1881–1971)
Novelist, short story writer. Born in Sorell, Tasmania where her mother's family had lived since 1834; educated at Scotch College. Wrote and published her first story 1919 after which she continued to write many novels and stories of a light, adventurous nature, some of which were for children. Was the sister of writer Roy Bridges with whom she lived from 1935 on the family property. Lived and wrote constantly in her brother's shadow, working as his amanuensis and keeping house for him while publishing her own work under male pseudonyms. Nevertheless, wrote over 400 stories and sketches and over 18 serials for magazines such as the *Australian Woman's Mirror.*

FICTION *Our Neighbours*, London, Hodder & Stoughton, 1922; *The Squatter's Daughter*, (adapted from the play by Bert Bailey and Edmund Duggan), Sydney, Bookstall, 1922; *Jock Whitehead, An Australian Fairy Tale*, Melbourne, Whitcombe & Tombs, 1922; *Bobby's First Term*, Melbourne, Whitcombe & Tombs, 1924; *The Lady of the Cavern*, Sydney, Bookstall, 1925; *Chinese Lacquer: An Australian Story*, London, Hodder & Stoughton, 1926; *Carnaby's Boy*, Melbourne, Whitcombe & Tombs, 1926; *The House of Make Believe*, London, Hodder & Stoughton, 1928; *House of Storms*, London, Wright & Brown, 1931; *Chinese Jade*, London, Wright & Brown, 1933; *Distant Fields*, London, Wright & Brown, 1936; *Ships of the Mist*, London, Wright & Brown, 1936; *Derelict Island*, London, Wright & Brown, 1937; *Conisby's Corner*, London, Wright & Brown, 1937; *Men Must Live*, London, Wright & Brown, 1938; *House with Black Blinds*, Melbourne, Popular Publications, 1940; *The Creaking Door*, London, Boardman, 1950.
MANUSCRIPTS University of Tasmania Archives: Personal Papers B 4/1.

Brinsmead, Hesba (1922–)
Novelist. Born in Bilpin in the NSW Blue Mountains. Educated by correspondence followed by private schooling. Trained as a teacher and worked as a governess during WWII, afterwards moving to Melbourne with her husband and family. Here taught kindergarten, acted in theatre, and, in the 1960s, began writing. Describes herself as a 'transition novelist', meaning that her books are for adolescents rather than children and address the problems of the teenager in modern society. *Pastures of the Blue Crane* was winner of the Mary Gilmore Award 1963 and the Children's Book of the Year Award 1965 and was adapted for television in 1971. *Longtime Passing* also won the Children's Book of the Year Award 1972. Her books have been translated into several other languages.

FICTION *Pastures of the Blue Crane*, London, OUP, 1964; *Season of the Briar*, London, OUP, 1965; *Beat of the City*, London, OUP, 1966; *A Sapphire for September*, London, OUP, 1967; *Isle of the Sea-Horse*, London, OUP, 1969; *Listen to the Wind*, London, OUP, 1970; *Who Calls from Afar?*, London, OUP, 1971. *Longtime Passing*, Sydney, A & R, 1971; *Echo in the Wilderness*, London, OUP, 1972; *Under the Silkwood*, Sydney, Cassell, 1976; *The Wind Harp*, Sydney, Cassell, 1977; *The Ballad of Benny Perhaps*, Sydney, Cassell, 1977; *The Honey Forest*, Sydney, Hodder & Stoughton, 1979; *Once there was a Swagman*, Melbourne, OUP, 1979; *High Dive, Free is Lovely*, Sydney, Hodder & Stoughton, 1979; *Time for Tarquinea*, Sydney, Hodder & Stoughton, 1981; *Longtime Dreaming*, Sydney, A & R, 1982; *Christmas at Longtime*, Sydney, A & R, 1983; *The Sand Forest*, Sydney, A & R, 1985; *Someplace Beautiful*, Sydney, A & R, 1985.
OTHER Stories and articles have appeared in various collections such as *This Australia* and *A Time of Dreaming*.
MANUSCRIPTS NL, Canberra: Hesba Brinsmead Papers MS 4557.

Brooks, Barbara (1947–)
Prose and short story writer. Born in Surfers Paradise and grew up in rural Queensland. Attended the University of Queensland 1966–9, then went to London, returning to Australia 1973. Since then has lived in Sydney and been employed part-time as a librarian, teacher and reviewer. A member of the 'No Regrets' Sydney Women Writers' Workshop, she has been involved in organising readings, small publications and community writing projects.

FICTION *Leaving Queensland*, Sydney, Sea Cruise Books, 1983.
OTHER Work has appeared in the anthologies, *Mother, I'm Rooted* (Outback Press, 1975), *No Regrets I, II, & III* (Sydney Women Writers,

Workshop, 1978, 1981, 1985), *Island in the Sun 2* (Sea Cruise Books, 1981) and *Transgressions* (Penguin, 1986).

Brooksbank, Anne (1943–)
Scriptwriter, playwright. Born in Melbourne; educated at the Melbourne Church of England Girls' Grammar School and the University of Melbourne, graduating MA honours 1965. Has written various television and film scripts and co-written films such as *Newsfront* 1978 and *Maybe This Time* 1980. Won five AWGIE Awards 1972–80 for best documentary script, best children's script, best original feature film, etc. Is married to writer and actor Bob Ellis.

DRAMA *Green Room*, Sydney, A & R, 1976; *Down Under* (with Bob Ellis), Sydney, A & R, 1977.
FICTION *Mad Dog Morgan* (with Bob Ellis), London, Corgi Books, 1976; *Archer*, Sydney, Bay Books, 1985; *On Loan*, Melbourne, McPhee Gribble/ Penguin, 1985.

Broome, Mary Anne, Lady (1831–1911)
Novelist, travel writer, children's author. Born Mary Anne Stewart in Jamaica. Educated in England. Married Captain G. R. Barker 1852 who died when she was 32; became Lady Barker by this marriage. Four years later married Frederick Napier Broome in England and departed for New Zealand to live upon a sheep station for 3 years. Returned to England before her husband entered Colonial Service and was appointed Governor of WA 1882. Her acclaimed book, *Station Life in New Zealand*, went into many editions and was translated into French and German.

NON-FICTION *Station Life in New Zealand*, London, Macmillan, 1870; *Travelling Over Old and New Ground*, London, George Routledge, 1872; *Station Amusements in New Zealand*, London, W. Hunt, 1873; *First Lessons in the Principles of Cooking*, London, Macmillan, 1874; *Letters to Guy*, London, Macmillan, 1885; *Colonial Memories*, London, Smith, Elder & Co., 1904.
FICTION *Sybil's Book*, London, Macmillan, 1874; *Stories About*, London, Macmillan, 1876; *A Christmas Cake in Four Quarters*, London, F. Warner, n.d.
SEE ALSO A. Hasluck, *Remembered with Affection* (new edition of *Letters to Guy*, OUP, 1963) and Lady Barker, *Family Life in New Zealand* (extracts for children from *Station Life*, etc, 1969).

'Broughton, Mary' *See:* **Dolling, Alison**

Brown, Lyn Ingoldsby (1918–)
Poet. Born in Fairfield and educated at Parramatta High and the University of Sydney graduating MA 1946. Worked for the CSIRO for 10 years

as an editor and librarian. Later taught modern languages with the NSW Department of Education. Since 1982 has been employed as an honorary tutor in French in a community service learning programme. Began writing at an early age and had juvenilia published in the *Australian Woman's Mirror* and the *Australian Journal* 1927–33 but did not publish her first collection of poetry until 1970. Received a commendation in the John Shaw Neilson Poetry Competition 1973.

POETRY *Late Summer*, Sydney, Wentworth Books, 1970; *Jacaranda and Illawarra Flame*, Sydney, English Teachers' Assocation, 1973; *Listen! It's Poetry, Give it a Go* (with Joan Baldwin), Sydney, the authors, 1973; *Going Home at Night*, UK, Hub Publications, 1979.
OTHER Poems have appeared in magazines in Australia and the UK, also in *A Spin of Gold Wattle*, (Society of Women Writers, 1982). Has published articles in the *Australian Author* and other journals, plus a bibliography of Marjorie Barnard and Flora Eldershaw in *Biblionews*, Vol. 43, No. 4 (1970).

Brown, Pamela (1948–)
Poet, prose writer. Born in Seymour, Victoria, and educated in Queensland. Has published consistently over the years since the appearance of her first book 1972, and has been committed to small publishing houses. Currently works part-time as a lecturer in film-making, a job she has held from time to time. In the last eight years her work has received support from the Literature Board through a number of awards. *Selected Poems* was a finalist in the NSW Premier's Literary Awards 1985.

POETRY/PROSE *Sureblock*, Melbourne, Pat Woolley, 1972; *Cocobola's Funny Picture Book*, Sydney, Tomato Press, 1973; *Automatic Sad*, Sydney, Tomato Press, 1974; *Cafe Sport*, Sydney, Sea Cruise Books, 1979; *Correspondences* (with Joanne Burns), Sydney, Red Press, 1979; *Country & Eastern*, Sydney, Never Never Books, 1980; *Small Blue View*, Adelaide, Magic Sam, 1982; *Selected Poems 1971–1982*, Sydney, Redress Press/Wild & Woolley, 1984.
OTHER Work has also appeared in the following anthologies: *Mother I'm Rooted* (Outback, 1975), *Hecate's Daughters* (Hecate, 1978), *Stories of Her Life* (Outback, 1979), *Poet's Choice* (Island, 1979), *Frictions* (Sybylla, 1982) and *Off the Record* (Penguin, 1985).

Bruce, Mary Grant (1878–1958)
Children's author, journalist. Born in Sale, Victoria, and left for Melbourne 1898 where she took her first job as a journalist, editing the children's page of the *Leader*. Also wrote articles and stories for the *Age*, *Lone Hand*, *Woman's World* and other journals and papers, and had her first novel serialised in the *Leader*, 1905–07. Went to England 1913

where she met her cousin George Bruce whom she married upon their return to Australia. Were stationed in Ireland after the outbreak of WWI and here had two sons. After the war returned to settle in Taralgon, Victoria 1919, but over the years continued to travel between Australia, Ireland and England, and died in England 1958. Became a best-selling author with the famous *Billabong* series, published over 40 years. Set in the northern Gippsland region of Victoria, they celebrate the idyllic and conservative haven of Australian pastoral life.

FICTION *A Little Bush Maid*, London, Ward Lock & Co., 1910; *Mates at Billabong*, London, Ward Lock & Co., 1911; *Timothy in Bushland* London, Ward Lock & Co., 1912; *Glen Eyre*, London, Ward Lock & Co., 1912; *Norah of Billabong*, London, Ward Lock & Co., 1913; *Gray's Hollow*, London, Ward Lock & Co., 1914; *From Billabong to London*, London, Ward Lock & Co., 1915; *Jim and Wally*, London, Ward Lock & Co., 1916; *'Possum*, London, Ward Lock & Co., 1917; *Dick*, London, Ward Lock & Co., 1918; *Captain Jim*, London, Ward Lock & Co., 1919; *Dick Lester of Kurrajong*, London, Ward Lock & Co., 1920; *Rossiter's Farm*, London, Whitcombe & Tombs, 1920; *Back to Billabong*, London, Ward Lock & Co., 1921; *The Cousin from Town*, London, Whitcombe & Tombs, 1922; *The Stone Axe of Burkamukk*, London, Ward Lock & Co., 1922; *The Twins of Emu Plains*, London, Ward Lock & Co., 1923; *Billabong's Daughter*, London, Ward Lock & Co., 1924; *The Houses of the Eagle*, London, Ward Lock & Co., 1925; *Hugh Stanford's Luck*, Sydney, Cornstalk, 1925; *Robin*, Sydney, Cornstalk, 1926; *The Tower Rooms*, London, Ward Lock & Co., 1926; *Billabong Adventurers*, London, Ward Lock & Co., 1927; *Anderson's Jo*, Sydney, Cornstalk, 1927; *Golden Fiddles*, London, Ward Lock & Co., 1928; *The Happy Traveller*, London, Ward Lock & Co., 1929; *Bill of Billabong*, London, Ward Lock & Co., 1931; *The Road to Adventure*, London, Ward Lock & Co., 1932; *Billabong's Luck*, London, Ward Lock & Co., 1933; *Seahawk*, London, Ward Lock & Co., 1934; *Wings above Billabong*, London, Ward Lock & Co., 1935; *Circus Ring*, London, Ward Lock & Co., 1936; *Billabong Gold*, London, Ward Lock & Co., 1937; *Told by Peter*, London, Ward Lock & Co., 1938; *Son of Billabong*, London, Ward Lock & Co., 1939; *Peter and Co.*, London, Ward Lock & Co., 1940; *Karalta*, London, Ward Lock & Co., 1941; *Billabong Riders*, London, Ward Lock & Co., 1942.

OTHER Also published a collection of radio talks, *The Power Within* (1940), plus numerous uncollected journalism and shorter fiction although some has recently appeared in Prue McKay (ed.) *The Peculiar Honeymoon and Other Writings by Mary Grant Bruce* (McPhee Gribble, 1986).

MANUSCRIPTS La Trobe Library, Melbourne: Mary Grant Bruce Papers MS 9975.

SEE ALSO A. Alexander, *Billabong's Author, the Life of Mary Grant Bruce* (A & R, 1979) and B. Niall, *Seven Little Billabongs* (MUP, 1979).

Bulcock, Emily Hemans (1877–1969)
Poet. Born in Tinana, Queensland, the sister of writer Vance Palmer. Became a schoolteacher and wrote regularly for newspapers in Brisbane. Wrote poetry celebrating national events, and sensitive and skilful nature poems. Was active in the Queensland Authors and Artists' Association.

POETRY *Jacaranda Blooms and Other Poems*, Brisbane, Queensland Book Depot, 1923; *From Quenchless Springs*, Brisbane, the author, 1944–5; *From Australia to Britain*, Brisbane, Smith & Paterson, 1961.
SEE ALSO H. Brotherton in *Salient*, Vol. 11, No. 1 (1961).

Bunn, Anna Maria, 'An Australian' (1808–1899)
Novelist. Born Anna Maria Murray in Ireland. Came to Australia 1827, married George Bunn, a shipowner, and remained here the rest of her life. Her only novel was published anonymously and the identity of its author remained a mystery for many years. Though not set in Australia, it was the first novel to be printed in NSW and the first novel by a woman to be published in Australia.

FICTION *The Guardian*, by An Australian, Sydney, J. Spilsbury, 1838.
SEE ALSO G. Wilson in *ALS*, Vol. 3, No. 2 (1967) and in *Murray of Yarralumla* (OUP, 1968).

Burchill, Dora (1908–)
Non-fiction writer. Born Elizabeth Burchill in Melbourne. Trained as a nurse and during her career completed several post-graduate certificates and was registered in seven countries. Worked in the pioneering Australian Inland Mission 1930–32 and in the Spanish Civil War 1937 and was a captain in the Australian Army Nursing Service during WWII 1940–46. Nursed in Darwin, Thursday Island, New Guinea, Europe, the USA and Canada, and has written about her experiences over the years. Was winner of the Litchfield Prize and the Bread and Cheese Club Literary Award 1979 for *The Paths I've Trod*.

NON-FICTION *Labrador Memories*, Shepparton Newspapers, 1947; *Innamincka*, Melbourne, Hodder & Stoughton, 1960; *New Guinea Nurse*, Adelaide, Rigby, 1967; *Thursday Island Nurse*, Adelaide, Rigby, 1972; *The Paths I've Trod*, Melbourne, Spectrum Publs, 1981.
OTHER Contributed to magazines such as *Walkabout* (1946) and the *Age Literary Supplement* (1961).

Burke, Colleen (1943–)
Poet, biographer. Born and educated in Sydney, graduating in arts from the University of Sydney 1974. An advocate of folk traditions and literature, has been actively involved in the promotion of folk music and poetry. Edited 1974–5 the *Cornstalk Gazette*, the magazine of the NSW Folk Federation and helped establish the Australian National Folk Trust 1974.

POETRY *Go Down Singing*, Sydney, Khasmick Press, 1974; *Hags, Rags and Scriptures*, Townsville, Cochon Press, 1977; *The Incurable Romantic*, Melbourne, Outback Press, 1979; *She Moves Moutains*, Sydney, Redress/Wild & Woolley, 1984.
NON-FICTION *Doherty's Corner, the Life and Work of Australian Poet Marie E. J. Pitt*, Sydney, Sirius, 1985.

Burke, Janine (1952–)
Art critic and historian, novelist. Studied fine arts at the University of Melbourne and La Trobe University. Was Research Officer and organiser for the touring exhibition of Australian Women Artists 1975, one of the first significant exhibitions of women's art in Australia. Was a founding member of the *Lip* collective 1976. Has contributed art criticism to various journals, and lectured in art history.

NON-FICTION *Australian Women Artists 1840–1940*, Melbourne, Greenhouse Publs, 1980; *Joy Hester*, Melbourne, National Gallery of Victoria, 1983.
FICTION *Speaking*, Melbourne, Greenhouse Publs, 1984; *Second Sight*, Melbourne, Greenhouse Publs, 1986.
OTHER Has also contributed to: *Art International, Meanjin, Art in Australia*, and the *National Times*.

Burns, Joanne (1945–)
Poet, prose writer. Born in Sydney and trained as a teacher. Has done many readings of her poems, and there is a strong emphasis upon performance in her work.

POETRY *Snatch*, 1972; *Ratz*, Sydney, Saturday Centre Books, 1973; *Adrenalin Flicknife*, Sydney, Saturday Centre Books, 1976; *Radio City 2AM* (with S. Bennet & R. Fondham), Townsville, Cochon International, 1976.
FICTION *Alphabetics*, Sydney, Saturday Centre Books, 1976; *Correspondences* (with P. Brown), Sydney, Red Press, 1979; *Ventriloquy: Monologues 1977–1980*, Sydney, Sea Cruise Books, 1981.
OTHER Short stories have also appeared in *Meanjin* (1977), *Stories of Her Life* (1979) and *Island in the Sun* (1980). Also edited *Hot to Trot: Poetry*

on the Move (with R. Harris & C. Smyth, Victorian Education Department, 1980).
SEE ALSO R. D. Jones (interview) in *Makar*, Vol. 13, No. 3 (1978).

'Bushwoman' *See:* **Palmer-Archer, Laura**

Byles, Marie Beuzeville (1900–1979)
Travel and non-fiction writer. Born in Ashton-on-Mersey, England. After coming to Australia was educated at the University of Sydney graduating in law 1924. Practised as a solicitor 1929–70 until retirement and was the first woman to practise law in NSW 1924. Her long interest and involvement in conservation and wildlife issues, and in Eastern religion and philosophy is reflected in her writings.

NON-FICTION *By Cargo Boat and Mountain*, London, Seeley, Service & Co., 1931; *Footprints of Gautama the Buddha*, London, Rider, 1957; *Journey into Burmese Silence*, London, Allen & Unwin, 1962; *The Lotus and the Spinning Wheel*, London, Allen & Unwin, 1963; *Paths to Inner Calm*, London, Allen & Unwin, 1965; *Stand Straight without Strain*, Romford, Eng., L. N. Fowler, 1978.

C

Caffyn, Kathleen, 'Iota' (1853–1926)

Novelist. Born in Ireland and came to Australia about 1880 with husband, writer Stephen Mannington Caffyn. Lived in Sydney and Melbourne, returning to London 1892. All her novels except the first were written after her return to England and mostly after the death of her husband 1896; consequently Australia features only marginally in two of her novels, *A Comedy of Spasms* and *Dorinda and her Daughter*. Also contributed articles and stories to newspapers while in Australia.

FICTION *A Yellow Aster*, by Iota, London, Hutchinson, 1894; *Children of Circumstance*, by Iota, London, Hutchinson, 1894; *A Comedy of Spasms*, by Iota, London, Hutchinson, 1895; *A Quaker Grandmother*, London, Hutchinson, 1896; *Poor Max*, London, Hutchinson, 1898; *Ann Mauleverer*, London, Methuen, 1899; *Miss Milne and I*, Chicago, Conkey, 189–?; *The Minx*, London, Hutchinson, 1900; *The Happenings of Jill*, London, Hutchinson, 1901; *He For God Only*, London, Hutchinson, 1903; *Patricia: A Mother*, London, Hutchinson, 1905; *Smoke in the Flame*, London, Hutchinson, 1906; *The Magic of May*, London, Nash, 1908; *Whoso Breaketh an Hedge*, London, Hurst & Blackett, 1909; *Dorinda and Her Daughter*, London, Hurst & Blackett, 1910; *The Fire-Seeker*, London, Nash, 1911; *Two Ways of Love*, London, Hurst & Blackett, 1913; *Mary Mirrilees*, London, Hurst & Blackett, 1916.
OTHER Also contributed to *Coo-ee: Tales of Australian Life by Australian Ladies* (ed. H. Patchett Martin, 1891) and *By Creek and Gully* (ed. L. Fisher 1899).

Calthorpe, Mena (1905–)

Novelist. Born in Goulburn, NSW. Was first encouraged to write by T. J. Hebblewhite, editor of the Goulburn *Evening Penny Post*, who had earlier helped Miles Franklin. Worked as a school teacher in the country and in a variety of other jobs ranging from fruit picking to office work. Settled in Sydney and joined the Sydney Modern Writers' Club. Her novels reflect social concerns, portraying the working lives of the urban lower classes. *The Dyehouse* has been translated into German and Czechoslovakian.

FICTION *The Dyehouse*, Sydney, Ure Smith, 1961; *The Defectors*, Sydney, Australasian Book Society, 1969.
OTHER Also contributed to *Summers Tales 3* (Macmillan, 1966).
SEE ALSO N. Keesing in *Southerly*, Vol. 22 (1962).

Cambell, Zora Mabel
Novelist. Wrote under the pseudonyms 'Aroz' and 'Aroz le Bam' (i.e. Zora and Zora Mabel). Published two known works; the second is a lightweight romance concerning the inmates of a suburban boarding house.

FICTION *Alcedama*, Sydney, W. Brooks, 188–?; *Mrs Button's Boarders, Their Adventures: A Sydney Romance*, Sydney, Edwards, Dunlop, 1890.

Cambridge, Ada (1844–1926)
Novelist, poet. Born in Norfolk, England, and published some early religious books inspired by a devout Anglicanism. Married clergyman George Cross in Ely 1870 and emigrated to Australia in the same year; lived in various country locations throughout Victoria before settling in Melbourne. A carriage accident in the 1870s forced ill-health on her for the rest of her life, however she enjoyed remarkable success as an author and was the first significant Australian woman poet. Began writing in earnest 1873 for amusement and to boost the family fortunes (according to her autobiography, *Thirty Years in Australia* 1903) and began to make money with the publication of *A Marked Man* 1890. Also contributed to journals such as the *Atlantis Monthly* and the *Australian Ladies' Annual;* several of her novels were serialised before being published in book form. Returned to visit England 1913, where her husband died 1917; she herself died in Victoria 1926. *A Marked Man* was reprinted by Pandora Press 1987, and *The Three Miss Kings* by Virago 1987.

FICTION *The Two Surplices*, London, Joseph Masters, 1865; *Little Jenny*, London, SPCK, 1867; *The Vicar's Guest*, London, Joseph Masters, 1869; *Up the Murray*, serialised in the *Australasian* 1875; *My Guardian: A Story of the Fen Country*, London, Cassell, 1878; *In Two Years' Time*, London, Bentley, 1879; *Dinah*, serialised in the *Australasian* 1879–80; *A Girl's Ideal*, serialised in the *Age* 1881; *Missed in the Crowd*, serialised in the *Australasian* 1881–2; *A Mere Chance*, London, Bentley, 1882; *Across the Grain*, serialised in the *Australasian* 1882; *Mrs Carnegie's Husband*, serialised in the *Australasian* 1884–5; *Against the Rules*, serialised in the *Australasian* 1885–6; *A Woman's Friendship*, serialised in the *Age* 1889; *A Marked Man: Some Episodes in His Life*, London, Heinemann, 1890; *The Three Miss Kings*, London, Heinemann, 1891; *Not all in Vain*, London Heinemann, 1892; *A Little Minx: A Sketch*, London, Heinemann, 1893; *A Marriage Ceremony*, London, Heinemann, 1894; *Fidelis*, London, Hutchinson, 1895; *A Humble Enterprise*, London, Ward Lock, 1896; *At Midnight and Other Stories*, London, Ward Lock, 1897; *Materfamilias*, London, Ward Lock, 1898; *Path and Goal*, London, Methuen, 1900; *The Devastators*, London, Methuen, 1901; *Sisters*, London, Hutchinson, 1904; *A Platonic Friendship*, London, Hurst & Blackett, 1905; *A Happy Marriage*,

London, Hurst & Blackett, 1906; *The Eternal Feminine*, London, Hurst & Blackett, 1907; *The Making of Rachel Rowe*, London, Cassell, 1914.
POETRY *Hymns on the Litany*, London, Parker, 1865; *Hymns on the Holy Communion*, London, Houlston & Wright, 1866; *The Manor House and Other Poems*, London, Daldy, Isbister, 1875; *Unspoken Thoughts* (anon.) London, K. Paul, 1887; *The Hand in the Dark and Other Poems*, London, Heinemann, 1913.
NON-FICTION *Thirty Years in Australia*, London, Methuen, 1903; *The Retrospect*, London, Stanley Paul, 1912.
SEE ALSO W. Birkett in *The Peaceful Army* (ed. F. Eldershaw, Sydney, 1938), J. Roe in *ALS*, Vol. 5, No. 4 (1972), C. Craig in *Refractory Girl* (March, 1979), S. Higgins in *Australia 1888 Bulletin*, No. 7 (1981) and E. Morrison in *Books, Libraries and Readers* (Monash University, 1985).

Campbell, Jean (1901–)
Novelist. Born in Melbourne. Educated at the Presbyterian Ladies' College. Worked for the Department of the Army during WWII. Had a large output of novels, the first few of which are set in and offer detailed views of Melbourne in the late nineteenth and early twentieth century.

FICTION *Brass and Cymbals*, London, Hutchinson, 1933; *Lest We Lose Our Edens*, London, J. Long, 1935; *Greek Key Pattern*, London, Hutchinson, 1935; *The Red Sweet Wine* London, Hutchinson, 1937; *The Babe is Wise*, London, Hutchinson, 1939.
OTHER The following novels are listed as being published by New Century Press, Sydney, between 1943–5: *Her Fate in the Stars*, *Folly's Fire*, *Bed of Roses*, *Tentacles of Temptation*, *Passion from Pekin*, *Midnight in Manilla*, *The Man Above Her*, *The Perfect Lady*, *Beware of Beauty*, *Dressmaker's Dream*, *Sailor's Sweetheart*, *Passport for Paradise*, *Beauty at Bay*. Also contributed the chapter, 'Literature in Australia Today' to N. Macgeorge, *The Arts in Australia* (Melbourne, Cheshire, 1948).
MANUSCRIPTS NL, Canberra: Papers 1930–55 MS 2897.

Campbell, Marion (1948–)
Novelist, short fiction writer. Born in Sydney. Educated at the University of NSW, then the University of WA, majoring in French. Received a Hackett Studentship to pursue post-graduate studies in France. Upon her return to Australia tutored in French and comparative literature; has also taught English. Her first novel reflects her interests in art and feminist cultural theory. Is currently working upon a second novel.

FICTION *Lines of Flight*, Fremantle, Fremantle Arts Centre Press, 1985.
OTHER Has also published fiction in *Westerly* (1977, 1979), *Decade* (Fremantle Arts Centre Press, 1982) and *Portrait* (Fremantle Arts Centre Press, 1986).

'Campion, Sarah' *See:* **Coulton, Mary**

Cappiello, Rosa
Novelist. Born in Naples, Italy and migrated to Australia 1971. Published an autobiographical novel about the experiences of migrants in Australia in the '70s in which themes such as feminism and working-class values are central. It was first published in Italy 1981 as *Paese Fortunata* and won the Italian Premio Calabria award 1982. Also published another novel in Italy, *I Semi Negri* (*The Black Seeds*) 1977.

FICTION *Paese Fortunata* (*Oh Lucky Country*) trans. G. Rando, St Lucia, UQP, 1984.

Carew, Elsie (1895–1971)
Poet. Born in Auckland, New Zealand, and came to Australia aged 19. Spent a lonely and independent life in Sydney travelling occasionally (e.g. to Moscow) but mainly living in apparently impoverished circumstances. Died at the Salvation Army's People's Palace, Sydney.

POETRY *Elsie Carew: Australian Primitive Poet*, by Nancy Keesing, Sydney, Wentworth Press, 1965; *The Passing Pageant: Poems and Prose* by Elsie Carew, Sydney, Wentworth Press, 1970.
SEE ALSO N. Keesing in *Southerly*, Vol. 22 (1962).

Carleton, Caroline (1820?–1874)
Poet. Born in England, migrated to Australia 1839. Author of the first book of poetry published by a woman in South Australia.

POETRY *The Song of Australia*, by C.L. Words by Mrs C. J. Carleton, Adelaide, Penman & Galbraith, 1859; *South Australian Lyrics*, Adelaide, J. H. Lewis, c. 1860.

Carlon, Patricia
Novelist. Born in Wagga Wagga, NSW. Educated in various NSW schools. Is a writer of crime fiction and thrillers who is published in seven countries besides England and whose books have also been translated into various languages.

FICTION *Circle of Fear*, London, Ward Lock, 1961; *Danger in the Dark*, London, Ward Lock, 1962; *Who are You, Linda Condrick?* London, Ward Lock, 1962; *The Price of an Orphan*, London, Hodder & Stoughton, 1964; *Crime of Silence*, London, Hodder & Stoughton, 1965; *The Unquiet Night*, London, Hodder & Stoughton, 1965; *Betray Me if You Dare*, London, Hodder & Stoughton, 1966; *The Running Woman*, London, Hodder & Stoughton, 1966; *Hush, It's a Game*, London, Hodder & Stoughton, 1967; *See Nothing, Say Nothing*, London, Hodder &

Stoughton, 1967; *Forty Pieces of Alloy*, London, Hodder & Stoughton, 1968; *The Whispering Wall*, London, Hodder & Stoughton, 1969; *Death by Demonstration*, London, Hodder & Stoughton, 1970; *The Souvenir*, London, Hodder & Stoughton, 1970.

Carmichael, Grace, 'Jennings Carmichael' (1868–1904)
Poet. Born in Ballarat, Victoria and grew up in the Gippsland region. Trained as a nurse at the Children's Hospital in Carlton, Melbourne in the early 1890s where she first began to write and publish poems in newspapers. Married Francis Mullis and left for England 1897, where she died a pauper leaving her three children in a London workhouse. Was the first woman poet born in Victoria, and expressed her love of the bush through her work.

POETRY *Poems*, by Jennings Carmichael, London, Longman's Green, 1895; *For Some One's Sake*, Melbourne, Lindsay Gordon Lovers' Society, 1955.
OTHER Also published *Hospital Children* (prose sketches, G. Robertson, 1891) and contributed to *Childhood in Bud and Blossom* (ed. J. Lake, Atlas Press, 1900).
SEE ALSO *Centennial Magazine* (Feb. 1890) and G. A. Hunter in *All About Books* (June, 1937).

Carnegie, Margaret (1910–)
Historical writer. Born in Melbourne; educated at schools in Melbourne and Switzerland and later completed a BA at Riverina CAE 1977. Has been involved in library committee and art archival work, establishing art records at the State Library of Victoria. Became a life member of the National Gallery 1975. Was awarded the Queen's Silver Jubilee Medal 1977.

NON-FICTION *Friday Mount*, Melbourne, Hawthorn Press, 1973; *Morgan the Bold Bushranger*, Melbourne, Hawthorn Press, 1974; *In Search of Breaker Morant: Balladist and Bushveldt Carbineer* (with Frank Shields), Armadale, H. H. Stephenson, 1979; *In Step with Sturt* (with Keith Swan), Graphic Books, 1979.

Casey, Maie, Lady (1892–1983)
Biographer, poet. Born in Melbourne, a fourth-generation Australian descended from early Victorian settlers. Married to Baron Casey of Berwick. Became an artist and qualified air pilot, and lived and worked in various parts of the world. Published autobiographical books and works concerning the history of her own family in Australia.

NON-FICTION *An Australian Story 1827–1907*, London, M. Joseph,

1961; *Tides and Eddies*, London, M. Joseph, 1966; *John Cotter's Birds of the Port Phillip District of NSW 1843–1849*, Sydney, Collins, 1974; *Melba Revisited*, Melbourne, the author, 1975; *Rare Encounters*, Melbourne, Nomad Press, 1980.
POETRY *Verses*, Melbourne, McLaren, 1963; *From the Night*, Berwick, Vic., the author, 1976.
OTHER Edited (with others) *Early Melbourne Architecture 1840–1888* (OUP, 1953), *A Company of Carols* (with J. Lindsay, R. Dobson & M. Bassett, Melbourne, 1967), *The Young Kabbarli* (Music by M. Sutherland, Albert, 1972).

Cash, Deirdre, 'Criena Rohan' (1925–1963)
Novelist. Born in Melbourne into a working-class Irish-Catholic family. Studied singing and later sung in nightclubs and taught ballroom dancing. Published only under the above pseudonym. Her two published novels are colloquial and humorous stories of the working class of the late 1950s, reflecting a world she knew well. The first was received with critical acclaim both in Australia and overseas, the second appeared shortly after her death. Both were written whilst in hospital or convalescing from an illness finally diagnosed as cancer. A third unpublished novel, *House With the Golden Door*, considered by Deirdre Cash to be her best, has disappeared.

FICTION *The Delinquents*, London, Victor Gollancz, 1962; *Down by the Dockside*, London, Victor Gollancz, 1963.
SEE ALSO J. Factor in *Meanjin*, Vol. 45, No. 3 (1986).

Castilla, Ethel
Poet, short story writer. Born Ethelritha Ramos de Castilla of Spanish heritage in Kyneton, Victoria. Published poetry, stories and articles in magazines and newspapers. Also worked as a teacher, then journalist, publishing in the *Centennial Magazine* and elsewhere. Lived most of her life in Melbourne. *The Australian Girl* has a preface by Rolf Boldrewood.

POETRY *The Australian Girl and Other Verses*, Melbourne, G. Robertson, 1900.
FICTION *The Red Kangaroo* (with others), *Sydney Mail*, 1904.

Cataldi, Lee (1942–)
Poet. Born in Sydney. Educated at the University of Sydney, graduating with honours and the University Medal 1963, and at Oxford University. Lectured in English at the University of Bristol 1967–73, and has since taught in secondary schools. Was awarded the Ann Elder Poetry Prize 1978 and the Red Earth Poetry Prize 1985.

POETRY *Invitation to a Marxist-Lesbian Party*, Sydney, Wild & Woolley, 1978.
NON-FICTION *A Handbook to Sixteenth-Century Rhetoric*, London, Routledge & Kegan Paul, 1966.

Cato, Nancy (1917–)
Novelist, poet. Born in Adelaide. Was a journalist and art critic for the *Adelaide News* 1936–58. Since then has worked as a full-time writer and been active in the literary world. In 1978 she rewrote the trilogy of historical novels published 1958–62, combining them under the one title, *All the Rivers Run*. Published simultaneously in Australia, England and the USA, it became a best-seller and in 1983 a highly successful television series. Was awarded the AM 1984.

FICTION *All the Rivers Run*, London, Heinemann, 1958; *Time, Flow Softly*, London, Heinemann, 1959; *Green Grows the Vine*, London, Heinemann, 1960; *But Still the Stream*, London, Heinemann, 1962; *North West by South*, London, Heinemann, 1964; *The Sea Ants and Other Stories*, Melbourne, Heinemann, 1964; *Brown Sugar*, London, Heinemann, 1974; *Nin and the Scribblies*, Brisbane, Jacaranda Wiley, 1978; *All the Rivers Run* (new ed.), London, New English Library, 1978; *Forefathers*, London, New English Library, 1983; *The Lady Lost in Time*, Sydney, Collins, 1986; *A Distant Island*, London, Collins, 1986.
NON-FICTION *Queen Trucanini* (with V. R. Ellis), London, Heinemann, 1976; *Mr Maloga: Daniel Matthews and His River Murray Mission to the Aborigines*, St Lucia, UQP, 1976; *The Noosa Story: A Study in Unplanned Development*, Brisbane, Jacaranda Wiley, 1979; *River's End* (with L. McLeay), Adelaide, 1985.
POETRY *The Darkened Window*, Sydney, Lyrebird Writers, 1950; *The Dancing Bough*, Sydney, A & R, 1957.
OTHER Also edited the *Jindyworobak Anthology* (Adelaide, 1950).
MANUSCRIPTS NL, Canberra: Nancy Cato Papers 1949–60 MS 757 & 1847.
SEE ALSO J. Hetherington in *Forty-Two Faces* (F. W. Cheshire, 1963).

Catts, Dorothy (1896–1961)
Novelist, biographer. Born in Sydney. Married James Howard Catts, politician and union secretary with whom she edited and published the *Australian Home Budget* for 25 years. *Cornerstone*, written in the form of a diary, draws heavily upon historical sources and shows her interest in Sydney's early history.

FICTION *Dawn to Destiny*, Sydney, Consolidated Press, 1946; *Cornerstone*, Sydney, Shakespeare Head, 1947; *Those Golden Years*, London, Hutchinson, 1956; *The Crathies of Killara*, London, Hurst & Blackett, 1957.

NON-FICTION *James Howard Catts, MHR*, Sydney, Ure Smith, 1953; *King O'Malley, Man and Statesman*, Sydney, Publicity Press, 1957.
OTHER Edited the *Australian Home Budget*.
MANUSCRIPTS NL, Canberra: Papers 1907–1960 MS 658.

Chads, Ellen Augusta, 'E.A.C.'
Short story writer. Wrote mystery and adventure stories; some have distinctly Gothic undertones such as the title story in *Tried as Pure Gold and Other Tales*, which has similarities to *Jane Eyre*. Also wrote rather pious prose offering conservative views on the role of women.

FICTION *Tried as Pure Gold and Other Tales*, Melbourne, Cameron Laing, 1882; *Dora's Repentance*, Melbourne, Radcliffe, Whitelaw, 1883; *The Snowdrop's Message and Other Tales*, Melbourne, G. Robertson, 1888; *Tracked by Bushrangers and Other Stories, with Work for the Master: A Series of Papers for Women*, Melbourne, G. Robertson, 1891.

Chapman, Jean
Children's author. Born and educated in Sydney and studied at the national Art School, NSW. Published both fiction and educational books for children and stories in anthologies and collections. Worked freelance for the ABC as a writer of educational scripts from 1957. Has been a member of the Children's Book Council since the early 1950s and worked as an adviser on children's literature. Some of her books have been translated into other languages and several have also won awards including the Austrian Children's Literature Award 1969; the *Sugar Plum Christmas Book* was commended as 'one of the most beautiful books in the world', 1980.

FICTION *Amelia Muddle*, Sydney, A & R, 1963; *Sandy the Cane Train*, Sydney, A & R, 1966; *The Wish Cat*, Sydney, A & R, 1966; *The Someday Dog*, Sydney, A & R, 1968; *Cowboy*, Sydney, A & R, 1969; *Do You Remember What Happened*, Sydney, A & R, 1969; *Wombat*, Sydney, A & R, 1969; *Tell Me a Tale*, Sydney, Hodder & Stoughton, 1974; *Tell Me Another Tale*, Sydney, Hodder & Stoughton, 1976; *Sugar Plum Christmas Book*, Sydney, Hodder & Stoughton, 1977; *Supermarket Thursday*, Melbourne, Nelson, 1977; *Beware, Take Care*, Sydney, Hodder & Stoughton, 1978; *Moon Eyes*, Sydney, Hodder & Stoughton, 1978; *Tales to Tell*, Sydney, Hodder & Stoughton, 1978; *Velvet Paws and Whiskers* Sydney, Hodder & Stoughton, 1979; *Pancakes and Painted Eggs*, Sydney, Hodder & Stoughton, 1981; *Pinecone Possum*, Sydney, Hodder & Stoughton, 1981.
NON-FICTION *James Ruse*, Sydney, Wentworth Press, 1969; *Some Australian Houses*, Sydney, Wentworth Press, 1969; *Sun, Wind and Coral: Australia's Great Barrier Reef*, Sydney, Wentworth Press, 1972.

Chauncy, Nan (1900–1970)
Children's author. Born in England and came to Australia as a child. Brought up and educated in Tasmania, training as a welfare worker. Most of her books are set in Tasmania. Three have won Children's Book of the Year Awards; some have been translated into other languages such as German, Swedish and French.

FICTION *They Found a Cave*, London, OUP, 1948; *World's End was Home*, London, S. Hughes, 1952; *A Fortune for the Brave*, Melbourne, OUP, 1954; *Tiger in the Bush*, London, OUP, 1957; *Devil's Hill*, London, OUP, 1958; *Tangara*, London, OUP, 1960; *Half a World Away*, London, OUP, 1962; *The Roaring 40*, London, OUP, 1963; *High and Haunted Island*, London, OUP, 1964; *The Skewbald Pony*, London, Nelson, 1965; *Beekeeping*, London, OUP, 1967; *Mathinna's People*, London, OUP, 1967; *Lizzie Lights*, London, OUP, 1968; *The Lighthouse Keeper's Son*, London, OUP, 1969.

Clacy, Ellen
Fiction, non-fiction writer. Born in England, visited Australia briefly 1852 during the gold rush and wrote one of the best contemporary accounts of life on the Victorian goldfields. Her fictional work consists of novellas and some short sketches dealing with bushranging, the blacks, gold-digging, and bush and city life.

NON-FICTION *A Lady's Visit to the Gold-Diggings of Australia in 1852–53*, London, Hurst & Blackett, 1853. (Republished, ed. P. Thompson, London, A & R; Melbourne, Lansdowne, 1963.)
FICTION *Lights and Shadows of Australian Life*, London, Hurst & Blackett, 1854.

Clare, Monica (1924–1973)
Novelist. Born in Mungindi, Queensland, of English and Aboriginal parents. After her mother died in her third childbirth, she spent an itinerant childhood before being taken from her father by the Child Welfare Department and sent to a Sydney home. Later became active in Aboriginal welfare and rights. Wrote an autobiographical account of the hardships of growing up as an Aboriginal girl which was published posthumously.

FICTION *Karobran: The Story of an Aboriginal Girl*, Sydney, Alternative Publ. Co., 1978.

Clark, Marjorie, 'Georgia Rivers' (c. 1897–)
Novelist, short story writer. Born in Melbourne, and educated at Milverton College. Went into business after school and wrote her first

novel surreptitiously while working in an office. Continued to publish all her work under her pseudonym, writing stories for the *Australian Woman's Mirror*, the *Triad*, and other magazines.

FICTION *Jacqueline*, London, Hodder & Stoughton, 1927; *Tantalego*, London, Skeffington, 1928; *The Difficult Art*, London, Skeffington, 1930; *She Dresses for Dinner*, London, Skeffington, 1933.
MANUSCRIPTS La Trobe Library, Melbourne: Marjorie Clark Papers.
SEE ALSO N. Palmer in *All About Books* (March, 1930).

Clark, Mavis Thorp
Children's author, non-fiction writer. Born in Melbourne and educated at the Methodist Ladies' College. Began to write while still at school although did not begin to publish until much later. Is widely travelled, and her books demonstrate a keen awareness of the Australian landscape. *The Brown Land was Green* was serialised by the author for the ABC. Won the Children's Book Council Book of the Year Award 1967 for *The Min-Min*, which has also been translated into other languages. Other books have also been published overseas, published in Braille, and received commendations in various awards.

FICTION *Dark Pool Island*, London, OUP, 1949; *The Twins from Timber Creek*, London, OUP, 1949; *Home Again at Timber Creek*, London, OUP, 1950; *Jingaroo*, London, OUP, 1951; *Missing Gold*, London, Hutchinson, 1951; *Gully of Gold*, London, Heinemann, 1958; *Pony from Tarella*, London, Heinemann, 1959; *They Came South*, London, Heinemann, 1963; *The Min-Min*, Sydney, Lansdowne Press, 1966; *Blue Above the Trees*, Sydney, Lansdowne Press, 1967; *Spark of Opal*, Sydney, Lansdowne Press, 1968; *Nowhere to Hide*, Sydney, Lansdowne Press, 1969; *Iron Mountain*, Sydney, Lansdowne Press, 1970; *New Golden Mountain*, Sydney, Lansdowne Press, 1973; *Wildfire*, Sydney, Hodder & Stoughton, 1973; *The Sky is Free*, Sydney, Hodder & Stoughton, 1974; *The Hundred Islands*, Sydney, Hodder & Stoughton, 1976; *Spanish Queen*, Sydney, Hodder & Stoughton, 1977; *The Boy from Cumeroogunga*, Sydney, Hodder & Stoughton, 1976; *The Lilly-Pilly*, Adelaide, Rigby, 1979; *A Stranger Came to the Mine*, London, Hutchinson, 1980; *Solomon's Child*, London, Hutchinson, 1981; *Soft Shoe*, Adelaide, Rigby, 1982; *Young and Brave*, Sydney, Hodder & Stoughton, 1984.
NON-FICTION *John Batman*, Melbourne, OUP, 1962; *Fishing*, Melbourne, OUP, 1963; *Pastor Doug*, Sydney, Lansdowne Press, 1965; *The Pack Tracker*, Melbourne, OUP, 1968; *The Opal Miner*, Melbourne, OUP, 1969; *Iron Ore Mining*, Melbourne, OUP, 1971; *Strolling Players*, Sydney, Lansdowne Press, 1972; *No Mean Destiny*, Melbourne, Hyland House, 1986.

SEE ALSO W. McVitty in *Innocence and Experience, Essays on Contemporary Australian Children's Writers* (Nelson, 1981).

Clarke, Coralie (1909–1972)
Travel writer, playwright. Born in Perth and educated at the University of WA. Published some early plays in the student paper *Black Swan*, edited by her future husband Leslie Rees. Moved to London and married 1931, returning to Australia 1936. Contributed to the *West Australian* and wrote for radio, and also wrote various travel articles for *Walkabout*.

NON-FICTION *Spinifex Walkabout* (with Leslie Rees), Sydney, Australasian Publ. Co., 1953; *Westward from Cocos* (with Leslie Rees), Sydney, Australasian Publ. Co., 1956; *Coasts of Cape York* (with Leslie Rees), Sydney, A & R, 1960; *People of the Big Sky Country* (with Leslie Rees), Sydney, Ure Smith, 1970; *Australia: The Big Sky Country* (with Leslie Rees), Sydney, Ure Smith, 1971.
OTHER *Silent His Wings* (poetry, Austr. Publ. Co., 1946); *Wait Till We Grow Up*, in *Australian Youth Plays* (ed. L. Rees, A & R, 1948).

Clarke, Doreen (1928–)
Playwright. Born in Manchester, England. Received an elementary education and left school at 14 to work in cotton mills and factories. Left England and settled in SA in 1958. Had her first play produced 20 years later in Adelaide. Since then has had plays produced all over Australia and been involved in writers' workshops in Adelaide since 1981. Was nominated for an AWGIE Award 1982 and received a Literature Board Fellowship 1983. In 1981 was writer-in-residence at the State Theatre of SA, and in 1985 at the Junction Theatre Company, Adelaide.

DRAMA *Farewell Brisbane Ladies*, Melbourne, Yackandandah Playscripts, 1981; *Roses in Due Season*, Sydney, Currency Press, 1982; *Bleedin' Butterflies*, Sydney, Currency Press, 1982.
OTHER Plays produced include *Missus Queen* (Adelaide, 1980); *Coppin & Co* (Adelaide, 1980); *The Sad Songs of Annie Sando* (Adelaide, 1981, Brisbane, 1982); *A Sort of Chimera* (Sydney, 1984); *Salt & Vinegar* (Adelaide, 1982); *Northern Line* (Adelaide, 1983); *My Blood for South Australia* (Adelaide, 1983) and *Hanging On* (Hobart, 1985). Is also represented in *After the Rage* (Tutu Press, 1984).

Clift, Charmian (1923–1969)
Novelist, journalist, short story writer. Born in Kiama, NSW; worked in the army during WWII and then on the Melbourne *Argus*. Married writer George Johnston 1947 with whom she collaborated on three novels, including *High Valley*, winner of the *Sydney Morning Herald* Literary

Competition 1948. Also adapted his novel *My Brother Jack* for television. Contributed regularly to the *Melbourne Herald*, amongst other papers and magazines, and wrote a weekly column for the *Sydney Morning Herald*. Lived in London and Greece for 14 years, leading a colourful, sometimes controversial life with her husband and their artistic and literary friends. Returned to Sydney 1964 where she died.

FICTION *High Valley* (with George Johnston), Sydney, A & R, 1949; *The Big Chariot* (with George Johnston), Sydney, A & R, 1953; *The Sea and the Stone* (with George Johnston), New York, Bobbs Merrill, 1955; *The Sponge Divers* (with George Johnston), London, Collins, 1956; *Walk to the Paradise Gardens*, London, Hutchinson, 1960; *Honour's Mimic*, London, Hutchinson, 1964; *Strong Man from Piraeus and Other Stories* (with George Johnston), selected by Gary Kinnane, Melbourne, Penguin, 1986.
NON-FICTION *Mermaid Singing*, London, M. Joseph, 1958; *Peel Me a Lotus*, London, Hutchinson, 1959; *Images in Aspic*, London, Horwitz, 1965; *The World of Charmian Clift*, Sydney, Ure Smith, 1970.
SEE ALSO C. Tolchard in *Walkabout*, Vol. 35, No. 1 (1969) and G. Kinnane in *George Johnston* (Nelson, 1986).

'Clyde, Constance' *See:* **Macadam, Constance**

Cole, Elsie
Poet. Born in Melbourne and educated at South Melbourne College. First published poems in the *Bulletin* when still a schoolgirl. Married 1926 to Alfred H. Angel, editor of the Victorian *Hansard*. Her poetry reflected her love of nature, particularly the landscape surrounding Melbourne. Also contributed poems and stories to the *Australian Woman's Mirror* and other magazines.

POETRY *Holiday Songs*, Melbourne, G. Robertson, 1912; *Children of Joy*, Melbourne, Lothian, 1928; *In Memoriam G. E. Green*, the author, 1930.

Collins, Betty
Novelist, journalist. Born in Sydney. Has published stories in Australia, England, Germany and Russia. Worked as a freelance journalist, travel writer and secretary. Was for some years an active member of the Communist Party. Her first novel is set in the remote NSW mining town of Mount Isa, where she lived briefly. Some of her short stories have been translated into Russian.

FICTION *The Copper Crucible*, Brisbane, Jacaranda, 1966; *The Second Step*, Sydney, Australasian Book Society, 1972.
OTHER Short stories also appeared in the *Realist Writer* (1962, 1965).

Compton, Jennifer (1949–)
Playwright, short story writer, poet. Born in Wellington, New Zealand and came to Australia 1973. Spent 2 years at drama school in Auckland and was an actor before becoming a writer. Met husband Matthew O'Sullivan during a production of Richard III. Now has two young children and lives in the NSW country. Was writer-in-residence at the University of Canterbury (NZ) 1980. Has received several awards for her plays including an AWGIE award for the radio play *A Goose's Bridle* 1976 and the Katherine Mansfield Memorial Award from the Bank of NZ and the NZ Women Writers' Society 1977. Many of her plays have been produced on Radio NZ and the ABC.

DRAMA *Crossfire*, Sydney, Currency Press, 1976; *They're Playing Our Song*, in *Can't You Hear Me Talking to You* (ed. A. Sykes), St Lucia, UQP, 1978.
OTHER Plays produced include: *Stream of Consciousness*, *All Good Children Go to Heaven*, *A Goose's Bridle* (1976), *Fantasies Between Bars: Adolf* (NZ, 1977), *All the Time in the World* (1986) and *Wingello Road* (1987). Short stories have appeared in: *Listener Short Stories 3* (NZ, 1984), *The New Fiction* (Lindon Publishing, 1985), *One Whale Singing* (The Women's Press, 1985) and poems and stories have also been published in: *Landfall*, *Island*, *Poetry Australia*, *Aspect*, *Cli(Mate)*, *Westerly*, *Southerly*, *Moreporks*, *Pol*, *Cleo* and the *NZ Listener*.

Costello, Moya (1952–)
Prose-fiction writer. Born in Sydney and educated at the University of Sydney and Teachers' College, graduating in history and English. In 1983 completed a graduate diploma in media studies at the Victoria State College. Has worked as a tutor in adult literacy, English and creative writing. Is currently working upon a novella and on scripts for theatre and film.

FICTION *Kites in Jakarta*, Sydney, Sea Cruise Books, 1985.
OTHER Is represented in the following anthologies: *No Regrets II* (Sydney Women Writers' Workshop, 1981), *Frictions* (Sybylla, 1983) and *Transgressions* (Penguin, 1986)

Cottrell, Dorothy (1902–1957)
Novelist. Born Ida Dorothy Wilkinson in Picton, NSW. Studied art at the Royal Art Society of NSW. Caught infantile paralysis as a child and was confined to a wheelchair all her life. Spent some time on a Queensland station and married American Walter Mackenzie Cottrell 1922. Went to live in the USA soon after where she worked as a writer and journalist, returning to Australia 1954–56. *The Singing Gold* was first serialised in the *Ladies' Home Journal* before publication in book form.

Set in pastoral Queensland, the novel was a great success, being twice reprinted within a month, although an Australian edition did not appear until 1956. *The Silent Reefs* was filmed in 1959.

FICTION *The Singing Gold*, Boston, Houghton Mifflin, 1928; *Earth Battle*, London, Hodder & Stoughton, 1930; *Winks: His Book*, London, Jarrolds, 1934; *Wilderness Orphan: The Life and Adventures of Chut the Kangaroo*, Sydney, A & R, 1936; *The Silent Reefs*, London, Hodder & Stoughton, 1954.

Couani, Anna (1948–)
Fiction writer, poet. Born in Sydney of Greek and Polish parents. Educated in Sydney, and is a qualified architect, art teacher, and teacher of English as a second language. Has held a variety of jobs and is presently working in an Intensive Language Centre. Is a founding member of the Sydney Women Writers' Workshop, an officer of the Poets' Union, a member of the NSW Association of Multicultural Writers and a member of the Red Spark publishing group. Was founder and co-editor of the small press publishing companies, Magic Sam and Sea Cruise Books. Since 1980 has operated Sea Cruise Books alone, concentrating upon publishing women writers.

FICTION *Italy*, Melbourne, Rigmarole, 1977; *Were all Women Sex-Mad?*, Melbourne, Rigmarole, 1982; *The Train*, Sydney, Sea Cruise Books, 1983.
OTHER Also edited (with D. White & T. Thompson) *Island in the Sun: An Anthology of Recent Australian Prose* (Sea Cruise Books, 1980).
SEE ALSO Author's statement in *ALS*, Vol. 10, No. 2 (1981) and S. Gunew in *Meanjin*, Vol. 42, No. 1 (1983).

Coulton, Mary, 'Sarah Campion' (1906–)
Novelist. Born Mary Rose Coulton in Eastbourne, England. Worked as a teacher in England, Canada and Germany; also lived and worked in South Africa and New Zealand. Visited Australia 1938–40 before marrying New Zealand writer Antony Alpers and settling in that country where she still lives. Although her connection with Australia was short, it provided her with rich material for a trilogy of novels set in Northern Queensland, *Mo Burdekin*, *Bonanza* and *The Pommy Cow*. These novels are colloquial, tragi-comical, and demonstrate an impressive familiarity with the northern Australian region.

FICTION *If She is Wise*, London, P. Davies, 1935; *Duet for Female Voices*, London, P. Davies, 1936; *Cambridge Blue*, London, P. Davies, 1937; *Thirty Million Gas Masks*, London, P. Davies, 1937; *Unhandsome Corpse*, London, P. Davies, 1938; *Makeshift*, London, P. Davies, 1940; *Turn*

Away No More, London, P. Davies, 1940; *Mo Burdekin*, London, P. Davies, 1941; *Bonanza*, London, P. Davies, 1942; *The Pommy Cow*, London, P. Davies, 1944; *Dr Golightly*, London, P. Davies, 1946; *Come Again*, London, P. Davies, 1951.

NON-FICTION *My Father: A Portrait of G. G. Coulton At Home*, London, M. Joseph, 1929.

OTHER Also published short stories in *Southerly* (1952, 1953).

SEE ALSO J. Mackellar in *Southerly*, Vol. 11, No. 2 (1950), J. Henzenroeder in *North*, Vol. 6 (1968) and R. Store in *Islands Review*, Vol. 1, No. 3 (1968).

Coungeau, Emily (1860–1936)

Poet. Born in Essex, England and came to Australia 1887 with her husband, finally settling in Brisbane 1889. As a young woman worked for a member of the Royal family and was widely travelled in Europe. Began to write 1913, contributing to the *Bulletin*, the *Brisbane Courier* and the *Australian Woman's Mirror*.

POETRY *Stella Australia: Poems, Verses and Prose Fragments*, Brisbane, Gordon & Gotch, 1914; *Princess Mona: A Romantic Poetical Drama*, Sydney, W. Brooks, 1917; *Rustling Leaves: Selected Poems*, Sydney, W. Brooks, 1920; *Palm Fronds: Poems and Verse*, Brisbane, Smith & Paterson, 1927; *Fern Leaves: Poems and Verse*, Brisbane, Smith & Paterson, 1934.

Couvreur, Jessie, 'Tasma' (1848–1897)

Novelist. Born Jessie Catherine Huybers in London of Anglo-French and Dutch parents, and brought to Tasmania in the 1850s. Grew up under her mother's artistic and literary influences. Married Charles Frazer 1867 and lived with him in Victoria until he sent her overseas 1874, the marriage having broken down through his gambling and other vices. She returned 1883 to discover his infidelity and received a divorce in December 1883. Returned to Europe, shortly afterwards marrying Belgian politician and journalist Auguste Couvreur. They settled in Brussels, although she travelled Europe lecturing upon Australia and displaying a great interest in political, social and philosophical causes. Became Brussels correspondent for the *Times* upon the death of Couvreur 1894 and held the position until her own death 3 years later. Although she took the name of her adopted state for a pseudonym, her books have little to do with Tasmania. They are mainly about the problems within marriages formed from two unequal partners, and in particular the plight of women thus trapped.

FICTION *Uncle Piper of Piper's Hill: An Australian Novel*, London, Trubner, 1889; *In Her Earliest Youth*, London, Heinemann, 1890; *A Sydney Sovereign and Other Tales*, London, Trubner, 1890; *The Penance of Portia James*, London, Heinemann, 1891; *A Knight of the White Feather: Incidents and Scenes in Melbourne Life*, London, Heinemann, 1892; *Not Counting the Cost* London, Heinemann, 1895; *A Fiery Ordeal*, London, Bentley, 1897.

OTHER Also contributed to the *Australasian* and the *Australian Journal*, and to *Australasia: An International Christmas Annual* (1878) and *Coo-ee: Tales of Australia by Australian Ladies* (1891).

MANUSCRIPTS NL, Canberra: Jessie Couvreur Biographical Notes MS 2499; ML, Sydney: Journal 1889–91 FM4/447.

SEE ALSO D. Byrne in *Australian Writers* (London, 1896), W. Birkett in *The Peaceful Army* (ed. F. Eldershaw, Sydney, 1938) and S. Higgins in *Australia 1888 Bulletin*, No. 7 (1981).

Craig, Ailsa (1917–)

Journalist. Born in Sydney. Educated at Loreto Convent and the University of Sydney, graduating in arts 1937 and later MA in German 1984. Has worked as a demonstrator at university, a secondary school teacher, and as a writer and editor for various newspapers and magazines including the *Sunday Sun* and the *Australian Women's Weekly*. Was London correspondent for the *Sydney Morning Herald* 1954–7 and edited and wrote in various capacities for the *Woman's Day* 1957–76. Her work includes a long-running radio serial, *The Intruders*, and the famous *Middletons* serial for the *Woman's Day*. While she has written plays and stories, most of her work has been in journalism, mainly from the necessity of raising three children without support.

FICTION *If Blood Should Stain the Wattle*, Sydney, Currawong, 1946; *Life with the Middletons*, serialised in the *Woman's Day* 1959– ; *Australia Album* (ed.), Sydney, Sungravure, 1974.

Crawford, Eugenie

Biographer. Born in Sydney of French descent. Educated at the Presbyterian Ladies' College, Pymble and later the University of Sydney. Has travelled widely and contributed regularly to ABC radio and television. Collaborated with her mother Eugenie McNeil to write the stories of her French forebears in Australia.

NON-FICTION *A Bunyip Close Behind Me, Recollections of the Nineties*, Melbourne, Hawthorn Press, 1972; *Ladies Didn't*, Melbourne, Penguin, 1984.

Cross, Zora (1890–1964)

Poet, novelist, journalist. Born Zora Bernice May Cross in Brisbane. Educated at Ipswich Girls' Grammar School followed by Sydney Teachers' College. Worked for the Department of Education for 3 years before leaving teaching for acting and then journalism. Worked for *Boomerang* and later freelanced. Published forthright poems dealing frankly with the subjects of love, sexuality and the feelings of motherhood. As Bernice May conducted a regular column of interviews with Australian women writers in the *Australian Woman's Mirror* during the 1930s.

POETRY *A Song of Mother Love*, Brisbane, Carter, Watson, 1916; *Songs of Love and Life*, Sydney, Tyrrell's, 1917; *The Lilt of Life*, Sydney, A & R, 1918; *The City of Riddle-mee-ree* (children's), Sydney, A & R, 1918; *Elegy on an Australian Schoolboy*, Sydney, A & R, 1921.
FICTION *Daughters of the Seven-Mile: The Love Story of an Australian Woman*, London, Hutchinson, 1924; *The Lute-Girl of Rainyvale: A Story of Love, Mystery and Adventure in North Queensland*, London, Hutchinson, 1925; *The Victor*, serialised in the *Sydney Morning Herald*, 1933; *This Hectic Age*, Sydney, London Book Co., 1944.
OTHER Also published *Introduction to the Study of Australian Literature* (Sydney Teachers' College Press, 1922) and *The Wonderland of the North* (nd). Is represented in Nettie Palmer (ed.) *An Australian Story Book* (A & R, 1928) and George Mackaness (ed.) *Australian Short Stories* (1928).

Crowley, Eena Marie, 'Esther Roland'
Novelist. Wrote a novel about Australian outback life set in the Depression. Noted for its characterisation and convincing realism, it won second prize in the *Sydney Morning Herald* literary competition 1946.

FICTION *I Camp Here*, Sydney, A & R, 1948.
OTHER A short story, *Fourth Generation*, also appeared in the *Bulletin* (1941). *Success My Penalty* was produced on ABC radio (1940s).

Cummins, Bettina (1914–)
Poet, short story writer, editor. Born in Tenterfield, NSW and educated at country schools followed by Sydney Girls' High. Has had a long association with the FAW, is President of its North Shore regional branch and in 1979 was awarded a plaque and certificate for services to the FAW. Was the NSW correspondent for *Artlook* for 4 years. Is an exponent of self-publication and has written upon the topic for other writers. Her poetry has attracted a number of regional awards.

POETRY *Psyche* (with J. Gale and G. King), Sydney, W. A. Cummins, 1979.
NON-FICTION *Marketing Lists for New Writers*, Sydney, W. A. Cummins, 1977; *How to Self Publish*, Sydney, W. A. Cummins, 1982; *No Place Like It*, Sydney, W. A. Cummins, 1983.

Cumpston, Amy (1921–)
Poet, playwright. Born in Melbourne. Has published several plays and collections of verse and has also written for television. Has also written about half a dozen other plays which remain unperformed and unpublished. Now lives in Sydney.

POETRY *Human My Race*, Sydney, Pacific Press, 1955; *Borrow the Spring*, Sydney, Edwards & Shaw, 1961; *The Towers of Earth: Poems of the Blue Mountains*, Sydney, Elizabethan Press, 1969.
DRAMA *This Fatal Island*, Sydney, the author, 1973; *Woodrow Wilson*, Sydney, the author, 1973.

Curlewis, Jean (1899–1930)
Children's author. Born in Sydney, daughter of writer Ethel Turner (q.v.) with whom she collaborated on *The Sunshine Family*. Also wrote novels for children, as well as editing the children's page of the *Daily Telegraph*. Died early from tuberculosis.

FICTION *The Ship that Never Set Sail*, London, Ward Lock, 1921; *Drowning Maze*, London, Ward Lock, 1922; *Beach Beyond*, London, Ward Lock, 1923; *The Sunshine Family* (with Ethel Turner), London, Ward Lock, 1923; *The Dawn Man*, London, Ward Lock, 1924.
NON-FICTION *Verse Writing for Beginners*, 1925.

Cusack, Dymphna (1902–1981)
Novelist, playwright. Born Ellen Dymphna Cusack in Wyalong, NSW. Educated in the country and at the University of Sydney graduating BA honours. Married Norman Freehill 1926. While a prolific writer of fiction and drama, also devoted herself to working for women's rights, the peace movement, and the socialist cause. Her novels were translated into fifteen languages and she achieved greatest fame in Russia where her sales went into the millions. Was a life-long member of the CPA. For many years suffered a crippling neuralgia which made her give up teaching 1944; most of her books after *Come in Spinner* were written via dictation. Won many awards for her novels and plays including the *Daily Telegraph* prize 1948 for *Come in Spinner*. Received the Queen's Silver Jubilee Medal 1977 and the AO 1981, amongst other honours.

DRAMA *Shallow Cups*, in *Eight Plays by Australians*, Melbourne, Dramatists' Club, 1934; *Red Sky at Morning*, Melbourne, MUP, 1942; *Morning Sacrifice*, Sydney, Mulga Publs, 1943; *Three Australian 3–Act Plays*, Sydney, Australasian Publ. Co., 1950; *The Golden Girls, a Play in Three Acts*, London, Deane, 1955; *Pacific Paradise, A Play in 13 Scenes*, in *Theatregoer*, Vol. 3, No. 1, 1963.
FICTION *Jungfrau*, Sydney, Bulletin, 1936; *Pioneers on Parade* (with Miles

Franklin), Sydney, A & R, 1939; *Come in Spinner* (with Florence James), London, Heinemann, 1951; *Say No To Death*, London, Heinemann, 1951; *Southern Steel*, London, Constable, 1953; *The Sun in Exile*, London, Constable, 1955; *Heatwave in Berlin*, London, Heinemann, 1961; *Picnic Races*, London, Heinemann, 1962; *Black Lightning*, London, Heinemann, 1964; *The Sun is Not Enough*, London, Heinemann, 1967; *The Half-Burnt Tree*, London, Heinemann, 1969; *A Bough in Hell*, London, Heinemann, 1971.

NON-FICTION *Chinese Women Speak*, Sydney, A & R, 1958, *Holidays among the Russians*, London, Heinemann, 1964; *Mary Gilmore – A Tribute* (with others), Sydney, Australasian Book Soc., 1965; *Illyria Reborn*, London, Heinemann, 1966.

OTHER Also edited and introduced *Caddie – The Story of a Sydney Barmaid*, (Constable, 1953), published a children's book, *Kanga-Bee and Kanga-Bo* (Botany House, 1945) and assisted in Norman Freehill's biography, *Dymphna* (Nelson, 1975). Contributed to *The Peaceful Army* (ed. F. Eldershaw, Sydney, 1938) and *China Reconstructs*, Vol. 6 (1957). Unpublished plays include: *Anniversary*, *His Honour Comes to Tea*, *Second Rhapsody* (in the Campbell Howard Collection, University of New England) and *Eternal Now* (Hanger Collection, University of Queensland).

MANUSCRIPTS NL, Canberra: Dymphna Cusack Papers MS 4621 (main collection; other papers at MS 718, 2449 & 3925).

SEE ALSO M. Sterling in *Meanjin*, Vol. 24 (1965).

D

Dale, Alice Mary
Novelist. Born in Sheffield, England and came to Australia in the 1880s. Was a contributor in England to *Household Words*, *All the Year Round*, etc.

FICTION *With Feet of Clay*, London, Sonneschein, 1895; *Marcus Warwick, Atheist*, London, Paul, 1897; *The Peril of a Lie*, London, Routledge, 1898; *Duncan Falconer's Revenge*, London, Routledge, 1909.

D'Alpuget, Blanche (1944–)
Novelist, biographer, journalist. Born in Sydney. As a journalist worked in England, Indonesia and Malaya. Her overseas experiences provided material for her fiction, notably the political thriller *Turtle Beach*. Has been a reviewer for the *Australian Financial Review* and the *National Times*. Has won various awards for her work including two FAW prizes for short stories 1975, the *Age* Novel of the Year Award 1981 with *Turtle Beach*, and the NSW Premier's Award for Non-fiction for the biography of the Prime Minister, Bob Hawke, in 1983. *Turtle Beach* is currently being translated into French.

FICTION *Monkeys in the Dark*, Sydney, Australasian Publ. Co., 1980; *Turtle Beach*, Melbourne, Penguin, 1981; *Winter in Jerusalem*, New York, Simon & Schuster, 1986.
NON-FICTION *Mediator, a Biography of Sir Richard Kirby*, Melbourne, MUP, 1977; *Robert J. Hawke, a Biography*, Melbourne, Schwartz, 1982.
MANUSCRIPTS NL, Canberra: Blanche D'Alpuget Notes & Transcripts.
SEE ALSO H. Tiffin in *ALS*, Vol. 11, No. 4 (1984), C. Baker (interview) in *Yacker* (Pan/Picador, 1986) and J. Ellison (interview) in *Rooms of their Own* (Penguin, 1986).

Dalziel, Kathleen (1881–1969)
Poet. Born in Durban and came to Australia as a child. Never attended school but was educated at home by her mother. Lived for a while in Tasmania then settled in Melbourne. Encouraged by J. F. Archibald, she first began to publish in the *Bulletin*. Wrote poetry about the bush.

POETRY *Known and Not Held*, Melbourne, Bread and Cheese Club, 1941.
SEE ALSO *Southerly*, Vol. 30, No. 3 (1970).

Daniels, Kay (1941–)
Historian, non-fiction writer. Born in Adelaide. Educated at the University of Adelaide graduating 1962. Later graduated DPhil from the

University of Sussex 1967. Has been a lecturer in history at the University of Tasmania since 1967 and senior lecturer since 1977. During 1975–7 was Director of the National Research Programme for International Women's Year. Has been a member of the Sisters Publishing company since 1979. From 1974–5 was author (with cartoonist Jenny Coopes) of *Superfem*, Australia's first feminist cartoon strip. Has been active in historical and heritage organisations in Tasmania, and in women's education and research programmes.

NON-FICTION *Women in Australia: An Annotated Guide to Records* (ed. with M. Murnane & A. Picot), Canberra, AGPS, 1977; *Uphill all the Way: A Documentary History of Women in Australia* (with M. Murnane) St Lucia, UQP, 1980; *So Much Hard Work: Women and Prostitution in Australian History* (ed.) Sydney, Fontana, 1984.

Dark, Eleanor, 'Patricia O'Rane' (1901–1985)
Novelist. Born Eleanor O'Reilly in Sydney. Educated at private schools. Published her first poems 1921 as 'Patricia O'Rane' in *Triad*, and continued to use this pseudonym for some years. Married Eric Payten Dark 1922 and moved to Katoomba, NSW, where she lived for most of her life. Claimed to dislike her first novel, *Slow Dawning*, written supposedly to make money. However shortly achieved critical recognition with subsequent works, winning the Australian Literary Society's Gold Medal 1934 and 1936 for *Prelude to Christopher* and *Return to Coolami*. Was a great correspondent of Nettie Palmer (q.v.), sharing her ideas concerning Australian cultural development. After her first two novels, began dealing with questions of class society, democracy and war, explored also in the later historical novels. Was described by M. Barnard Eldershaw (q.v.) as an 'unwilling romantic'. Received the first Alice Award from the Society of Women Writers 1978, and the AO 1977. *The Timeless Land* was adapted for ABC television 1979.

FICTION *Slow Dawning*, London, John Lane, 1932; *Prelude to Christopher*, Sydney, Stephenson, 1934; *Return to Coolami*, London, Collins, 1936; *Sun Across the Sky*, London, Collins, 1937; *Waterway*, London, Collins, 1938; *The Timeless Land*, Sydney, Collins, 1941; *The Little Company*, Sydney, Collins, 1945; *Storm of Time*, Sydney, Collins, 1948; *No Barrier*, Sydney, Collins, 1953; *Lantana Lane*, London, Collins, 1959.
OTHER Also published poems and short stories in the *Bulletin*, the *Australian Woman's Mirror*, etc 1921–46. Contributed a chapter on Caroline Chisholm to *The Peaceful Army* (ed. F. Eldershaw, Sydney, 1938). Is represented in several anthologies including *Tales by Australians* (British Authors' Press, 1939) and *Modern Australian Short Stories* (Georgian House, 1965).

MANUSCRIPTS ML, Sydney: Eleanor Dark Collection 1849–1980 ML MSS 4545.
SEE ALSO M. Barnard Eldershaw in *Essays in Australian Fiction* (MUP, 1938), A. K. Thomson, *Understanding the Novel The Timeless Land* (Jacaranda, 1966), A. Grove Day, *Eleanor Dark* (Twayne, 1977. Also has a bibliography) and L. Hergenhan in *Unnatural Lives: Studies in Australian Fiction about the Convicts from James Tucker to Patrick White* (UQP, 1983).

David, Mary Edgeworth (1888–1987)
Biographer. Born in Maitland, NSW. Educated privately and at Kambala girls' school, Sydney. Was the daughter of Sir Edgeworth David, explorer and professor of geology at the University of Sydney; her mother was state Commissioner of the Girl Guides. Was known for her remarkable rural life in the middle of suburban Hornsby. Here she lived almost self-sufficiently, spinning wool from her own sheep and growing her own food. *Passages of Time*, her autobiography and biography of her parents, received a special commendation from the National Book Council.

NON-FICTION *Professor David, the Life of Sir T. W. E. David*, London, Arnold, 1937; *Passages of Time: An Australian Woman 1890–1974*, St Lucia, UQP, 1975.

Davidson, Robyn (1950–)
Travel writer. Born in Queensland on a cattle station. Educated in Brisbane and studied biology at the University of Queensland before moving to Sydney where she studied music. Returned to Queensland for further studies before moving to Alice Springs, Central Australia. In 1977 made an extraordinary journey across the desert from Alice Springs to the coast of WA accompanied only by camels and her dog. *Tracks*, a compelling book, describes that journey and her preparations for it; it was translated into French 1982. Has also published articles and reviews in the *National Times* and the *Sydney Morning Herald* and is presently working on a second book.

NON-FICTION *Tracks*, London, Jonathon Cape, 1980.

Davis, Beatrice Deloitte (1909–)
Editor, publisher. Born in Bendigo, Victoria and educated at North Sydney Girls' High and the University of Sydney. Spent many years in the publishing world, was general editor at Angus & Robertson 1937–73 and, following that, editor at Thomas Nelson 1974–81. Was made MBE and AM 1981 for her services to Australian publishing, and in 1977 was awarded Bookman of the Year by the National Book Council.

EDITED *Coast to Coast*, Sydney, A & R, 1943; *Short Stories of Australia:*

The Moderns, Sydney, A & R, 1967; *Best Australian Short Stories* (with Douglas Stewart), Melbourne, Lloyd O'Neil, 1971; *The Illustrated Treasury of Australian Verse*, Melbourne, Nelson, 1974.

Davis, Norma L. (1905–1945)
Poet. Born in Tasmania and educated at state schools. Published her poetry in the *Bulletin* and the *Australian Woman's Mirror*. Her poems published during the war express some wartime feeling but are largely characterised by their fondness for and detail of nature. Douglas Stewart claimed her poems were 'the best nature poetry we have had', comparing her favourably to William Wordsworth. Published little due to her early death.

POETRY *Earth Cry*, Sydney, A & R, 1943; *I, the Thief*, Melbourne, Arura Writers, 1944.
SEE ALSO D. Stewart in *The Flesh and the Spirit* (A & R, 1948. Reprinted from the *Bulletin* 'Red Page') and J. K. Ewers in *Creative Writing in Australia* (Georgian House, 1962).

Deamer, Dulcie (1890–1972)
Novelist, poet, journalist, actor. Born Mary Elizabeth Kathleen Dulcie Deamer in Christchurch, New Zealand. Became an actor and toured with Hugh Ward's company. Was married to Albert Goldie who had been a manager at J. C. Williamson's. Travelled in Asia, Europe, and the USA before returning to Sydney where she began to write. The title story of *In the Beginning* was awarded a prize in a *Lone Hand* competition 1907. Was known as the 'Queen of Bohemia', having associations with the Lindsay literary and artistic circle, with Kings Cross bohemianism and with vaudeville and club entertainment. Her work was strongly influenced by her interest in the ancient world.

FICTION *In the Beginning: Six Studies of the Stone Age and Other Stories*, Melbourne & Sydney, Day, 1909; *The Suttee of Safa: A Hindoo Romance*, New York, Dillingham, 1913; *Revelation*, London, Unwin, 1921; *The Street of the Gazelle*, London, Unwin, 1922; *The Devil's Saint*, London, Unwin, 1924; *As it was in the Beginning* (illust. Norman Lindsay), Melbourne, Frank Wilmot, 1929; *Holiday*, Sydney, Frank Johnson, 1940.
POETRY *Messalina*, Sydney, Frank Johnson, 1932; *The Silver Branch*, Sydney, Swinbourne Press, 1948.
OTHER *Easter, a Morality Play* appeared in *Best Australian One-Act Plays* (A & R, 1937). Unpublished plays include: *That by Which Men Live* (1936) and *Victory* (1938).
MANUSCRIPTS NL, Canberra: Dulcie Deamer Unpublished Manuscripts MS 1539; ML, Sydney: Dulcie Deamer Papers ML DOC 2313 (papers also in the Frank Johnson Papers ML MSS 1214).

De Groen, Alma (1941–)
Playwright. Born Alma Mathers in New Zealand and came to Australia 1964, settling in Sydney. Married artist Geoffrey de Groen 1965, had one daughter, and later divorced. Began writing for the theatre in the late 1960s and most of her early plays were performed at the new Nimrod Theatre, Sydney. Has had plays produced throughout Australia, in London, and Canada. Also writes scripts for television, and received an AWGIE award 1985 for the best television adaptation.

DRAMA *Chidley*, in *Theatre Australia*, Vol. 1, No. 6, Jan-Feb 1977; *Going Home; The Joss Adams Show; Perfectly All Right*, Sydney, Currency, 1977; *Going Home; Vocations*, Sydney, Currency, 1983.
OTHERS Plays produced include: *The Sweat-Proof Boy* (Nimrod, 1972); *The After Life of Arthur Craven* (Sydney, Jane St, 1973); *Decade* (1980); *Man of Letters* (adapted from the book by Glen Tomasetti, q.v., ABC television, 1984) and *The Rivers of China* (Sydney Theatre Company, 1987).
MANUSCRIPTS Fryer Library, University of Queensland: unpublished Mss in the Hanger Collection.
SEE ALSO 'People are talking about . . .' in *Vogue Australia* (April, 1973) and D. Carroll in *Australian Contemporary Drama 1909–1982* (Peter Lang, 1985).

Derham, Enid (1882–1941)
Poet, academic. Born in Melbourne. Educated at the University of Melbourne graduating MA with first class honours. Later also studied at Oxford. Although a brilliant student, had a fairly unremarkable academic career, lecturing in English at the University of Melbourne and briefly holding the position of Acting Professor. Her poetry was strongly influenced by her classical studies, although she was one of the earliest Australian writers to appreciate the poetry of Emily Dickinson. Died unexpectedly of a cerebral haemorrhage and her second volume of poetry was published posthumously.

POETRY *The Mountain Road and Other Verses*, Melbourne, Osboldstone, 1912; *Poems*, Melbourne, MUP, 1958.
OTHER Edited (with A. Ellis) *Two Centuries: Selections from English Prose and Poetry of the 18th and 19th Centuries* (Melville & Mullen, 1904); *Empire: A Morality Play for Children* (Osboldstone, 1912).

Devanny, Jean (1894–1962)
Novelist. Born Jean Crook in New Zealand, the daughter of a miner. Married miner and unionist Hal Devanny at the age of 17. Had three children within as many years and published five books before coming to Sydney 1929 at the beginning of the Depression. Found work as a

general hand on a station in north-west NSW before returning to Sydney 1930 to support her family. Joined the CPA 1931 and worked unpaid for the party, at the same time writing to earn a living. Worked for the CPA for the rest of her life, making a stand for the rights of women and of writers within its ranks and at times suffering because of her convictions. Was briefly expelled in the 1940s and resigned 1950 over the lack of support for her novel *Cindie*. However her commitment to the communist cause was unequivocal and took first place before her writing. Some of her best work came out of her party work, notably *Sugar Heaven*, based upon her experience as an organiser for the North Queensland canecutters' strike 1935.

FICTION *The Butcher Shop*, London, Duckworth, 1926; *Lenore Divine*, London, Duckworth, 1926; *Old Savage and Other Stories*, London, Duckworth, 1927; *Dawn Beloved* London, Duckworth, 1928; *Riven*, London, Duckworth, 1929; *Bushman Burke*, London, Duckworth, 1930; *Devil Made Saint*, London, Duckworth, 1930; *Unchastened Youth*, New York, Macaulay, 1930; *All for Love*, New York, Macaulay, 1932; *Poor Swine*, London, Duckworth, 1932; *Out of Such Fires*, New York, Macaulay, 1934; *The Virtuous Courtesan*, New York, Macaulay, 1935; *The Ghost Wife*, London, Duckworth, 1935; *Sugar Heaven*, Sydney, Modern Publishing Co., 1936; *Paradise Flow*, London, Duckworth, 1938; *The Killing of Jacqueline Love*, Sydney, Frank Johnson, 1942; *Roll Back the Night*, London, Hale, 1945; *Cindie*, London, Hale, 1949.
NON-FICTION *Of Tropic Sea and Jungle*, Sydney, A & R, 1944; *Bird of Paradise*, Sydney, Frank Johnson, 1945; *Travels in North Queensland*, London, Jarrolds, 1951; *Point of Departure: The Autobiography of Jean Devanny* (ed. C. Ferrier), St Lucia, UQP, 1986.
MANUSCRIPTS James Cook University Library, Qld: Jean Devanny Papers (An extensive collection including unpublished novels, correspondence and autobiographical mss).
SEE ALSO C. Ferrier in *LiNQ*, Vol. 8, No. 3 (1980) and in *Gender Politics and Fiction* (ed. C. Ferrier, UQP, 1985).

Dick, Charlotte Isabel
Novelist. Born in Tasmania of an old pioneer family. Began writing for an income after the death of her husband and published stories and serials in Australian newspapers, writing as 'Isabel Dick'. *Wild Orchard* was based upon her family history, and her other works were also about Tasmania.

FICTION *The Veil of Discretion*, Melbourne, A. McCubbin, 1920; *Garden Peace and Christmas Tales*, Hobart, Monotone Printers, 1927; *Huon Belle*, London, Stockwell, 1930; *Wild Orchard: A Story of Early Tasmania*, New

York, Crowell, 1945; *Country Heart*, Sydney, Australasian Publ. Co., 1946.
POETRY *The Year's Happiness to You*, by C.I.D., Hobart, Monotone Printers, 1932.

Diesendorf, Margaret (1912–)
Poet, translator, editor. Born in Vienna, Austria and spent part of her childhood in Hungary. Had a distinguished school and university career, reading philosophy, philology, psychology and educational theory. Was awarded two French scholarships upon completion of her doctoral thesis 1936. However left Europe because of the political situation and arrived in Australia 1939. Taught French and German in schools, then worked as a translator for the Commonwealth Office of Education and for radio and later television. Worked for South Head Press 1964 and was associate editor of *Poetry Australia* 1967–81. Was winner of the Borestone Mountain Poetry Award 1974 and 1976. In 1984 was awarded Personality of the Year by *Personaggi Contemporanei* (Italy).

POETRY *Light*, Sydney, Edwards and Shaw, 1981.
EDITED *Poetry Magazine, No. 4/5* (with L. Dautheuil) Translations into French of 16 Australian Poets; *L'Enfant au Cacatoès*, by Rosemary Dobson (trans. with L. Dautheuil), Paris, Pierre Seghers, 1967; *New Poetry from Australia* (with S. Amanuddin), USA, Poetry Eastwest, 1973; *Australian Women Poets*, USA, Creative Moment, 1980.
OTHER Articles, reviews, etc have appeared in many journals including *Poetry Magazine, Poetry Australia, Arena, Journal of South Asian Literature* and *Southern Review*. Poems have been published in numerous magazines and journals and in the anthologies: *Best Poems of 1973* (Pacific Books, 1974); *Within the Hill* (ANU, 1975); *The Electrical Imagination* (Vancouver, 1975); *Best Poems of 1975* (Pacific Books, 1976); *Making Love* (Picador, 1978) and *Joseph's Coat* (Hale & Iremonger, 1985).

Dixson, Miriam (1930–)
Historian. Born in Melbourne. Educated at the University of Melbourne and at the Australian National University. Has taught history at primary and secondary levels and lectured in history at four universities, and is presently Associate Professor of History at the University of New England, Armidale, NSW. Her work includes reasearch into national identity with particular reference to the role of women and the influence of gender. In 1975 taught Australia's first tertiary courses on women in Australian history. Was founder of the Women's Caucus of the Australian Historical Association, is a member of the Federation of University Women, the WEL, and the Movement for the Ordination of Women in

Australia. Currently is employed upon a project entitled *Women and Identity: America and Australia from Colonial Times to the Present.*

NON-FICTION *The Real Matilda, Women and Identity in Australia 1788 to the Present*, Melbourne, Penguin, 1976; *Greater than Lenin? Lang and Labour 1916–1932*, Melbourne, Politics Monographs, 1976.
OTHER Has contributed chapters to several books including *Australian Society* (Longman Cheshire, 1977) and *Australian Women: New Feminist Perspectives* (OUP, 1976). Articles have appeared in various journals including *Historical Studies, Australia and New Zealand; Politics, Journal of the Australasian Political Studies Association*, and *Labour History*.

Dobson, Rosemary (1920–)
Poet. Born in Sydney. Educated at Frensham School, Mittagong, and later the University of Sydney but did not take a degree. Studied design with artist Thea Proctor and later worked as an art teacher. Joined publishers Angus & Robertson in the early 1940s and worked as an editor. Married A. T. Bolton and continued with freelance work related to poetry. Travelled in England and Europe 1966–71, developing the life-long interest in art seen in her poetry. Has received a number of distinguished awards including the *Sydney Morning Herald* Poetry Prize 1948 for *The Ship of Ice*, the Christopher Brennan Award from the FAW 1979, and the Victorian Premier's Award for poetry 1985. Her work appears in many anthologies, including almost every volume of the annual *Australian Poetry*, and has been translated into French and other languages.

POETRY *In a Convex Mirror*, Sydney, Dymocks, 1944; *The Ship of Ice*, Sydney, A & R, 1948; *Child with a Cockatoo*, Sydney, A & R, 1955; *Selected Poems*, Sydney, A & R, 1963; *Cock Crow*, Sydney, A & R, 1965; *L'Enfant au Cacatoès* (trans. M. Diesendorf & L. Dautheuil), Paris, Pierre Seghers, 1967; *Selected Poems*, Sydney, A & R, 1973; *Greek Coins: A Sequence of Poems*, Canberra, Brindabella Press, 1977; *Over the Frontier*, Sydney, A & R, 1978; *The Continuance of Poetry*, Canberra, Brindabella Press, 1981; *The Three Fates and Other Poems*, Sydney, Hale & Iremonger, 1984.
NON-FICTION *Focus on Ray Crooke*, St Lucia, UQP, 1971; *Moscow Trefoil* (trans. with D. Campbell and N. Staples), Canberra, ANU Press, 1975; *Seven Russian Poets* (trans. with D. Campbell), St Lucia, UQP, 1979.
OTHER Also edited: *Australian Poetry 1949–1950* (A & R, 1950); *Songs for all Seasons, 100 Poems for Young People* (A & R, 1967); *Australian Voices, Poetry and Prose of the 1970s* (ANU Press, 1975) and *Sisters Poets 1* (Sisters, 1979).
MANUSCRIPTS NL, Canberra: Rosemary Dobson Papers.
SEE ALSO J. F. Burrows in *Southerly*, Vol. 30, No. 3 (1970), J. McAuley

in *ALS*, Vol. 6, No. 1 (1973), R. S. Heales in *ALS*, Vol. 6, No. 3 (1974) and J. Tulip in *Southerly*, Vol. 45, No. 1 (1985).

Dolling, Alison, 'Mary Broughton' (1917–)
History writer, journalist. Born in Adelaide. Educated at private schools then studied music at the Elder Conservatorium. After studying American history and literature at three American universities, returned to Adelaide to complete an arts degree, majoring in classics. Also studied English language and literature at King's College, London. Taught English and Latin in independent schools in SA and NSW. Has tutored migrants in English and has lectured in Australian literature and history at a tertiary level. For nine years was editor of the women's pages of the Adelaide paper *The Chronicle*, contributing weekly articles and miscellaneous pieces.

NON-FICTION *Chronicle Cameos*, by Mary Broughton, Jamestown, Nadjuri, 1977; *The History of Marion on the Sturt*, Frenville, Peacock Publications, 1981.
OTHER Edited and wrote 1962–71 for *Opinion*, S.A. English Teachers' Association Journal; edited 1977–9 *Bulletin*, journal of the National Council of Women; currently preparing a book on South Australian women writers.

Donkin, Nance (1915–)
Children's author, journalist. Born in Maitland, NSW, and began her career as a journalist with the *Maitland Daily Mercury* and the *Newcastle Morning Herald*. Worked for many years freelancing for the ABC, both in radio and television. Is currently tutor with the Council for Adult Education, Melbourne. Was President, Children's Book Council, Victoria, for eight years, and twice judge for the Book of the Year Award. Received the AM in 1986 for services to children's literature and to adult education. Stories, articles, and reviews have been published in many Australian magazines.

FICTION *Araluen Adventures*, Melbourne, Cheshire, 1946; *No Medals For Meg*, Melbourne, Cheshire, 1947; *Julie Stands By*, Melbourne, Cheshire, 1948; *Blue Ribbon Beth*, Melbourne, OUP, 1957; *House by the Water*, Sydney, A & R, 1967; *Johnny Neptune*, Sydney, A & R, 1971; *A Friend of Petros*, London, Hamish Hamilton, 1974; *Patchwork Grandmother*, London, Hamish Hamilton, 1975; *Yellowgum Gil*, London, Hamish Hamilton, 1976; *A Handful of Ghosts*, London, Hodder & Stoughton, 1976; *The Best of the Bunch*, Sydney, Collins, 1978; *The Maidens of Pefka*, Sydney, Methuen, 1979; *Green Christmas*, London, Hamish Hamilton, 1979; *Nini*, Adelaide, Rigby, 1979; *Stranger and Friend*, Melbourne, Dove, 1983; *We of the Never-Never* (retold for children), London, Hutch-

inson, 1984; *Two at Sullivan Bay*, Kenthurst, NSW, Kangaroo Press, 1985; *Blackout*, London, Macmillan, 1986.
NON-FICTION *Sheep*, Melbourne, OUP, 1967; *Sugar*, Melbourne, OUP, 1967; *An Emancipist*, Melbourne, OUP, 1968; *A Currency Lass*, Melbourne, OUP, 1969; *An Orphan*, Melbourne, OUP, 1970; *Margaret Catchpole*, Sydney, Collins, 1974.

Dowling, Dorothea Helena
Poet, children's author. Born and educated in Sydney. With her sister Mavis Dowling published several books for children. They both contributed articles, poems and short stories to various Australian journals and periodicals.

POETRY *When I am Free*, Sydney, G. B. Philip, 1940; *Proud Heritage*, Sydney, Streatfield Press, 1947; *The Open Road* (with M. Dowling), Adelaide, Jindyworobak, 1945; *Twenty-one Poems*, Sydney, Brogg & Sons, 1954; *Selected Poems* (with M. Dowling), Hull, Guild Press, 1958; *More Poems* (with M. Dowling), Leicester, Leslie Weston, 1961; *Candles are for Christmas*, Driffield, Yorkshire, Poetry Guild, 1963; *Bunny Slippers and Other Poems*, Sydney, Highway Press, 1968; *Poems for Recitation*, Sydney, the author, 1972; *Let's Recite*, Sydney, the author, 1975; *My Holiday Book*, Sydney, the author, 1975; *Here and There*, Sydney, the author, 1978.

Downes, Marion Grace
Novelist, poet. Born in Australia. Was secretary to an Australian minister whose life she described in *Swayed by the Storm*. Wrote poems celebrating the Australian landscape and life, as well as poems of a spiritual nature, and was published in several journals both here and overseas. Her second volume of poetry was published posthumously.

FICTION *Swayed by the Storm: A Story of Australia Today*, London, Drane; Melbourne, Lothian, 1911; *A Brave Bush Girl*, London, Bateman, 1912; *Flower o' the Bush*, London, Ward Lock, 1914; *In the Track of the Sunset: An Australian Story for Girls*, Melbourne, Modern Printing Co., 1919.
POETRY *Wayside Songs for Women*, Melbourne, A. McCubbin, 1921; *Wayside Songs*, London, Simpkin Marshall, 1927.

Dowrick, Stephanie (1947–)
Novelist, non-fiction writer. Born in Wellington, New Zealand and left her native land as a teenager to work in London. Followed a successful career in publishing and editing during which time she was managing editor of the New English Library and Triad Paperbacks. In 1977 founded the London feminist publishing house The Women's Press. For her work in feminist publishing and for her contribution to the 'positive

image of women' she received the inaugural Pandora Award 1982. Afterwards returned to Sydney where she published her first novel. Combines her job as a mother with freelance editing and writing reviews and articles. Currently is working on a non-fiction book entitled *Intimacy and Silence.*

FICTION *Running Backwards Over Sand*, Melbourne, Viking, 1985.
NON-FICTION *Land of Zeus*, London, New English Library, 1974; *Greek Island Mythology*, New York, Doubleday, 1974; *Classic Tales of Horror* (ed.) London, Constable, 1976; *Why Children?* (ed. with Sibyl Grundberg) London, The Women's Press, 1980; *The Handbook of Non-Sexist Writing* by Casey Miller & Kate Swift (revised), London, The Women's Press, 1981.

Dowse, Sara (1938–)
Novelist, journalist. Born in Chicago, USA. Lived in New York and Los Angeles before coming to Sydney 1958. Completed a BA at the University of Sydney and moved to Canberra 1968 to work in the public service. Became inaugural head of the Women's Affairs Unit of the Department of Prime Minister and Cabinet 1974. Since resigning 1977 has worked as a freelance writer, editor, journalist, lecturer and reviewer, concentrating upon fiction writing in recent years. Was awarded the AIPS/APSA Women in Politics Prize 1982. *West Block* was adapted for ABC television 1987.

FICTION *West Block*, Melbourne, Penguin, 1983; *Silver City*, Melbourne, Penguin, 1984.
OTHER Stories have appeared in *Muse* (1981, 1982) and *POL* (1980). Poems have appeared in *Canberra Poetry, Programme* and *Vashti*. Has contributed articles and chapters on a number of topics related to women's welfare to works such as *Worth Her Salt: Women at Work in Australia* (Hale & Iremonger, 1982); *Australian Quarterly* (Summer, 1982); *Leaving School: It's Harder for Girls* (YWCA, 1983); *Women, Social Welfare and the State* (Allen & Unwin, 1983) and *Sisterhood is Global* (1984). Reviews have appeared in the *National Times*, the *Canberra Times*, *ABR*, the *Sydney Morning Herald*, the *Age* and *Island*.
MANUSCRIPTS NL, Canberra: Sara Dowse Mss & Papers.
SEE ALSO J. Ellison (interview) in *Rooms of their Own* (Penguin, 1986).

Drake-Brockman, Henrietta (1902–1968)
Playwright, novelist, historian. Born in Perth, the daughter of Roberta Jull, doctor and campaigner for women's health. Educated at Frensham, NSW, but returned to WA where she lived almost all her life. Married Major Geoffrey Drake-Brockman, also from one of Perth's established families. Spent many years travelling in the outback of WA where she

gained material for her fiction and drama. Wrote as 'Henry Drake' for the *West Australian* and was active in the WA branch of the FAW. *Men Without Wives* won the drama section of the NSW sesquicentenary literary competition 1938.

DRAMA *The Man from the Bush*, in *Eight Plays by Australians*, Melbourne, Dramatists' Club, 1934; *Dampier's Ghost*, in *Best Australian One Act Plays*, Sydney, A & R, 1937; *Men Without Wives: A North Australian Play in 3 Acts*, Perth, Paterson's Printing Press, 1938; *The Lion Tamer: A Comedy in 1 Act*, Sydney, A & R, 1948; *Men Without Wives and Other Plays*, Sydney, A & R, 1955.

FICTION *Blue North*, Sydney, Endeavour Press, 1934; *Sheba Lane*, Sydney, A & R, 1936; *Younger Sons*, Sydney, A & R, 1937; *The Fatal Days*, Sydney, A & R, 1947; *Sydney or the Bush*, Sydney, A & R, 1948; *The Wicked and the Fair*, Sydney, A & R, 1957.

NON-FICTION *Education for Life*, Perth, FAW, 1941; *On the North-west Skyline*, Perth, Paterson's Printing Press, 1947; *Voyage to Disaster, the Life of Francis Pelsaert*, Sydney, A & R, 1963; *Katharine Susannah Prichard*, Melbourne, OUP, 1967.

OTHER Also edited: *Australian Short Stories* (with W. Murdoch, 1951); *Australian Legendary Tales*, by K. Langloh Parker (A & R, 1953); *Coast to Coast* (A & R, 1956) and *West Coast Stories* (A & R, 1959).

MANUSCRIPTS Battye Library, Perth: Henrietta Drake-Brockman Papers Acc. Nos. 1300A & 1311A.

SEE ALSO G. Drake-Brockman, *The Turning Wheel* (1960), J. Hetherington in *Forty Two Faces* (F. W. Cheshire, 1963) and A. Hasluck in *Of Ladies Dead* (A & R, 1970).

Dreyer, Marien (1911–1980)

Playwright, journalist. Born in Victoria and later lived in King's Cross, Sydney. Wanted to become an actor but after losing a leg turned to secretarial work followed by journalism in the 1940s. Published articles in newspapers and magazines such as *Voice*, and had a regular column in *New Idea*. Had her first short story published at the age of 16 and continued to write stories as well as drama, especially for radio. Won several awards for her plays including a Playwright's Advisory Board Award for *Wish No More* 1960 and a Journalists' Club Award for *Bandicoot on a Burnt Ridge* 1965. Few of her plays, however, were published. Tied for a Walkley Award for journalism 1959.

DRAMA *The Hard Way Back in*, *A.M.* August 1953.

OTHER Unpublished plays include: *Bandicoot on a Burnt Ridge*, *Coffee for Sixpence*, *Don't Forget Barney*, *Hangover*, *No Need for Tinkers*, *Return of the Tinker*, *A Touch of the Dark*, *Wish No More*, *Charles was There*, *The Power*

of a Woman and *Too of a Kind.* Short stories appeared in *The Man Storyteller* (1945) and *Summer's Tales* I (1964).
MANUSCRIPTS Some playscripts held in the Campbell Howard Collection, the University of New England.
SEE ALSO J.C. Kelly in *Australian Quarterly*, Vol. 32, No. 1 (1960).

Dumas, Grace, 'Louise'
Short story writer. Born in Australia. Published a small volume of sketches and poems largely recounting sad tales of individuals struggling in Australian life, but meant to convey both the 'sunshine' and the 'showers' of life.

FICTION *Sunshine and Showers:* Australian Sketches, Melbourne, Cameron Laing, 1882.

Duncan, Catherine (1915–)
Playwright. Born in Tasmnia. During the 1930s and 1940s was a popular radio and stage actor before taking up writing. Also worked as a film-maker and joined the Australian National Film Board 1946. Edited the Derwent Series of One-Act Plays for the Tasmanian Adult Education Board 1958. Wrote both for stage and radio and several of her plays won awards; *The Sword Sung* won the New Theatre League Competition 1937, *Path of the Eagle* an ABC award 1943 and *Sons of the Morning* (based upon an original radio play of the same name about the war) the Playwrights' Advisory Board Competition 1945.
DRAMA *Sons of the Morning, A Verse Play in Three Acts*, Sydney, Mulga Publs, 1946; *Path of the Eagle*, in *Australian Radio Plays*, Sydney, A & R, 1946; *Some New Moon*, Hobart, Tasmanian Adult Education Board, 1958.
OTHER Plays produced include: *The Sword Sung* (1937) and *We the Living.*
SEE ALSO A. Ashbolt in *Focus*, Vol. 1, No. 11 (1946–7).

Durack, Mary, Dame (1913–)
Children's author, historian, novelist. Born in Adelaide, a member of the pioneering Durack family who settled in the north-west of WA. Educated at Loreto Convent, Perth. Afterwards lived and worked on the family station in the Kimberleys, returning to Perth about 1937. Began working as a journalist for WA Newspapers Ltd, and conducted a regular column for country women. Wrote some fiction for adults, notably *Keep Him My Country* 1955, but became more interested in her family's history in works such as *Kings in Grass Castles* and *Sons in the Saddle.* Most of her children's books were produced in collaboration with her sister, artist Elizabeth Durack. Was created OBE 1966, DBE 1978, and awarded an honorary DLitt from the University of WA 1978.

FICTION *Chunuma*, Sydney Bulletin-Endeavour Press, 1936; *Son of Djaro*, Perth, R. S. Sampson, 1938; *The Way of the Whirlwind*, Sydney, Consolidated Press, 1941; *Piccaninnies*, Sydney, Offsett Press, 1943; *The Magic Trumpet*, Sydney, Cassell, 1944; *Keep Him My Country*, London, Constable, 1955; *Kookanoo and Kangaroo*, Adelaide, Rigby, 1963; *To Ride a Fine Horse*, Melbourne, Macmillan, 1963; *Tjakamurra, Boy Between Two Worlds* Perth, Vanguard Service Printing Co., 1977.
NON-FICTION *All-About, the Story of a Black Communtiy of Argyle Station, Kimberley*, Sydney, Bulletin-Endeavour Press, 1935; *Time and Tide*, Perth, Imperial Printing Co., 1946; *Child Artists of the Australian Bush* (with F. Rutter), London, Harrap, 1952; *Kings in Grass Castles*, London, Constable, 1959; *The Courteous Savage: Yagan of the Swan River*, Edinburgh, Nelson, 1964; *A Pastoral Emigrant*, Melbourne, OUP, 1964; *The Rock and the Sand*, London, Constable, 1969; *The End of Dreaming* (with I. Drysdale), Adelaide, Rigby, 1974; *Swan River Saga* (with N. Pannell), Perth, Vanguard Service Printing Co, 1975; *To be Heirs Forever*, London, Constable, 1975; *Sons in the Saddle*, London, Constable, 1983.
OTHER Also published the opera libretto *Dalgerie* (music by James Penberthy, 1966), a play, *The Ship of Dreams* (1968) and *The Aborigines in Australian Literature* (Perth, WAIT, 1978) and *A Legacy of Love* (with B. Mulholland, Artlook Books, 1981).
SEE ALSO J. Hetherington in *Forty Two Faces* (F. W. Cheshire, 1963) and B. E. Richardson in *Westerly* No. 4 (Dec. 1971).

Dwyer, Vera
Novelist. Born in Tasmania and worked in journalism, contributing to the children's pages of newspapers. Wrote her first book under the encouragement of Ethel Turner (q.v.) when only in her teens. Spent some years travelling abroad, returning to Sydney 1933. Was married to Captain Warwick Coldham-Fussell, whose diaries she used for *The Banished Lovers*.

FICTION *With Beating Wings: An Australian Story*, London, Ward Lock, 1913; *Mona's Mystery Man*, London, Ward Lock, 1914; *A War of Girls*, London, Ward Lock, 1915; *Conquering Hal*, London, Ward Lock, 1916; *The Kayles of Bushy Lodge, An Australian Story*, London, OUP, 1922; *The Marches Disappear*, New York, Robert McBride, 1929; *In Pursuit of Patrick*, Sydney, Endeavour Press, 1933; *House of Conflict*, Sydney, A & R, 1937; *The Stolen Ghost*, London, Quality Press, 1943; *The Banished Lovers*, Sydney, Peter Huston, 1947.
MANUSCRIPTS NL, Canberra: Papers MS 3949 (Misc. short stories).

E

Elder, Anne (1918–1976)
Poet. Born in Auckland, New Zealand and came to Australia as a child. Became a ballet dancer and worked with the Borovansky Ballet Company. Although widely represented in journals and magazines, only published two volumes of poetry, the second posthumously; it was commended in the National Book Council awards 1977. The Anne Elder Trust Fund was established in her honour 1977 and is annually awarded for the first best book of poetry published by an Australian writer.

POETRY *For the Record*, Melbourne, Hawthorn Press, 1972; *Crazy Woman and Other Poems*, Sydney, A & R, 1976.
OTHER Short story, *The Problem* appeared in *Meanjin*, Vol. 38, No. 3 (1979).

Eldershaw, Flora (1897–1956)
Novelist, historian. Born in Sydney and brought up in the NSW country. Educated at the University of Sydney graduating 1918 and became a teacher. Was senior mistress at the Presbyterian Ladies' College, Croydon, before moving to Canberra to take up a government position 1941. Transferred to Melbourne 1943, working for the Department of Labour and National Service before branching out into private practice in industrial consultancy. Her collaboration with Marjorie Barnard (q.v.), whom she met while at university, ended after she left Sydney, but she continued to maintain a high literary profile. Was the first woman president of the FAW 1935, and an active member of the CLF especially during the 1940s.

NON-FICTION *Contemporary Australian Women Writers*, Sydney, Australasian Medical Publ. Co., 1931; *Australian Literary Society Medallists*, Sydney, Australasian Medical Publ. Co., 1935; *Australian Writers' Annual* (ed.), FAW, 1936; *The Peaceful Army: A Memorial to the Pioneer Women of Australia 1788–1938* (ed.) Sydney, Australian 150th Anniversary Celebration Women's Executive Committee, 1938.

'Eldershaw, M. Barnard' *See also:* **Barnard, Marjorie and Eldershaw, Flora**
Novelists, historians. Pseudonym of writers Marjorie Barnard and Flora Eldershaw, a remarkable literary collaboration. Began writing together at the instigation of the *Bulletin* prize 1928 for an Australian novel which their first book, *A House is Built*, shared with Katharine Susannah Prichard's (q.v.) *Coonardoo*. The partnership extended beyond fiction to

history, criticism and biography. After the discouraging reception of the highly original, futuristic *Tomorrow and Tomorrow* 1947, they abandoned fiction as a team. The collaboration ended after Flora Eldershaw left Sydney for good. The first uncensored edition of *Tomorrow and Tomorrow and Tomorrow* (also its full title) was published by Virago 1983.

FICTION *A House is Built*, London, Harrap, 1929; *Green Memory*, London, Harrap, 1931; *The Glasshouse*, London, Harrap, 1936; *Plaque with Laurel*, London, Harrap, 1937; *Tomorrow and Tomorrow*, Melbourne, Georgian House, 1947.
NON-FICTION *Essays in Australian Fiction*, Melbourne, MUP, 1938; *Phillip of Australia: An Account of the Settlement of Sydney Cove 1788–1792*, London, Harrap, 1938; *The Life and Times of Captain John Piper*, Sydney, Limited Editions, 1939; *My Australia*, London, Jarrolds, 1939.
OTHER Also published a play, *The Watch on the Headland*, in *Australian Radio Plays* (A & R, 1946).
SEE ALSO R. Burns in *Meanjin*, Vol. 29, No. 3 (1970), L. E. Rorabacher, *Marjorie Barnard and M. Barnard Eldershaw* (Twayne, 1973) and J. Roe in *Meanjin*, Vol. 43, No. 2 (1984).

Eldridge, Marian (1936–)
Short story writer. Born in Victoria where she grew up on a farm. Educated by correspondence and later at the University of Melbourne. Lives and works in Canberra where she reviews for the *Canberra Times*. Has published stories in many magazines and anthologies and has won a number of literary competitions.
FICTION *Walking the Dog*, St Lucia, UQP, 1984.
OTHER Stories have also appeared in *Coast to Coast* (1968), *Westerly* (1968, 1971, 1976), *Festival* (1974) and *Australian Voices* (1975).

Ercole, Velia, 'Margaret Gregory' (1903–1978)
Novelist. Born in White Cliffs, NSW, into an Italian family. Brought up in Grenfell, where her father was a doctor, and educated at the Dominican Convent, Moss Vale. Worked as a journalist for the *Sunday Sun*. Married Eric Gregory whose last name she adopted as her pseudonym, and travelled in France, finally settling in England where she lived ever since. All but the first two of her novels were published under her pseudonym; these two also remain her best. *No Escape* won the *Bulletin* novel competition 1932.

FICTION *No Escape*, London, T. Butterworth, 1932; *Dark Windows*, London, T. Butterworth, 1934; *Marriage Made on Earth*, London, Hutchinson, 1939; *Marriage by Ordeal*, London, Hutchinson, 1941; *This Life to Live*, London, Hutchinson, 1946; *Summer Tempest*, London, Hutchinson, 1947; *Interference*, London, Hutchinson, 1949; *Winds of Autumn*, London,

Hutchinson, 1950; *At the Hotel Revera*, London, Hutchinson, 1952; *Two Summers*, London, Hutchinson, 1954.

Evans, Matilda Jane, 'Maud Jeanne Franc' (1827–1886)
Novelist. Born Matilda Jane Congreve in Surrey, England and came to Australia with her family 1849. Settled in South Australia where, writing always under a combination of the names Maud Jeanne Franc, she was to become South Australia's second woman novelist. Worked as a governess and was headmistress of the girls' school Angaston House 1868 before becoming a deacon in the Baptist church. Was married to Baptist minister, the Reverend E. Evans. Most of her writing was designed for young people. It conveyed the message of the gospels combined with Baptist morality and was very popular. Several novels ran into other editions and a collected edition of her complete works was reprinted in 13 volumes as *Australian Tales* 1888.

FICTION *Maria, or The Light of Some One's Home: A Tale of Australian Bush Life*, London, Sampson Low, 1861; *Vermont Vale, or Home Pictures in Australia*, London, Sampson Low, 1861; *Emily's Choice: An Australian Tale*, London, Sampson Low, 1867; *Minnie's Mission: An Australian Temperence Tale*, London, Sampson Low, 1869; *Golden Gifts: An Australian Tale*, SA, Scandrett & Elliot, 1889; *Silken Cords and Iron Fetters*, SA, Whaley, Austin, 1870; *John's Wife: A Story of Life in South Australia*, London, Sampson Low, 1874; *Hall's Vineyard*, London, Sampson Low, 1875; *Little Mercy, or For Better, For Worse*, London, Sampson Low, 1877; *Beatrice Melton's Discipline*, London, Sampson Low, 1880; *Christmas Bells* (with W. J. Evans), Adelaide, G. Collis, 1882; *No Longer a Child*, Adelaide, G. Collis, 1882; *Two Sides to Every Question: From a South Australian Standpoint*, Adelaide, G. Collis, 1883; *Into the Light*, Adelaide, G. Collis, 1885; *Master of Ralston*, Adelaide, G. Collis, 1885; *Rhymes Without Reason* (ed. W. J. Evans), Adelaide, G. Collis, 1898.

F

Fahey, Diane (1945–)
Poet, short story writer. Born and educated in Melbourne, graduating with an MA in literature. Is both a writer and a teacher, and her work has appeared in many magazines in Australia and overseas. Her poems have attracted various awards and commendations including the John Shaw Neilson Poetry Prize 1976 (second prize), the McGregor Poetry Award 1978 and the Mattara Poetry Prize 1985. In Ireland she won third prize in the Writers' Week Poetry Competition 1982.

POETRY *Voices from the Honeycomb*, Brisbane, Jacaranda, 1987.
OTHER Poems have appeared in the following journals: *Meanjin, Southerly, Westerly, Island, Helix, Aspect, Patterns, LiNQ, Southern Review*, and the *Age*. In England has been published in: *Other Poetry*, *Resurgence, Outposts, The Green Book, Ambit* and *Writing Women*, in Ireland in *Cyphers*, and in Denmark in *Kunapipi*. Short stories have also appeared in *Australian Short Stories* and the *South East Arts Review*.

Falkiner, Suzanne (1952–)
Fiction, non-fiction writer. Born in Sydney and grew up in the NSW country. Educated at the University of NSW graduating BA 1974. Afterwards spent three years travelling in Asia, Europe and South America. Returned to Australia 1977 and has worked both full-time and freelance in writing, editing and publishing. In 1980 started the publishing imprint Valadon Publishing, producing small editions of special-interest books.

FICTION *Rain in the Distance*, Melbourne, Penguin, 1986.
NON-FICTION *Australian Aborigines, Shadows in a Landscape* (with L. le Guay), Sydney, Globe, 1979; *Haddon Rig, the First Hundred Years*, Sydney, Valadon, 1980; *Australians Today* (with L. Graham), Sydney, Allen & Unwin, 1984.
OTHER Edited *Room to Move, the Redress Press Anthology of Women's Short Stories* (Redress/Unwin, 1985). Published a short story in *Home and Away* (ed. R. Cresswell, Penguin, 1986).

'Fane, Margaret' *See:* **Osborn, Beatrice**

Farmer, Beverley (1941–)
Short story writer. Born in Melbourne and educated at MacRobertson Girls' High and the University of Melbourne. Has worked in a variety of jobs including waitressing and secondary school teaching. Lived in Greece for three years where she taught English and was a partner in a

restaurant. Her stories have been widely published and have attracted several awards including first prize in the *Canberra Times* National Short Story Award 1980 and the NSW Premier's Award for Fiction 1984 for the collection, *Milk.* Was writer-in-residence at the University of Tasmania 1985. Now writes full-time.

FICTION *Alone*, Melbourne, Sisters, 1980; *Milk*, Melbourne, McPhee Gribble/Penguin, 1983; *Home Time*, Melbourne, McPhee Gribble/Penguin, 1985.
SEE ALSO J. Ellison (interview) in *Rooms of Their Own*, (Penguin, 1986).

Faust, Beatrice (1939–)
Non-fiction writer. Born in Melbourne; her mother died in childbirth and her difficult childhood was compounded by illness. Educated at various schools and the University of Melbourne graduating MA 1965. Initially qualified as a teacher, and taught while studying part-time. Married Clive Faust 1963; later divorced. Has worked as a freelance writer and journalist and been especially active in the women's movement. Was a founder of WEL 1972 and one of the first women to campaign for abortion law reform, sex education, and civil liberties. Remarried 1970 and lived in London 1978–80. In 1986 was Battye Lecturer at the University of WA.

NON-FICTION *Women, Sex and Pornography*, London, Melbourne House, 1981; *Natural Childbirth*, Adelaide, Rigby, 1982.
OTHER Has contributed regularly to the *Age* since 1975 and to other papers such as *Nation Review, Penthouse, ABR* and the *Sydney Morning Herald;* has contributed chapters to many publications including *Women in Australia* (Nelson, 1969), *Republic Australia* (Sun Books, 1977), *Popular Culture in Australia* (Penguin, 1977), *The Half-Open Door* (Hale & Iremonger, 1982) and *The Betrayal of Youth* (London, 1986).

Filson, Minnie Agnes, 'Ricketty Kate' (1898–1971)
Poet. Born in Wyalong, NSW. Her pseudonym referred self-critically but good-humouredly to a paralysing illness which forced her to dictate all her poetry. A religious person, she worked for the *Church Standard* for some years. However her poetry expresses less orthodox, more spiritualistic attitudes to life, especially the natural world.

POETRY *Rhymes and Whimsies*, Sydney, Lawson & Bray, 193–?; *Out of the Dust*, Sydney, Lawson & Bray, 1939; *Bralgah: A Legend*, Adelaide, Jindyworobak Publs., 1944.
MANUSCRIPTS La Trobe Library, Melbourne: Minne Agnes Filson Letters MS 6244.
SEE ALSO R. Wilson in *Southerly*, Vol. 11, No. 3 (1950).

Finnin, Mary (1906–)
Poet. Born in Geelong, Victoria and educated at the University of Melbourne. Trained as an artist and art teacher and taught at the Church of England Boys' Grammar School in Geelong. Also exhibited her paintings and has been an art critic. Her poetry includes comments upon contemporary events such as WWII, as well as reflecting interest in her native Victorian landscape and history.

POETRY *A Beggar's Opera*, Melbourne, W. A. Hamer, 1938; *Look Down, Olympians*, Melbourne, W. A. Hamer, 1939; *Royal*, Melbourne, W. A. Hamer, 1941; *The Book of Bauble* (children's), Melbourne, W. A. Hamer, 1945; *Alms for Oblivion*, Melbourne, W. A. Hamer, 1947; *The Shield of Place*, Sydney, A & R, 1957; *Off Shears 1958–1978*, Melbourne, Hawthorn Press, 1979.
SEE ALSO M. Haley in the *Advocate* (Feb. 27, 1958).

'Firenze' *See:* **Hayward, Florence**

Fisher, Lala (1872–1929)
Poet, editor. Born Mary Lucy Fisher in Rockhampton, Queensland and became a journalist before going to London 1897. Here she published her poetry and the expatriate anthology *By Creek and Gully*, which included such writers as Hume Nisbet, Harriet Martin, Rosa Praed (q.q.v.) and Louis Becke. Returned to Australia 1901 and worked for *Steele Rudd's Magazine* and *Theatre Magazine*, which she then bought and edited herself. Her advanced social views are expressed in some of her best poems.

POETRY *A Twilight Teaching and Other Poems*, London, Unwin, 1898; *Grass Flowering*, Sydney, Caxton Printing Works, 1915; *Earth Spiritual*, Sydney, Caxton Printing Works, 1918.
OTHER Edited: *By Creek and Gully, Stories and Sketches Mostly of Bush Life, Told in Prose and Rhyme, by Australian Writers in England* (London, Unwin, 1899); *Queensland Gems* (reprinted from *Steele Rudd's Magazine*, Brisbane, Powell & Co., 1906).

Fitzpatrick, Kathleen (1905–)
Historian, biographer, critic. Born in Victoria; educated in Melbourne and at Oxford University. Taught history at the University of Melbourne 1932–62 and was Associate Professor in the history department there. *Solid Bluestone Foundations* is an autobiographical account of her childhood and education.

NON-FICTION *Sir John Franklin in Tasmania 1837–1843*, Melbourne, MUP, 1949; *Martin Boyd and the Complex Fate of the Australian Novelist*,

Canberra, C.U. College, 1953; *Australian Explorers* (ed), London, OUP, 1958; *Martin Boyd*, Melbourne, OUP, 1963; *PLC Melbourne, the First Century 1875–1975*, Melbourne, PLC, 1975; *Solid Bluestone Foundations and Other Memories of a Melbourne Girlhood 1908–1923*, Melbourne, Macmillan, 1983.

Fletcher, Jane Ada (c. 1871–1956)
Nature writer, children's author. Born at Penshurst, Victoria and became a teacher in the Education Department of Tasmania. Was also a naturalist and ornithologist and a member of the Royal Australian Ornithologists' Union.

NON-FICTION *Nature and Adventure, for Boys and Girls*, London, Macmillan, 1916; *A Brochure of Nature Study*, 1933.
FICTION *Stories from Nature* (illust.), London, Macmillan, 1915.
OTHER Contributed to the *Fernland Story Book* (ed. Donald Barr, 1922). Also wrote a series of small booklets on Tasmanian flora and history for children.
MANUSCRIPTS John Oxley Library, Brisbane: Jane Ada Fletcher Literary MSS OM 67–2.

Foott, Bethia (Grace Gwendoline Bethia)
Non-fiction, fiction writer. Born in Sydney, the daughter of Ethel Anderson (q.v.). Wrote a fictionalised account of her great-great-grand-mother Leonora Bridgman who came to Australia in the 1830s. Also wrote the story of Australia's first political dismissal, and a description of her encounters with the American Army during WWII.

FICTION *Leonora, an Indomitable Woman*, Sydney, Currawong, 1958.
NON-FICTION *We Drove the Americans* (with M. Mann), Sydney, A & R, 1944; *Dismissal of a Premier, the Philip Game Papers*, Sydney, Morgan Publs, 1968.

Foott, Mrs James
Non-fiction writer. Born in Scotland. Emigrated to Melbourne with her husband and lived there some time before departing for the bush in 1860. Lived on the banks of the Darling River, and published an account of her life there.

NON-FICTION *Sketches of Life in the Bush, or Ten Years in the Interior*, Sydney, Gibbs, Shallard & Co., 1873.

Foott, Mary Hannay (1846–1918)
Poet, editor. Born Mary Hannay Black in Glasgow, Scotland of a literary family on her mother's side. Came to Australia 1853 and was educated in

Melbourne, attending the National Gallery Art School. Married Thomas Wade Foott 1874 and went to live on his station on the Paroo River, Queensland, remaining there until his death 1884. Afterwards lived in Brisbane where she worked as a journalist, becoming literary editor of the *Queenslander* 1887, a position she held for nearly 10 years before retiring to Bundaberg where she died. Is best remembered for the poem, *Where the Pelican Builds*.

POETRY *Where the Pelican Builds and Other Poems*, Brisbane, Gordon & Gotch, 1885; *Morna Lee and Other Poems*, London, Gordon & Gotch, 1890.
SEE ALSO H. A. Kellow, in *Queensland Poets* (Harrap, 1930, ch. 5).
MANUSCRIPTS John Oxley Library, Brisbane: First edition of *Where the Pelican Builds*, etc and notes.

Forrest, Mabel (1872–1935)
Novelist, poet. Born Helena Mabel Checkley Mills in the Darling Downs region of Queensland. Wrote popular poetry and fiction characterised by conventional romance and sentiment; set many of her works in rural Queensland. First published at the age of 10, and published poems and stories in the *Bulletin* and the *Australasian*. The best of her work is perhaps to be seen in *The Wild Moth* 1924.

FICTION *The Rose of Forgiveness and Other Stories*, Brisbane, W. Brooks, 1904; *A Bachelor's Wife*, Sydney, Bookstall, 1914; *The Wild Moth*, London, Cassell, 1924; *The Luck Bringer*, London, Hutchinson, 1925; *Gaming Gods*, London, Hutchinson, 1926; *Hibiscus Heart*, London, Hutchinson, 1927; *Reaping Roses*, London, Hutchinson, 1928; *White Witches*, London, Hutchinson, 1929.
POETRY *Alpha Centauri*, Melbourne, Lothian, 1909; *The Green Harper* (prose & verse), Brisbane, Gordon & Gotch, 1915; *Streets and Gardens*, Brisbane, Gordon & Gotch, 1922; *Poems*, Sydney, Cornstalk, 1927.

Forshaw, Thelma (1923–)
Short story writer, reviewer. Born in Sydney; educated at convent and state schools and at Sydney Teachers' College. Since WWII (when she served in the WAAAF) has worked in advertising, and as a freelance reviewer for such publications as the *Age*, the *Australian*, the *Bulletin* and the *Sydney Morning Herald. An Affair of Clowns* collects stories published in various journals over some years, the best of which are those based upon the members of her mother's family.

FICTION *An Affair of Clowns*, Sydney, A & R, 1967.

Fortune, Mrs Mary, 'Waif Wander', 'W.W.'
Story writer. The first woman writer of detective fiction in Australia. Was praised by Henry Mitchell (see below) for her outstanding originality and for her 'unequalled' status as a fiction writer of Australia; unfortunately his article did not reveal details of her life. *The Detectives' Album*, the first book of detective stories published in Australia, is six stories originally published in the *Australian Journal.*

FICTION *The Detectives' Album*, by W. W., Melbourne, Clarson Massina, 1871; *Navvie's Tales: Retold by the Boss*, in the *Australian Journal* (1874–5); *The Secrets of Balbrooke*, in the *Australian Journal* (1866?); *Twenty-six Years Ago, or the Diggings from '55* in the *Australian Journal* (1882–3); *The Moffat Mystery*, in *Town and Country Journal* (Nov. 5–19, 1887); *'Bride' of the Mountain*, in *Town and Country Journal* (Nov.-Dec. 1887); *A Sister of the King's Guild* (no imprint, n.d.); *A Memory of a White Dove* (no imprint, n.d.).
OTHER Short stories were published in the *Australian Journal* (1865 to 1920), the *Sydney Mail* (May 1881) and the *Illustrated Australian Annual for Christmas and New Year's Day* (ed. W. H. Williams 1869–68)
SEE ALSO H. W. Mitchell in the *Australian Journal*, Vol. 15, May 1880 (pp. 487–8).

Foster, Lynn (1913–)
Playwright, novelist. Born in Sydney and wrote for radio during the 1930s and 1940s in Sydney. Also lived and worked in England writing for radio and television. She shared the Playwrights' Advisory Board Prize 1946 for *And the Moon Will Shine; The Exiles* is based upon her television play cycle of the same name.

DRAMA *There is no Armour: A Play in Three Acts*, Sydney, Mulga Publs, 1945.
FICTION *The Exiles*, London, Hodder & Stoughton, 1960; *Blow the Wind Southerly*, London, Robert Hale, 1969.
OTHER Plays produced include *And the Moon Will Shine* (1946).
SEE ALSO A. Ashbolt in *Focus*, Vol. 1, No. 2 (1946–7).

'Franc, Maud Jeanne' *See:* **Evans, Matilda Jane**

Franklin, Miles, 'Brent of Bin Bin' (1879–1954)
Novelist, journalist. Born Stella Maria Sarah Miles Franklin near Tumut, NSW, and grew up at Brindabella in the Monaro region, and in the Goulburn district of NSW. Became well known for *My Brilliant Career* 1901, which broke new ground in Australian fiction but which provoked an ambivalent response both in its critics and author. Lived and worked in Sydney after its publication, working as a journalist, establishing literary

contacts, and beginning an involvement with the feminist cause. Travelled to the USA 1905 where she lived 9 years working for the women's labour movement and editing the magazine *Life and Labour*. Also travelled to England and worked as a volunteer during WWI in England and Macedonia. Remained abroad until 1927 and returned permanently to Australia 1932. Six of her novels were published under the pseudonym 'Brent of Bin Bin'. Was awarded the S.H. Prior Memorial Prize 1936 for *All that Swagger*, and again in 1939, with Kate Baker, for the then unpublished biography of Joseph Furphy. In 1948 established the annual Miles Franklin awards for Australian fiction from her family estate. Some of her work was published posthumously and her extensive manuscript collection includes at least 20 other unpublished novels. *My Brilliant Career* was made into a highly successful film 1979.

FICTION *My Brilliant Career*, Edinburgh, Blackwood & Sons, 1901; *Some Everyday Folk and Dawn*, Edinburgh, Blackwood & Sons, 1909; *Up the Country*, Edinburgh, Blackwood & Sons, 1928; *Ten Creeks Run*, Edinburgh, Blackwood & Sons, 1930; *Back to Bool Bool*, Edinburgh, Blackwood & Sons, 1931; *Old Blastus of Bandicoot*, Melbourne, Lothian, 1932; *Bring the Monkey*, Sydney, Endeavour Press, 1933; *All that Swagger*, Sydney, Bulletin, 1936; *Pioneers on Parade* (with Dymphna Cusack), Sydney, A & R, 1939; *My Career Goes Bung*, Melbourne, Georgian House, 1946; *Sydney Royal*, Sydney, Shakespeare Head, 1947; *Prelude to Waking*, Sydney, A & R, 1950; *Cockatoos*, Sydney, A & R, 1954; *Gentlemen at Gyang Gyang*, Sydney, A & R, 1956; *On Dearborn Street* (ed. Roy Duncan), St Lucia, UQP, 1981.

NON-FICTION *Joseph Furphy: The Legend of a Man and his Book* (with Kate Baker), Sydney, A & R, 1944; *Laughter, Not for a Cage*, Sydney, A & R, 1956; *Childhood at Brindabella*, Sydney, A & R, 1963.

OTHER Published countless journal articles, reviews, etc in Australia and overseas; also plays, e.g. *No Family* in *Best Australian One-Act Plays* (A & R, 1937).

MANUSCRIPTS ML, Sydney: Miles Franklin Papers ML MSS 364. A huge collection (see *Guide to the Papers and Books of Miles Franklin in the Mitchell Library*, Library Council of NSW, 1980), including correspondence, diaries, literary papers, mss, etc. NL, Canberra: Miles Franklin Papers MS 477, 681 and 1558 (Contents list available). La Trobe Library, Melbourne: Articles, papers, letters in the J. K. Moir Collection.

SEE ALSO M. Barnard, *Miles Franklin* (Hill of Content, 1967), J. Roe in *Meanjin*, Vol. 39, No. 1 (1980), V. Coleman, *Her Unknown (Brilliant) Career: Miles Franklin in America* (Sirius, 1982), F. McInherny in *Who Is She? Images of Woman in Australian Fiction* (ed. S. Walker, UQP, 1983) and S. Gardner and V. Kent in *Gender, Politics and Fiction* (ed. C. Ferrier, UQP, 1985).

Friend, Robyn (1942–)
Fiction writer, biographer. Born in Melbourne. Qualified as a teacher, but has wide experience of other occupations ranging from acting to factory work. Has travelled extensively, and lived 4 years in Idi Amin's Uganda. After publishing a number of short stories began writing with serious intent after meeting Eva, the subject of her first book 1983, and developing the technique of 'reconstructive biography'. Presently is working upon a novel with the aid of a Literature Board Grant and now regards herself as a full-time writer.

FICTION/BIOGRAPHY *Eva*, Melbourne, McPhee Gribble/Penguin, 1984.
OTHER Short stories have also appeared in *Island, Inprint* (1979, 1980), the *Canberra Times* and *Nation Review* between 1970–83.

Fullerton, Mary, 'E', 'Alpenstock', etc (1868–1946)
Poet, novelist. Born at Glenmaggie, in the North Gippsland region of Victoria. Was a strong feminist who wrote for journals and papers before leaving for England 1921 where she died. Published under many pseudonyms due to her belief in the prejudice against women writers. Was a great friend of Miles Franklin (q.v.), who arranged for the publication of her poetry in 1942 and 1946; *Rufus Sterne* was dedicated to 'Brent of Bin Bin'. Her later poetry was noted for its succinct, often satirical, lucidity.

POETRY *Moods and Melodies: Sonnets and Lyrics*, Melbourne, Lothian, 1908; *The Breaking Furrow*, Melbourne, Endacott, 1921; *Moles Do So Little with their Privacy*, by 'E', Sydney, A & R, 1942; *The Wonder and the Apple: More Poems* by 'E', Sydney, A & R, 1946.
FICTION *Bark House Days*, Melbourne, Endacott, 1921; *Two Women: Clare, Margaret* (anon.) London, Philpot, 1923; *The People of the Timber Belt*, London, Philpot, 1925; *A Juno of the Bush*, London, Heath Cranton, 1930; *Rufus Sterne*, by Robert Gray, Edinburgh, Blackwood, 1932; *The Murders at Crabapple Farm*, by Gordon Manners, London, Jenkins, 1933.
NON-FICTION *The Australian Comic Dictionary of Words*, by Turner O. Lingo, 1916; *The Australian Bush*, Dents Outward Bound Library, 1928.
MANUSCRIPTS ML, Sydney: Mary Fullerton Papers ML MS 2342; La Trobe Library, Melbourne: Mary Elizabeth Fullerton Papers in the J. K. Moir Collection.
SEE ALSO Miles Franklin in the *Bulletin*, 15 May, 1946.

G

Gage, Mary (1940–)
Playwright, author. Born in London; educated at Salisbury and at Cambridge University graduating from Girton College as History masters 1967. Trained as a journalist on the *Times*, London, and has worked for most of the major newspapers in Australia. Has also worked in public relations (e.g. for the Festival of Perth), and produced a variety of literature. *The Price of Pearls* won the West Australian 150th anniversary playwriting competition 1979; *Praise the Egg* won the A & R Fellowship 1980. Was Playwright-in-Residence at Perth Playhouse 1979.

DRAMA *The New Life*, Sydney, Currency Press, 1977; *My Name is Pablo Picasso*, Sydney, Currency Press, 1984.
NON-FICTION *The Overlanders' Handbook*, Id Press, 1976; *Praise the Egg*, Sydney, A. & R. 1981.
OTHER Plays produced include *The Catalyst* (1972); *Supermarket* (1975); *Everyone's a General* (1976); *The Same Square of Dust* (Perth 1980); *The Price of Pearls* (1980) and *C.Y.* (1981). Drama for television includes *Deadwater* (1976); *Clara's Story* (1983/4) and *Pipedreams* (1985/6). Short stories have appeared in *Argosy* and *Quadrant* and have been broadcast on the BBC.

Gallagher, Katherine (1935–)
Poet. Born in Maldon, Victoria, and grew up in a small farming community. After leaving school took various jobs until 1960 when she enrolled at the University of Melbourne, completing a BA 1964. Taught high school before leaving for Europe. Lived in Paris 1971–9 teaching English; met and married Frenchman Bernard Londeix. Returned in 1979 with her family to London, where she still lives, teaching and writing. Began writing poetry in 1965, and short stories about 1970, but is basically a poet and has won a number of awards for her work including third prize in the John Shaw Neilson Poetry Award of the FAW 1971, and first prize in the Brisbane Warana Festival Poetry Awards 1981.

POETRY *The Eye's Circle*, Melbourne, Rigmarole, 1974; *Tributaries of the Love-Song*, Sydney, A & R, 1978; *Passengers to the City*, Sydney, Hale & Iremonger, 1985.
OTHER Poems have appeared in: *Applestealers* (Outback Press, 1974); *Mother I'm Rooted* (Outback Press, 1975); *Poet's Choice* (Island, 1976); *Faith in Life* (Community Arts Centre, 1982); *A Time to Choose* (Backyard Press, 1984); *Friendly St Poets Anthology* (1985); and in numerous journals and magazines including: *Luna, Overland, Meanjin*, the *Age, Quadrant,*

Contempa, Poetry Australia, New Poetry, Magic Sam, and the *Realist*. Short stories have appeared in: the *Sun* (1975), *Inprint* (1980), *Tabloid Story* (1980) and *Australian Short Stories* (1985).

Gantner, Neilma, 'Neilma Sidney' (1922–)
Short story writer, novelist. Born in San Francisco, USA, a daughter of the Myer family of Melbourne. Educated at the University of Melbourne and Stanford University, USA, graduating 1954. Has lived and worked overseas, including in India, for international welfare agencies. Has been a member of the Executive of International Social Service since 1955 and is currently its honorary Vice President.

FICTION *Saturday Afternoon*, Melbourne, Cheshire, 1959; *Beyond the Bay*, Melbourne, Cheshire, 1966; *The Eye of the Needle*, Melbourne, Lloyd O'Neil, 1970; *The Return*, Melbourne, Nelson, 1976; *Journey to Mourilyan*, Melbourne, Dent, 1986.
OTHER Also published for children, *Beaches* (OUP, 1964). Short stories have also appeared in *Australian Signpost* (1950), *Meanjin* (1961) and *Two Ways Meet* (1969). Articles appeared in the *Age Literary Supplement* 1958–60.

Gardner, Silvana (1942–)
Poet, artist. Lives in Brisbane where she has been a teacher of creative writing and participated in several art-in-education projects. Her art is represented in various galleries both in Australia and overseas.

POETRY *When Sunday Comes*, St Lucia, UQP, 1982; *Hacedor*, Broadway, Qld, Planet Press, 1983; *With Open Eyes*, Brisbane, Qld Community Press, 1983; *Children of the Dragon*, Brisbane, Jacaranda, 1985.

Gare, Nene (1919–)
Novelist, short story writer, artist. Born in Adelaide and educated at the Adelaide Art School and later Perth Technical College; in later years returned to study Arts at Murdoch University, Perth. Is active in the Perth branch of the FAW. Has had several exhibitions of her paintings and won the Canning Art Award four times. Is best known for *The Fringe Dwellers*, which joins the slender body of fiction by white Australians written from the point of view of the Aborigines; it was filmed by Bruce Beresford and released 1986. Her short stories have appeared in several anthologies.

FICTION *The Fringe Dwellers*, London, Heinemann, 1961; *Green Gold*, London, Heinemann, 1963; *Bend to the Wind*, Melbourne, Macmillan, 1978; *A House with Verandahs*, Melbourne, Macmillan, 1980; *An Island Away*, Melbourne, Macmillan, 1981.

SEE ALSO M. Smith in *Gender, Politics and Fiction* (ed. C. Ferrier, UQP, 1985).

Garner, Helen (1942–)
Novelist, short story writer. Born in Geelong, Victoria. Educated at the University of Melbourne, graduating with honours 1965 to become a secondary school teacher. Taught for 5 years with time off for travelling and having a daughter, to be sacked in 1972 by the Education Department for her controversial use of language. Since then has worked on newspapers and magazines, lived on a supporting mother's pension in various collective households and undergone a second marriage. Has also received three writers fellowships from the Literature Board and been writer-in-residence at Griffith University, Brisbane, and the University of WA. *Monkey Grip* received wide acclaim for its portrayal of a heroin addict, winning the National Book Council Book of the Year Award 1978; it was made into a film in 1982 and has been translated into French. *Postcards from Surfers* won the NSW Premier's Award for Fiction 1986.

FICTION *Monkey Grip*, Melbourne, McPhee Gribble/Penguin, 1977; *Honour and Other People's Children*, Melbourne, McPhee Gribble/Penguin, 1980; *Moving Out* (with Jennifer Giles), Melbourne, Sphere Books, 1984; *The Children's Bach*, Melbourne, McPhee Gribble/Penguin, 1984; *Postcards from Surfers*, Melbourne, McPhee Gribble/Penguin, 1985.
SEE ALSO P. Craven in *Meanjin*, Vol. 44, No. 2 (1985), C. Baker (interview) in *Yacker* (Pan/Picador, 1986) and D. K. Burns in *Meanjin*, Vol. 45, No. 3 (1986).

Gaskin, Catherine (1929–)
Novelist. Born in County Louth, Ireland. Was brought to Australia when a baby, her family settling in Sydney. Made her mark by publishing her first novel, which was a great success, at the age of 16 while still at school. Published a second novel in Sydney before returning to Britain 1948 with her sister and mother, to seek medical help for her sister in London. Continued to write to support herself and her sister. Her Australian connections were reinforced with her most successful book, *Sara Dane*, published when she was 25, loosely based upon the story of convict Mary Reiby. Shortly after met and married American Sol Cornberg and lived with him in New York, the Caribbean, Ireland and finally the Isle of Man. Has for many years been a best-selling romantic novelist, the appeal of her books lying in their interesting plots and historical backgrounds. All the novels since *All Else is Folly* have been

translated into other languages; *Sara Dane* has been published in 14 other languages and was serialised on Australian television 1982.

FICTION *This Other Eden*, Sydney, Collins, 1946; *With Every Year*, Sydney, Collins, 1947; *Dust in Sunlight*, London, Collins, 1950; *All Else is Folly*, London, Collins, 1951; *Daughter of the House*, London, Collins, 1952; *Sara Dane*, London, Collins, 1955; *Blake's Reach*, London, Collins, 1958; *Corporation Wife*, London, Collins, 1960; *I Know My Love*, London, Collins, 1962; *The Tilsit Inheritance*, New York, Doubleday, 1963; *The File on Devlin*, London, Collins, 1965; *Edge of Glass*, London, Collins, 1967; *Fiona*, London, Collins, 1970; *A Falcon for a Queen*, New York, Doubleday, 1972; *The Property of a Gentleman*, New York, Doubleday, 1974; *The Lynmara Legacy*, London, Collins, 1975; *The Summer of the Spanish Woman*, New York, Fawcett Crest, 1977; *Family Affairs*, London, Collins, 1980; *Promises*, London, Collins, 1982; *The Ambassador's Women*, London, Collins, 1985.

Gaunt, Mary (1861–1942)
Novelist, short story writer, travel writer, journalist. Born at Chiltern, Victoria, the daughter of Judge W. H. Gaunt. Educated at Grenville College, Ballarat and then became one of the first two women students at the University of Melbourne. Married Dr Hubert Miller 1894 and lived at Warrnambool, Victoria. After his death 1900 went to live in London where most of her novels were written and published. Began writing c. 1888, publishing reviews and articles for a living in various papers such as the *Age*, the *Argus* and the *Australasian*, and published her first short story in the *Sydney Mail*. As well as romances and short stories (at which she was particularly skilled) also wrote descriptive works based upon her extensive travels throughout Africa, China and the West Indies; took and developed her own photographs for her travel books. In later years lived in Italy and died at Cannes 1942.

FICTION *Dave's Sweetheart*, London, Edward Arnold, 1894; *The Moving Finger*, London, Methuen, 1895; *Kirkham's Find*, London, Methuen, 1897; *Deadman's*, London, Methuen, 1898; *The Arm of the Leopard* (with J. R. Essex), London, Grant Richards, 1904; *Fools Rush In* (with J. R. Essex), London, Heinemann, 1906; *The Silent Ones* (with J. R. Essex), London, T. Werner Laurie, 1909; *The Mummy Moves*, London, T. Werner Laurie, 1910; *The Uncounted Cost*, London, T. Werner Laurie, 1910; *Every Man's Desire*, London, T. Werner Laurie, 1913; *The Ends of the Earth*, London, T. Werner Laurie, 1915; *A Wind from the Wilderness*, London, T. Werner Laurie, 1919; *The Surrender and Other Happenings*, London, T. Werner Laurie, 1920; *As the Whirlwind Passeth*, London, John Murray, 1923; *The Forbidden Town*, London, T. Fisher Unwin, 1926; *Saul's Daughter*, London, T. Fisher Unwin, 1927; *The Lawless*

Frontier, London, Ernest Benn, 1929; *Joan of the Pilchard*, London, Ernest Benn, 1930; *Harmony: A Tale of the Old Slave Days of Jamaica*, London, Ernest Benn, 1933; *Worlds Away*, London, Hutchinson, 1934.
NON-FICTION *Alone in West Africa*, London, T. Werner Laurie, 1912; *A Woman in China*, London, T. Werner Laurie, 1914; *A Broken Journey*, London, T. Werner Laurie, 1919; *Where the Twain Meet*, London, John Murray, 1922; *George Washington and the Men Who Made the American Revolution*, London, A & C Black, 1926; *Reflection – In Jamaica*, London, Ernest Benn, 1932.
OTHER Also contributed to E. E. Morris (ed.) *Cassell's Picturesque Australasia* (Cassell, 1887, 9 chapters), *Picturesque New Zealand* (Cassell, 1895) and Joshua Lake (ed.) *Childhood in Bud and Blossom* (Atlas Press, 1900).
SEE ALSO Joan Gillison in *Victorian Historical Journal*, Vol. 51, No. 2 (May, 1980). For a full bibliography see Ian F. McLaren, *Mary Gaunt, A Cosmopolitan Australian* (University of Melbourne Library, 1986).

Gibbs, May (1877–1969)
Children's author and illustrator. Born Cecilia May in Kent, England and came to Australia as a child. Studied art in London, then returned to Australia and lived in Sydney. Published her first Australian children's book, *Gumnut Babies*, 1916. It exploited the unique Australian flora and fauna in an appealing formula that ensured her popularity and success as a children's author for generations. Apart from the many books, she also illustrated a long-running comic strip for various newspapers 1924–67 featuring the characters 'Bib and Bub', 'Snugglepot and Cuddlepie', etc., who were so popular in her books.

FICTION *About Us*, London, Nister, 1912; *Gumnut Babies*, Sydney, A & R, 1916; *Gum Blossom Babies*, Sydney, A & R, 1916; *Boronia Babies*, Sydney, A & R, 1917; *Flannel Flowers and Other Bush Babies*, Sydney, A & R, 1917; *Wattle Babies*, Sydney, A & R, 1918; *Snugglepot and Cuddlepie, Their Adventures Wonderful*, Sydney, A & R, 1918; *Little Ragged Blossom*, Sydney, A & R, 1920; *Little Obelia and Further Adventures of Ragged Blossom, Snugglepot and Cuddlepie*, Sydney, A & R, 1921; *Nuttybub and Nittersing*, Melbourne, Osboldstone, 1923; *Chucklebud and Nunkeydoo*, Melbourne, Osboldstone, 1924; *Bib and Bub, Their Adventures*, Sydney, Cornstalk, 1925; *Further Adventures of Bib and Bub*, Sydney, Cornstalk, 1927; *More Funny Stories*, Sydney, Cornstalk, 1928; *Bib and Bub in Gumnut Town*, Waterloo, Halstead Printing Co., 1929; *Two Little Gumnuts*, Sydney, Cornstalk, 1929; *Scotty in Gumnut Land*, Sydney, A & R, 1941; *The Complete Adventures of Snugglepot and Cuddlepie*, Sydney, A & R, 1942; *Mr & Mrs Bear and Friends*, Sydney, A & R, 1943.
SEE ALSO Maureen Walsh, *Mother of the Gumnuts, Her Life and Work*, in *The May Gibbs Collection* (A & R, 1985).

Giles, Barbara (1912–)
Poet, children's novelist. Born in England and attended school there before coming to Australia where she took a degree and qualified as a teacher. Was a primary and secondary school teacher for nearly forty years until 1977. Amongst many other activities has taught creative writing, been a book reviewer, and an editor of the women's literary magazine *Luna*. Since retiring from teaching in 1978 has also lectured on the craft of writing, been a member of Pariah Press, and continued to write, mostly for children. Was awarded the John Shaw Neilson Poetry Prize 1972.

POETRY *Eve Rejects Apple*, Sydney, A & R, 1978; *Earth and Solitude*, Melbourne, Pariah Press, 1984.
FICTION *Bicycles Don't Fly*, Melbourne, Penguin, 1982; *Jack in the Bush*, Melbourne, Penguin, 1983; *Upright, Downfall* (with R. Fuller & A. Rumble), London, OUP, 1983; *Alex is My Friend*, Melbourne, Penguin, 1984; *Flying Backwards*, Melbourne, Penguin, 1985.
OTHER Poems, articles and reviews have appeared in a number of journals and papers including the *Age, ABR, Quadrant, Meanjin*, and *Compass*.

Gilmore, Mary, Dame (1865–1962)
Poet. Born Mary Jean Cameron near Goulburn, NSW. Worked as a school teacher before joining Willian Lane in the socialist experiment which led to the setting up of a community in Paraguay, South America. There married William Gilmore 1897. Returned to Australia 1902 following the failure of the experiment. Spent some years upon a farm in Victoria before moving to Sydney where for 23 years she wrote and edited the women's page of the Sydney *Worker*. Her life-long interest in the state of the workers, the needy and the dispossessed was reflected both in her journalism and her poetry. Her humane and sympathetic nature was especially stirred by the plight of the Australian Aborigines. Was created DBE 1936 and by the time of her death had achieved virtually legendary status in Australia.

POETRY *Marri'd and Other Verses*, Melbourne, G. Robertson, 1910; *The Tale of Tiddley Winks*, Sydney, Bookfellow, 1917; *The Passionate Heart*, Sydney, A & R, 1918; *The Tilted Cart: A Book of Recitations*, Sydney, *Worker*, 1925; *The Wild Swan*, Melbourne, Robertson & Mullens, 1930; *The Rue Tree*, Melbourne, Robertson & Mullens, 1931; *Under the Wilgas*, Melbourne, Robertson & Mullens, 1932; *Battlefields*, Sydney, A & R, 1939; *The Disinherited*, Melbourne, Robertson & Mullens, 1941; *Pro Patria Australia and Other Poems*, Sydney, W. H. Honey, 1945; *Selected Verse*, Sydney, A & R, 1948; *Fourteen Men*, Sydney, A & R, 1954; *Mary Gilmore*, selected by R. D. Fitzgerald, Sydney, A & R, 1963.
NON-FICTION *The Worker Cookbook*, Sydney, The Worker Trustees,

1915; *Hound of the Road*, Sydney, A & R, 1921; *Old Days, Old Ways*, Sydney, A & R, 1934; *More Recollections*, Sydney, A & R, 1935.
MANUSCRIPTS ML, Sydney: Dame Mary Gilmore Collection A 3293 (restricted indefinitely). Other papers held at: Archives Office of Tasmania NS 399, La Trobe Library, Melbourne (in the J. K. Moir Collection) and NL, Canberra (miscellaneous papers in several holdings).
SEE ALSO *Mary Gilmore: A Tribute* (Australasian Book Soc., 1965. Also has a bibliography); S. Lawson, *Mary Gilmore* (OUP, 1966); W. H. Wilde in *Three Radicals* (OUP, 1969); W. H. Wilde & T. Inglis Moore (eds) *The Letters of Mary Gilmore* (MUP, 1980) and D. Modjeska in *Meanjin*, Vol. 41, No. 2 (1982).

Gordon, Nancy (1918–)
Poet. Born in Melbourne and educated at St Margaret's School for Girls. Over the years has tutored in Workers' Education Association classes and at colleges of advanced education. Was recently awarded grants by the South Australian government and the Literature Board to conduct poetry workshops at Adelaide's Festival Theatre.

POETRY *Not Crab But Butterfly*, Adelaide, Raphael Arts, 1978.
OTHER Work is included in the *Friendly Street* anthologies, *The Orange Tree* (Wakefield, 1985) and *The Penguin Book of Australian Women Poets* (Penguin, 1986), and in *Meanjin, Hemisphere, Luna*, the *Canberra Times* and *Expression*.

Goyder, Margot *See:* **'Neville, Margot'**

Gray, Oriel (1920–)
Playwright. Born in Sydney into a politically active family. Joined the CPA and the Sydney New Theatre in 1937. Led an interesting, sometimes controversial life, writing plays for radio and television (including scripts for *Bellbird* and *Rush*), but mostly for the stage. *Lawson* was one of the first dramatisations of the life of Henry Lawson. *The Torrents* shared equal first prize with Ray Lawler's *Summer of the Seventeenth Doll* in the Playwright's Advisory Board Competition 1954, but did not share its glory. All her plays between 1943–60 were produced at the New Theatre, but remain unpublished. *Burst of Summer* won a prestigious J. C. Williamson's Theatre Guild Award 1959. *Exit Left* recounts her involvement with the Communist Party and the New Theatre; while a lively sketch of her 'wryly amusing life', it is also a fascinating account of the left-wing movement in Sydney and the Australian political scene during the war years.

DRAMA *Drive a Hard Bargain*, Hobart, Tasmanian Adult Education Board, 1960; *The Golden Touch*, in *Drama in Action Book I*, Melbourne,

Nelson, 1965; *The Ghost of Dog Leg Creek*, in *Drama in Action Book II*, Melbourne, Nelson, 1967; *Baiame and the Mahdi, Noah's Deluge, The Ink-Smeared Lady* (adaptations) and *Belle and the Bushranger*, in *Setting the Stage Book I*, Adelaide, Rigby, 1969; *The Three Good Witches and the Bad Bad Prince*, in *Plays for Young Players*, Adelaide, Rigby, 1970; *The Pot of Gold, The Monstrous Spider* (adaptations) and *Lawson*, in *The Living Stage Book II*, Adelaide, Rigby, 1970.
NON-FICTION *Exit Left, Memoirs of a Scarlet Woman*, Melbourne, Penguin, 1985.
OTHER Plays produced include: *Lawson* (1943); *Had We But World Enough* (1948); *Sky Without Birds* (1950); *The Torrents* (1954); *Burst of Summer* (1959) (unpublished mss in the Hanger and Campbell Howard Collections); *The King's Wouldn't* (1952) and *Western Limits* (1954).
SEE ALSO K. Brisbane in the *National Times*, Sept. 13–18, 1976 (pp. 26–7).

Green, Dorothy (Dorothy Auchterlonie) (1915–)
Poet, critic, essayist. Born Dorothy Auchterlonie in Durham, England. Educated at North Sydney Girls' High and the University of Sydney. Has worked as a teacher, as a journalist with the ABC, as an academic, and an essayist and reviewer for many journals and newspapers over the last thirty years. Was senior lecturer in English and Australian Literature at Monash University, Melbourne, at the Australian National University, Canberra, and Honorary Visiting Fellow at the former Royal Military College, Duntroon. Retired 1980 to write full-time. Her articles and essays offer analyses of texts in their historical and cultural context, and are noted for their uncompromising views. Married librarian and critic H. M. Green 1944. Recently published a revised edition of his *History of Australian Literature* and is currently preparing a third volume to bring the history up to 1980. Received the Barbara Ramsden Award 1973 and the James Cook University Literary Award 1973. Was awarded OAM 1984.

POETRY (As Dorothy Auchterlonie): *Kaleidoscope*, Sydney, Viking Press, 1940; *The Dolphin*, Canberra, ANU Press, 1967; *Something to Someone*, Canberra, Brindabella Press, 1984.
NON-FICTION *Australian Poetry* (ed.), Sydney, A & R, 1968; *Ulysses Bound: Henry Handel Richardson and her Fiction*, Canberra, ANU Press, 1973; *The Music of Love, Critical Essays on Literature and Life*, Melbourne, Penguin, 1984; *A History of Australian Literature 1789–1950* Vols I & II (revised), Sydney, Angus & Robertson, 1985.
OTHER Over 150 articles, book reviews and essays have appeared in journals and newspapers. For a full bibliography see J. Hooton and S. Burchill in *The Music of Love* (Penguin, 1984).

Greene, Abigail (c. 1873–1935)
Playwright. Born Abigail Marshall in Melbourne. Became an actor working with George Rignold's Shakespearian company before going to the USA. Won the Players Club of Philadelphia prize for the play *Accomplice*. Returned to Australia 1929.

DRAMA *Plays for Australian Children*, Sydney, Shakespeare Head Press, 1933.

Greer, Germaine, 'Rose Blight' (1939–)
Feminist writer, broadcaster, journalist. Born in Melbourne. Educated at Catholic schools and at the Universities of Melbourne, Sydney and Cambridge. In 1970 achieved fame with the landmark feminist study, *The Female Eunuch*. Has tutored and lectured in English at Warwick University, England, been Visiting Professor of the University of Tulsa, Oklahoma, and Director of the Tulsa Centre for the Study of Women's Literature. Was columnist for the London *Sunday Times* 1971–3, and has contributed articles to many other magazines including *Harpers*, the *Listener*, the *Spectator* and *Esquire*. Since the controversial and sometimes hostile reception of *The Female Eunuch* in her homeland, Greer has not found Australia congenial; has spent most of the last 12 years in Tuscany, Italy, and now lives in England. *The Female Eunuch* enjoyed immense worldwide popularity and sales, has been translated into 12 languages, and has influenced a generation of women. *The Obstacle Race* is an account of the history of women artists; *Sex and Destiny* refines Greer's views on women.

NON-FICTION *Darling Say You Love Me*, 1965; *The Female Eunuch*, London, MacGibbon & Kee, 1970; *The Revolting Garden*, London, *Private Eye*, 1979; *The Obstacle Race*, London, Secker & Warburg, 1979; *Slade Women*, 1979; *Shakespeare*, London, OUP, 1981; *Sex and Destiny, the Politics of Human Fertility*, London, Secker & Warburg, 1984; *The Madwoman's Underclothes, Essays and Occasional Writings 1968–1985*, London, Picador, 1986.
OTHER Also published the Foreword to the *Autobiography of Anna Kollontai* (1970), the Introduction to Christina Rossetti's *Goblin Market* (Stonehill, 1971) and the chapter 'Women and Power in Cuba' in *Women: A World Report* (1985).

'Gregory, Margaret' *See:* **Ercole, Velia**

Greig, Maysie, 'Jennifer Ames' (c. 1901–1971)
Novelist. Born in Sydney. Worked on the *Sydney Morning Herald* before moving to England where she worked for several newspapers. Married journalist Max Murray in New York 1937; later married Jan Sopoushek.

Returned to Australia and journalism in the 1950s and became active in PEN Australia, helping revive that organisation. After a few years returned to London where she died. Wrote popular romances which underwent many reprints and various translations.

FICTION From 1920 published approximately 200 novels, too many to list here; the Mitchell Library, Sydney, holds about 100 of them. Her main publishers were Hodder & Stoughton (London, 1932–42 and Collins (London) 1946–70.
SEE ALSO M. Greig, 'The Way I Wrote my First 170 Novels', *Observer*, Feb.18, 1961 (pp.9–10).

Grenville, Kate (1950–)
Novelist, short story writer. Born in Sydney. Educated at the University of Sydney graduating with honours in arts 1972. Later graduated MA from the University of Colorado, USA. Has worked as a film editor, journalist, typist, teacher and subtitles editor for multicultural television. Currently writes full time and has received fellowships in Australia and the USA. Was runner up in the Vogel/*Australian* Award 1983 and winner 1984 with *Lilian's Story*, a novel based on the life of Sydney identity Bea Miles. Her stories have been published overseas as well as in Australia.

FICTION *Bearded Ladies*, St Lucia, UQP, 1984; *Lilian's Story*, Sydney, Allen & Unwin, 1985; *Dreamhouse*, St Lucia, UQP, 1986.
OTHER Stories have also appeared in *Southerly, Quadrant, Forum* and the *Bulletin Literary Supplement*, and in the anthologies *Room to Move* (Redress/Unwin, 1985) and *The State of the Art* (Penguin, 1985).
SEE ALSO G. Mercer in *Southerly*, Vol. 45, No. 3 (1985) and J. Ellison (interview) in *Rooms of their Own* (Penguin, 1986).

Grimshaw, Beatrice (1870–1953)
Novelist. Born in Ireland, educated in France and at the University of London. Afterwards travelled around the South Pacific and lived for some years in New Guinea before settling in NSW where she died. While in New Guinea published reports and pamphlets concerning that country for the Australian government. Gained popularity with her novels and stories based upon her knowledge and experience in the South Pacific region.

FICTION *Broken Away*, London, Lane, 1897; *Vaiti of the Islands*, London, Newnes, 1907; *When the Red Gods Call*, London, Mills & Boon, 1911; *Guinea Gold*, London, Mills & Boon, 1912; *The Sorcerer's Stone*, London, Hodder & Stoughton, 1914; *Red Bob of the Bismarcks*, London, Hurst & Blackett, 1915; *Nobody's Island*, London, Mills & Boon, 1917; *Kris-Girl*, London, Mills & Boon, 1917; *The Coral Queen*, Sydney, Bookstall, 1919;

White Savage Simon, Sydney, Bookstall, 1919; *The Terrible Island*, London, Hurst & Blackett, 1920; *Queen Vaiti*, Sydney, Bookstall, 1920; *The Coral Palace 'Twixt Capricorn and Cancer*, London, Mills & Boon, 1920; *Little Red Speck and Other South Sea Stories*, London, Hurst & Blackett, 1921; *My South Sea Sweetheart*, London, Hurst & Blackett, 1921; *Conn of the Coral Seas*, London, Hurst & Blackett, 1922; *The Valley of the Never-come-back and Other Stories*, London, Hurst & Blackett, 1923; *Sands of Oro*, London, Hurst & Blackett, 1924; *Helen of Man-o'-War Island: A Story of the South Seas*, London, Hurst & Blackett, 1924; *The Candles of Katara and Other Stories*, London, Hurst & Blackett, 1925; *Eyes in the Corner and Other Stories*, London, Hurst & Blackett, 1927; *The Wreck of the 'Red Wing'*, London, Hurst & Blackett, 1927; *Black Sheep's Gold*, London, Hurst & Blackett, 1927; *The Paradise Poachers*, London, Hurst & Blackett, 1928; *My Lady Far-Away*, London, Cassell, 1929; *The Star in the Dust*, London, Cassell, 1930; *The Beach of Terror and Other Stories* London, Cassell, 1931; *The Mystery of Tumbling Reef*, London, Cassell, 1932; *The Long Beaches and Other South Sea Stories*, London, Cassell, 1933; *Rita Regina*, London, Jenkins, 1939; *Lost Child*, London, Jenkins, 1940; *South Sea Sarah; Murder in Paradise*, Sydney, New Century Press, 1940; *The Island Queen*, London, Vallencey, 1944; *The Missing Blondes*, Sydney, Invincible Press, 1945.
NON-FICTION *From Fiji to the Cannibal Islands*, London, George Bell, 1907; *In the Strange South Seas*, London, Hutchinson, 1907; *The New New Guinea*, London, Hutchinson, 1910; *Adventures in Papua, With the Catholic Mission*, Melbourne, ACTS, 1913; *Isles of Adventure*, Boston, Houghton Mifflin, 1930.

Grimstone, Mary Leman (c. 1800–187–?)
Novelist. Born Mary Leman Rede in Hamburg, Germany. Published poetry in London under the pseudonym 'Oscar'. Came to Australia 1826 for health reasons and lived with her sister in Tasmania for 3 years. Here wrote *Woman's Love*, the first novel in all probability to be written in Australia, though neither published nor set in Australia. Returned to England 1829. In London published a letter about Tasmania which caused some controversy in Hobart. Contributed to the *Colonial Times* and published short stories set in Tasmania. In London was a member of Caroline Norton's *La Belle Assemblée* literary circle. As Mary Gillies also published children's books. *Woman's Love*, like most of her fiction, is partly concerned with the position of women.

FICTION *Woman's Love*, London, 1832; *Louisa Egerton*, London, 1830; *Character, or Jew and Gentile*, London, C. Fox, 1833; *Cleone*, London, 1834; *The Beauty of the British Alps, or Love at First Sight*, London, H. Fisher, 1840.

POETRY *Zayda, a Spanish Tale, and Other Poems*, London (n.d.)
OTHER Published articles and stories in the *People's Journal* (1846) as Mary Leman Gillies.
SEE ALSO E. Morris Miller, 'Australia's First Two Novels', in *Papers and Proceedings of the Tasmanian Historical Research Association*, Vol. 6, Nos. 2 & 3 (1957).

Gunn, Jeannie (1870–1961)
Prose writer. Born Jeannie Taylor in Melbourne and educated at the University of Melbourne. Conducted a private school with her sister for some years before marrying Aeneas Gunn 1901. Accompanied him to the Elsey cattle station on the Roper River, south-east of Katherine in the Northern Territory. After his death there 1903, returned to Melbourne and wrote her autobiographical account of her sojourn in the 'never-never'. Both of her books have always had wide popular appeal both in Australia and overseas. Jack London considered *We of the Never-Never* to be one of the best books written on Australian pioneering life. Jeannie Gunn was awarded the OBE 1939. *We of the Never-Never* was made into a film 1982.

NON-FICTION *The Little Black Princess*, London, De La More Press, 1905; *We of the Never-Never*, London, Hutchinson, 1908.
MANUSCRIPTS NL, Canberra: Jeannie Gunn Papers 1905–55 MS 82–84, 2323, 4908 (manuscripts, correspondence, photographs, etc). La Trobe Library, Melbourne: Mrs Aeneas Gunn Papers MS 562571 (similar).
SEE ALSO J. L. Rossiter, *Handbook to We of the Never-Never* (G. B. Philip, 1922), S. Musgrove in *Southerly*, Vol. 6, No. 2 (1945), I. Nesdale, *The Little Missus, Mrs Aeneas Gunn* (Lynton Publications, 1977) and M. Bosworth in *JRAHS*, Vol. 70, Pt 2 (Oct. 1984)

Gwynne, Agnes
Novelist, playwright. Wrote sentimental romances set in and describing aspects of Australia such as station life and the convict period. Received some recognition for her drama including a prize for *A Social Experiment* 1908.

FICTION *The Mistress of Windfalls*, Melbourne, Cole's Book Arcade, 1921; *The Mystery of Lakeside House*, Melbourne, G. Robertson, 1925; *An Emergency Husband*, London, M. G. Maurice, 192?; *High Dawn*, Melbourne, Robertson & Mullens, 1935.
DRAMA *A Social Experiment, A Comedy in Three Acts*, Melbourne, Lothian, 1908; *The Capitalist, An Original Play in One Act*, Melbourne, F. Wilmot, 1931.

Gwythr, Michaela, 'Kayla Seymour'; 'Hazel Blair' (1920–)
Poet, short story writer. Born in Buckinghamshire, England. Educated to matriculation at the Trowbridge School of Domestic Science. In England worked as an actor, singer, freelance journalist, secretary, housekeeper and hotel manager. In Australia her occupations have ranged from bookselling and lecturing to broadcasting and breeding of terrier dogs. Began publishing poetry in the late 1960s, and also completed a BA through external studies at Deakin University, Victoria. Has won a number of awards for her work including a National Book League award in the UK. Short stories have appeared in magazines in England, America and Australia and her poems are represented in several anthologies. Lately has been writing plays and pantomimes for children.

POETRY *Nova*, Melbourne, Nova Press, 1973; *Tweed*, NSW, Shelters Press, 1974; *Trams*, Melbourne, Spectrum Press, 1978.
OTHER Poems have also appeared in the anthologies *Winchester Poets* Series (Winchester Press 1968–70), *Autumn Anthology*, (Regency Press 1969) and *New Poetry* (Cathay Press, 1971).

H

Hackett, Patricia (1908–1963)
Poet, actor. Born in Perth, the daughter of Sir John Winthrop Hackett, newspaper editor and benefactor of the University of WA. Studied law in London, returning to practise in Adelaide. Bought her own theatre, the Torch, 1934 and produced many plays there. The Patricia Hackett Prize for poetry was established in her memory 1965.

POETRY *These Little Things*, Adelaide, Hunkin Ellis & King, 1938.
SEE ALSO 'Patricia Hackett: An Appreciation' in *Westerly*, Vol. 1 (May, 1965).

Hadow, Lyndall (1903–1976)
Editor, journalist, short story writer. Born in Kalgoorlie, WA, of a socialist family. Her mother Florence Stuart organised the first Women's Labour League on the goldfields and her father edited the *Westralian Worker;* her brother Donald Stuart also became a writer. Worked as a commercial traveller in WA in the 1930s, and later edited the magazine *Our Women*. Wrote numerous critical and review articles as well as short fiction. Also edited a book of her father's writings, *Part of the Glory*. A second book of her short stories was completed but not published before her death. The Lyndall Hadow Award for short stories was created by the WA branch of the FAW 1977 in her memory.

FICTION *Full Cycle and Other Stories*, Sydney, Collins, 1969.
OTHER *Part of the Glory* (ed. Australasian Book Society, 1967).
SEE ALSO *She Too is Part of the Glory: Lyndall Hadow 1903–1976* (FAW, 1976).

Haenke, Helen (1916–1978)
Poet, playwright, short story writer. Born in Newcastle, NSW. Educated at the Methodist Ladies' College, Burwood, and East Sydney Technical College where she studied commerical art. Worked as a commercial artist in Sydney until her marriage c. 1938 when she moved to Brisbane. Lived in Melbourne (where she studied painting with artist Max Meldrum), Blackheath, NSW, and Ipswich, Queensland, during WWII, afterwards remaining in Queensland until her death. Had earlier published poems in newspapers but, occupied with children and painting, did not begin writing seriously until the 1960s. Published many stories and articles in magazines and later plays and poetry, and has left much unpublished material, including novels. At the time of her death from

cancer had almost completed an arts degree. *Firebug* won an award in the Warana Writers' Convention 1973.

POETRY *The Good Company*, Melbourne, Hawthorn Press, 1977; *Prophets and Honour*, Melbourne, Hawthorn Press, 1979.
DRAMA *Firebug*, in *Three Queensland One-Act Plays for Festivals*, Brisbane, Playlab Press, 1978; *The Bottom of a Birdcage, an 'Anti-thriller' in Two Acts*, Brisbane, Playlab Press, 1978.
OTHER Plays produced include: *Truth to Tell*, *Golden Sword*, *Black Out* and *The Passage*. A short story appeared in *Southerly* (1967).

Halinbourg, Beryl (1900–)
Poet, essayist. Born in Melbourne, into a Jewish family of French and Greek origins. Was a gifted musician who trained as a singer but was prevented from making singing her professional career due to financial difficulties. Worked as a secretary for over thirty years and began to write poetry in her spare time. Was never in a position to become a full-time writer but her poems were widely published in journals both in Australia and overseas and received various awards and prizes. *Testament*, a long poem affirming a credo of religious and secular love, was published with a Foreword by the poet Bernard O'Dowd. *In the Poet's Eye*, a verse-play, attracted a glowing tribute from Martin Boyd.

POETRY *Prologue and Other Poems*, Melbourne, Robertson & Mullens, 1939; *New Weapons of the Spirit*, Melbourne, the author, 1945; *Testament*, Melbourne, Ramsay Ware, 1946; *This Wonderful Age*, Melbourne, Ramsay Ware, 1958; *In the Poet's Eye*, London, Mitre Press, 1964; *Domestic Opus*, Redcliffe, Qld, Refulgence Publs., 1974.
NON-FICTION *Let's Look at Literature, an Essay in Dialogue*, Melbourne, the author, 1962; *In Homage to Music and its Creators*, Redcliffe, Qld, Refulgence Publs., 1970; *Musical Mimeographs*, Melbourne, Swinburne Press, 1980.
OTHER Early fiction such as sketches and short stories appeared in journals and papers, e.g. the *Age*.
MANUSCRIPTS La Trobe Library, Melbourne: Beryl Halinbourg Papers MS 8917 and in the Rosa N. Jonnes Papers MS 10864.

Halls, Geraldine, 'Charlotte Jay' (1919–)
Novelist. Born Geraldine Melville in Adelaide; adopted her mother's last name as a pseudonym under which she has published thrillers. Educated at the University of Adelaide. Worked as a shorthand typist in Australia and England and as a court stenographer in New Guinea 1942–50. Married to Albert Halls, an Oriental specialist, and has dealt in Oriental antiques in England and Australia. Won the Edgar Allen Poe Award from the Mystery Writers of America 1952 for *Beat not the Bones*.

FICTION *The Knife is Feminine*, London, Collins, 1951; *Beat not the Bones*, London, Collins, 1952; *The Yellow Turban*, New York, Harper, 1955; *The Feast of the Dead*, London, R. Hale, 1956; *The Man Who Walked Away*, London, Collins, 1958; *Arms for Adonis*, London, Collins, 1960; *The Fugitive Eye*, London, Collins, 1961; *A Hank of Hair*, New York, Harper, 1964; *The Silk Project*, London, Collins, 1964; *The Cats of Benares*, New York, Harper, 1967; *The Cobra Kite*, London, Constable, 1971; *The Voice of the Crab*, London, Constable, 1974; *The Last Summer of the Men Shortage*, London, Constable, 1976; *The Felling of Thawle*, London, Constable, 1979; *Talking to Strangers*, London, Constable, 1982.

Hampton, Susan (1949–)
Poet. Born in Inverell, NSW. Attended Newcastle Teachers' College 1966–7 and became a primary school teacher before studying for her BA at Newcastle and Macquarie Universities. Was joint winner of the Patricia Hackett Award 1977 and was also awarded the Dame Mary Gilmore Prize for Poetry 1979. Now lives in Sydney with her son, and is presently co-writing *Ruby's Story* with Ruby Langford.

POETRY *Costumes*, Sydney, Transit Poetry, 1981; *White Dog Sounds*, Sydney, Fab Press, 1987; *The Penguin Book of Australian Women Poets* (ed. with Kate Llewellyn), Melbourne, Penguin, 1986.
NON-FICTION *About Literature* (with Sue Woolfe), Melbourne, Macmillan, 1984.
OTHER Is represented in *Sisters Poets I* (Sisters, 1979), *The Last Poets' Choice* (1979), *No Regrets* and journals and magazines (e.g. *Southerly*) since 1975.

Handford, Nourma (1911–)
Novelist, editor. Born into a pioneering family in the Darling Downs region of Queensland. Spent some years travelling in Asia. Worked as a freelance writer, contributing short stories to magazines in Australia, Canada and England. Edited the *Australian Women's Digest*, and wrote novels both for adults and children.

FICTION *Three Came from Britain* (children's), Sydney, Pratten, 1945; *High River*, Sydney, Shakespeare Head Press, 1947; *Cottontrees*, London, Collins, 1948; *Murder for Tea*, London, Collins, 1949; *Carcoola: A Story for Girls*, Sydney, Dymocks, 1950; *Carcoola Adventure* (children's), Sydney, Dymocks, 1952; *Carcoola Holiday* (children's), Sydney, Dymocks, 1953; *Blood on the Leaves*, Sydney, Dymocks, 1953; *Coward's Kiss*, Sydney, Dymocks, 1954; *Carcoola Backstage: A Career Novel for Girls*, Sydney, Dymocks, 1956; *Fools of Time*, London, Robert Hale, 1958.

Hanger, Eunice (1911–1972)
Playwright. Born in Rockhampton, Queensland and educated at the University of Queensland where she later taught. Was active in the theatre world in Brisbane, producing and acting in plays. Collected unpublished plays which are now in the Fryer Library of the University of Queensland, known as the Hanger Collection. *Flood* (in *2D and Other Plays*) won an award in the Playwrights' Advisory Board Competition 1955.

DRAMA *Upstage*, 1952; *An Actor Prepares*, in *Never Kill a Dolphin*, 1959; *Flood* and *The Frogs*, in *2D and Other Plays* (ed. Alrene Sykes), St Lucia, UQP, 1978.
EDITED *Australian One Act Plays*, Adelaide, Rigby, 1962; *Khaki, Bush and Bigotry*, St Lucia, UQP, 1968; *Three Australian Plays*, Minneapolis, University of Minneapolis Press, 1968; *Six One Act Plays*, St Lucia, UQP, 1970; *Drama for High Schools*, St Lucia, UQP, 1971.
OTHER Plays produced include: *Tragedy* (1948); *The Dolls* (1952); *A House is Built* (1954); *Well Well* (1954); *For Love or Money* (1961); *Foundations* (1961); *Short Street* (1962); *A Sandwich for the Teacher* (1967); *The Lawn Mower* (1976) and *Ring the Changelings* (1976).
SEE ALSO 'Forebears of the Doll' in *Southerly*, Vol. 18, No. 1 (1951) and 'Place in Australian Plays' in *Australian Quarterly*, Vol. 34 (June, 1962).

Hanrahan, Barbara (1939–)
Novelist, short story writer, artist. Born in Adelaide. Was brought up by her mother (a commercial artist) and grandmother following the early death of her father. Attended Adelaide Teachers' College and the SA School of Arts. Began printmaking in the early 1960s before leaving for London 1963 to study at the Central School of Art. Over the years has travelled between London and her home city, teaching and lecturing; now lives in Adelaide with Jo Steele. Her paintings and prints have been exhibited in 24 shows in Australia, London and Florence since 1964. She is represented in the collections of the Australian National Gallery and most state galleries. Began writing in earnest 1968 when the death of her grandmother prompted childhood memories, resulting in the autobiographical *The Scent of Eucalyptus*. Some early stories were published in *Torch*, the Adelaide Teachers' College magazine.

FICTION *The Scent of Eucalyptus*, London, Chatto & Windus, 1973; *Sea-green*, London, Chatto & Windus, 1974; *The Albatross Muff*, London, Chatto & Windus, 1977; *Where all the Queens Strayed*, St Lucia, UQP, 1978; *The Peach Groves*, St Lucia, UQP, 1979; *The Frangipani Gardens*, St Lucia, UQP, 1980; *Dove*, St Lucia, UQP, 1982; *Kewpie Doll*, London, Chatto & Windus, 1984; *Annie Magdalene*, London, Chatto & Windus, 1985; *Dream People*, London, Grafton, 1987.

SEE ALSO J. Mott (interview), and A. Sykes in *ALS*, Vol. 11, No. 1 (1983), B. Walker in *Who is She? Images of Woman in Australian Fiction* (ed. S. Walker, UQP, 1983) and C. Baker (interview) in *Yacker 2* (Pan/Picador, 1987).

Harford, Lesbia (1891–1927)
Poet. Born Lesbia Keogh in Melbourne and educated at the University of Melbourne, graduating in arts and law 1916. Worked in a variety of jobs from teaching to clerical and factory work, the latter to gain an understanding of the conditions of working-class women. Her poems, collected and published by Nettie Palmer well after her death, are noted for their honesty, openness and simple lyricism.

POETRY *Poems*, Melbourne, MUP, 1941.
FICTION *The Invaluable Mystery*, Melbourne, McPhee Gribble/Penguin, 1987.
SEE ALSO *The Poems of Lesbia Harford* (ed. Drusilla Modjeska and Marjorie Pizer, Sirius, 1985).

Harrower, Elizabeth (1928–)
Novelist. Born in Sydney and spent her childhood in industrial Newcastle. Worked as a clerk and studied psychology before taking up writing. Between 1951–59 lived in London. Returned to Sydney where she has worked as a reviewer for the *Sydney Morning Herald*, for the ABC, and in publishing. All her novels demonstrate a psychological fascination with deep-seated human motivations, fears and obsessions.

FICTION *Down in the City*, London, Cassell, 1957; *The Long Prospect*, London, Cassell, 1958; *The Catherine Wheel*, London, Cassell, 1960; *The Watch Tower*, London, Cassell, 1966.
OTHER Short stories have appeared in: *Australian Letters* (1961); *Summer's Tales I & II* (1964, 1965); *The Penguin Book of Australian Short Stories* (1976); *Overland* (1977); *Australian Short Stories* (1983) and *The Oxford Anthology of Australian Literature* (1985).
SEE ALSO R. Claremont in *Quadrant* (Nov. 1979), S. Gunew and F. McInherny in *Hecate*, Vol. 9 (1983), C. Ferrier in *Who is She? Images of Woman in Australian Fiction* (ed. S. Walker, UQP, 1983) and D. R. Burns in *Meanjin*, Vol. 45, No. 3 (1986).

Harry, J. S. (1939–)
Poet. Born in Adelaide and now lives in Sydney. Has published poems in many literary journals and magazines. Was awarded the Harri Jones Prize 1971 for her first volume of poetry.
POETRY *The Deer Under the Skin*, St Lucia, UQP, 1971; *Hold for a Little*

While and Turn Gently, Sydney, Island Press, 1979; *A Dandelion for Van Gogh*, Sydney, Island Press, 1986.
SEE ALSO J. Tulip in *Southerly*, Vol. 32 (1972).

Hart, Gertrude
Novelist, children's author. Born in Melbourne and grew up in Stawell, Victoria. Published her first story at the age of 14 and her first book in London when still in her teens. With Bernard Cronin founded the Derelicts' Club which later became the Melbourne Society of Australian Authors.

FICTION *At the Bend of the Creek* (with A. Hart), London, Partridge, 190?; *Clouds that Pass*, London, Partridge, 190?; *The Dream Girl*, Melbourne, G. Robertson, 1912; *The Laughter Lady: A Story for Children of Different Ages*, Melbourne, Melbourne Publ. Co., 1918; *Chubby*, London, Hutchinson, 1937.
OTHER Poems were published in *The Little Track and Other Verses* (1922).

Harwood, Gwen (1920–)
Poet, librettist. Born in Brisbane. Studied music and for a time was organist at All Saints' Church. Married 1945 and moved to Tasmania where she has lived ever since. Began writing poetry as a response to pain during a period of hospitalisation when in her 30s. Her work is characterised by the use of masking personas, possibly connected to the number of pseudonyms (e.g. 'Walter Lehman', 'Miriam Stone', etc) under which she originally published work in literary magazines. Her poetry has also been influenced by the philosopher Wittgenstein. Has received various distinguished awards including the *Meanjin* Poetry Prize 1958 and 1959, the Robert Frost Award 1977 and the Patrick White Literary Award 1978.

POETRY *Poems*, Sydney, A & R, 1963; *Poems: Volume 2*, Sydney, A & R, 1968; *Selected Poems*, Sydney, A & R, 1975; *The Lion's Bride*, Sydney, A & R, 1981.
OTHER Has also written libretti for Larry Sitsky: *Fall of the House of Usher* (1965); *Lenz* (1972); *Fiery Tales* (1976); *Voices in Limbo* (1978) and *The Golem* (1979); for James Penberthy: *Commentaries on Ling* and *Choral Symphony;* and for Ian Cugley: *Sea Changes*.
SEE ALSO N. Talbot in *ALS*, Vol. 7, No. 3 (1976); J. Strauss in *Meanjin*, Vol. 38, No. 3 (1979); E. Lawson in *Southerly*, Vol. 43, No. 1 (1983) and P. Makeham, *The Poetry of Gwen Harwood: An Introduction* (English Teachers' Association of NSW, 1983. Includes bibliography).

Hasluck, Alexandria, Dame (1908–)
Historian, biographer. Born into an established Perth family. Educated at Perth College and the University of WA. After completing a BA, was a

teacher before her marriage to Sir Paul Hasluck (politican and Governor-General of Australia 1969–74). Despite the demands of public and political life, has produced various histories, biographies and editions of letters of other public figures. Was awarded an honorary D.Litt by the University of WA 1970, and in 1978 was created Dame of the Order of Australia.

NON-FICTION *Portrait with Background: A Life of Georgiana Molloy*, London, OUP, 1955; *Unwilling Emigrants*, London, OUP, 1959; *Remembered with Affection*, London, OUP, 1964; *Evelyn Hill: A Memoir*, Perth, the author, 1963; *Thomas Peel of Swan River*, London, OUP, 1965; *To Guide and Guard*, Guide Dogs for the Blind Association, 1967; *Of Ladies Dead*, Sydney, A & R, 1970; *Royal Engineer, A Life of Sir Edmund DuCane*, Sydney, A & R, 1973; *Victorian and Edwardian Perth in Photographs*, Perth, National Trust, 1977; *Audrey Tennyson's Vice-Regal Days*, Canberra, Australian National Library, 1977; *Portrait in a Mirror* (autobiography), London, OUP, 1981.

Hawker, Ruth
Children's author. Born in England, but of a pioneer SA family. Came to Australia with her parents as a child in 1906, and was sent back to England to finish her education. After living in the outback, she returned to Adelaide to teach at Woodlands Church of England Girls' Grammar School. *An Emu in the Fowl Pen*, later published as *Growing Up in the Outback* (1977), is an autobiographical account of station life.

FICTION *Us Three Outback*, Adelaide, Harman, 1932; *Yesterday: Being the Adventures of Us Three with the Early Colonists*, Adelaide, F. W. Preece, 1936; *Treasure at Prince's Point*, Melbourne, OUP, 1949; *Two New Australians*, Melbourne, OUP, 1949; *Heather at Magpie Creek*, Melbourne, OUP, 1950; *The Warrens of Wombat Flat*, Melbourne, OUP, 1950; *An Emu in the Fowl Pen*, Adelaide, Rigby, 1967; *Volcano Cottage*, Adelaide, Rigby, 1970.
POETRY *Fantasy and Reality*, Adelaide, Mail Newspapers, 1918; *Heritage and Other Poems*, Adelaide, Gillingham, 1923; *Us Three*, Adelaide, McGrath, 1930.

Hay, Agnes Grant, 'Anglo-Australian' (1838–1910)
Fiction and memoir writer. Born Agnes Gosse in London and came to Australia at the age of 12 with her family; her father practised medicine in Adelaide. Met colonist and politician Alexander Hay when she was 34, and then became his second wife 1872. Was the mother of novelist William Gosse Hay. Wrote books of memoirs and family history, although her discretion meant that biographical details in such works as *After Glow Memories* were so heavily disguised as to appear fictional.

FICTION *After Glow Memories*, by Anglo-Australian, London, Methuen, 1905; *Malcolm Canmore's Pearl*, London, Hurst & Blackett, 1907.
NON-FICTION *Footprints, a Memoir of the Late Alexander Hay*, London, Elliot Stock, 1899; *Ober-Ammergau and its Great Passion Drama of 1901*, London, Elliot Stock, 1902.
SEE ALSO Fayette Gosse, *The Gosses: An Anglo-Australian Family* (Brian Clouston, 1981).

Hayball, Doris
Playwright, travel writer. Born Ada Doris Hayball. Lived and worked in Melbourne but also spent much of her life travelling, visiting Asia, North America, Europe and Great Britain. Her manuscript collection is extensive and contains much unpublished material; some of her work appeared in Braille.

DRAMA *The Grotesque*, in *Eight Plays by Australians*, Melbourne, Dramatists' Club, 1934; *Out of a Clear Sky*, in *Playbill*, No. 3, May, 1935; *Blue Willow Pattern: A Play with Music*, Melbourne, Sunsphere Press, 1944; *Opening Movement: Two Comedies from Australia's Beginnings*, Melbourne, Sunsphere Press, 1944.
NON-FICTION *Sidelights on the Soviet, a Trip to Russia and its Great Theatre Festival*, Melbourne, G. Batchelor, 1939; *Strawberries in the Jam*, Melbourne, Sunsphere Press, 1940.
OTHER Also published poetry, *Field of Opal* (Sunsphere Press, 1965) and an American diary, *From Coast to Coast.*
MANUSCRIPTS La Trobe Library, Melbourne: Ada Doris Hayball Papers 1909–48 MS 7058–7074.

Hayward, Florence, 'Firenze'
Poet, children's author. Born Florence Burden. Was later married to William Thornborough. Lived and wrote in Adelaide where she published several books of verse, some of which were for children.

POETRY *Old Blues and Reds and Other Verses*, Adelaide, Pritchard Bros, 1915; *The Voice in Rama*, Adelaide, Pritchard Bros, 1916; *Tales and Tales of Tails and No Tails*, Adelaide, Pritchard Bros, 1920; *Vagabond Verses*, Adelaide, Pritchard Bros, 1924; *The Orchestra of Life*, Adelaide, the author, 1926; *Why the Laughing Jackass Laughed*, Adelaide, Rigby, 19–?.
OTHER Is represented in *Lady Galway Belgium Book* (1916). Also published essays in *Literary Jaunts and Jolts* (Pritchard Bros, 1925).

Hazzard, Shirley (1931–)
Novelist, short story writer. Born and educated in Sydney. After travelling since 1947 in the Far East, New Zealand and Italy, is now an American citizen. Worked for the United Nations in New York for ten years but

resigned in 1962 to devote herself to writing. *Deafeat of an Ideal* is an account of the UN's failures and weaknesses. Although she continues to revisit Australia, and wrote a long account of her impressions of her native country for the *New Yorker* in 1976, Australia does not feature largely in her fiction. Many of her short stories have appeared in the *New Yorker*. Won the USA National Book Critics' Award 1980 for the Best Novel of 1980, *The Transit of Venus*. Hazzard lives in New York and Capri with her husband, writer Francis Steegmuller.

FICTION *Cliffs of Fall*, London, Macmillan, 1963; *The Evening of the Holiday*, London, Macmillan, 1966; *People in Glass Houses*, Melbourne, Macmillan, 1967; *The Bay of Noon*, London, Macmillan, 1970; *The Transit of Venus*, London, Macmillan, 1980.
NON-FICTION *Deafeat of an Ideal: A Study of the Self-destruction of the United Nations*, London, Macmillan, 1973.
SEE ALSO R. Sellick in *ALS*, Vol. 9. No. 2 (1979); J. Wieland in *Kunapipi*, Vol. 5, No. 2 (1983); C. Rainwater & W. J. Scheick in *Texas Studies in Literature and Language*, Vol. 25 (1983. Interview, article & bibliography); P. Kavanagh (interview) in *Southerly*, Vol. 45, No. 2 (1985) and B. Levy in *Gender, Politics and Fiction* (ed. C. Ferrier, UQP, 1985).

Heddle, Enid Moodie (1904–)
Poet, critic. Born in Victoria and educated at the University of Melbourne. Worked as a teacher 1927–34, spending some time in England. Worked for publishers Collins for over 30 years and in that time produced many books. Is best remembered for the *Boomerang* series of Australian literature.

POETRY *Solitude and Other Vagaries*, Adelaide, Hassell Press, 1937; *Sagitta Says*, Adelaide, Hassell Press, 1943.
NON-FICTION *The Poet's Way* (edited), 1942, 1943, 1944; *Some Australian Adventurers*, Melbourne, Longmans Green, 1944; *Modern English Literature*, Melbourne, Cheshire, 1947; *Australian Literature Now: A Reader's Survey*, Melbourne, Longmans Green, 1949; *Discovering Poetry* (edited), 1956, 1957; *The Boomerang Book of Australian Poetry*, London, Longmans Green, 1956; *The Boomerang Book of Legendary Tales*, Melbourne, Longmans Green, 1957; *Boy on a Horse, The Story of Adam Lindsay Gordon* (with H. J. Samuel), Melbourne, Cheshire, 1957; *The Times We Live In, 24 BBC Talks*, Melbourne, Longmans Green, 1958; *Story of a Vineyard: Chateau Tahbilk*, Melbourne, Cheshire, 1960; *How Australian Literature Grew*, Melbourne, Cheshire, 1962; *Poets and Poetry, Books 1–4*, Melbourne, Longmans, 1966–7.
OTHER Also published articles in *Meanjin* (1943, 1947, 1959) and *Walkabout* (1953).

Hellyer, Jill (1925–)
Poet, fiction writer. Born in Sydney. Educated at North Sydney Girls' High. Was co-founder and first Executive Secretary of the ASA 1963–71. Although as a writer she has been restricted by the pressures of having two handicapped sons, has contributed numerous poems, stories and articles to various literary magazines over the years. Won the Grenfell Henry Lawson Award 1963, the *Poetry Magazine* Award 1965, and has received several literary fellowships.

POETRY *The Exile*, Sydney, Alpha Books, 1969; *Song of the Humpbacked Whales*, Melbourne, Sisters, 1981.
FICTION *Not Enough Savages*, Sydney, Alpha Books, 1975.
OTHER Edited a biographical work, *Fifty Years in Psychiatry: D. W. H. Arnott* (1980). Poems, stories, articles have appeared in the *Sydney Morning Herald*, the *Age*, *Meanjin*, *Overland*, *Westerly*, *Southerly*, the *Australian*, *Poetry Magazine*, and *Luna*.

Heney, Helen (1907–)
Novelist, social historian. Born in Sydney, the daughter of journalist Thomas Heney. Educated at the University of Sydney. Lived mainly in Poland 1929–35, working as a translator and teacher. During WWII worked for the Red Cross and was a social worker in Europe. After publishing five novels and a biography, her interest turned to history with an emphasis upon women, such as in her study of Australian women between 1788 and 1822, *Australian's Founding Mothers*. *Dear Fanny*, the collection of letters by Australian women, is considered by Heney to be her most useful contribution to Australian social history. Is presently working upon another historical book, *A River Flows Through Parramatta*.

FICTION *The Chinese Camellia*, London, Collins, 1950; *The Proud Lady*, London, Collins, 1951; *Dark Moon*, Sydney, A & R, 1953; *This Quiet Dust*, Sydney, A & R, 1956; *The Leaping Blaze*, Sydney, A & R, 1962.
NON-FICTION *In A Dark Glass: The Biography of Sir Paul Strzelecki*, Sydney, A & R, 1961; *Australia's Founding Mothers*, Melbourne, Nelson, 1978; *Dear Fanny, Letters From Australian Women*, London, Pergamon Press, 1985.
MANUSCRIPTS ML, Sydney: Helen Heney Mss & Papers.

Henning, Rachel (1826–1914)
Letter-writer. Born in Bristol, England, and came to Australia to join her family 1854. Stayed two years before returning to England, but arrived again 1861 to settle permanently. Joined her brother and sister on their property in Queensland. Married 1866 and eventually moved to a property near the NSW south coast. Her now famous letters, first published in the *Bulletin* 1951–2, were written to various members of

her family in England and Australia. They are valued for their vivid portrayal of station life in the second half of the nineteenth century and for her own humour and frankness about the life she led.

NON-FICTION *The Letters of Rachel Henning*, ed. David Armstrong, illust. Norman Lindsay, Sydney, Bulletin, 1952.
MANUSCRIPTS ML, Sydney: M/film copies of original letters.
SEE ALSO D. Jones in *Span*, No. 21 (Oct. 1985).

Henry, Alice (1857–1943)
Journalist, suffragist. Born in Richmond, Victoria. Became prominent in the 1890s and published articles in the *Australasian*, the *Argus*, the *Daily Herald* and the *Triad* upon an enormous range of subjects related to women's welfare. Departed for England and the USA 1905 and spent nearly 30 years overseas lecturing on women's suffrage and working in the trade union movement. Returned to Australia permanently 1933.

NON-FICTION *The Trade Union Woman*, New York, Appleton & Co., 1915; *Women and the Labour Movement*, New York, Macmillan, 1927; *Memoirs of Alice Henry* (ed. Nettie Palmer) Melbourne, the author, 1944.
MANUSCRIPTS NL, Canberra: Alice Henry Misc. Papers MS 1066; ML, Sydney: Alice Henry File QA 824/H; plus: 'Bibliography of the Works of Australian Women Writers' (t/script) QA 820.3/H.

Hepburn, Edith, 'Anna Wickham' (1883–1949)
Poet. Born in London and brought to Australia as a child. After publishing two plays for girls, she returned to London 1903; here she remained and published the rest of her work, mostly under the pseudonym 'Anna Wickham'. Enjoyed some success among her literary peers.

POETRY *Songs*, by John Oland, London, Women's Printing Society, 1903; *The Contemplative Quarry*, by Anna Wickham, London, Poetry Bookshop, 1915; *The Man with a Hammer*, Verses by Anna Wickham, London, Grant Richards, 1916; *The Little Old House* by Anna Wickham, London, Poetry Bookshop, 1921; *The Contemplative Quarry and the Man with a Hammer*, New York, Harcourt Brace, 1921; *Poems* (ed. J. Gawsworth) London, Richards Press, 1936.
DRAMA *The Seasons: A Speaking Tableau for Girls*, Sydney, Pepperday, 1902; *Wonder Eyes: A Journey to Slumbertown*, Sydney, Pepperday, 1903.
SEE ALSO *Selected Poems by Anna Wickham*, introduced by D. Garnett (Chatto & Windus, 1971).

Herron, Margaret (? – 1968)
Novelist. Born Olive Herron. Became the wife of poet C. J. Dennis whom she met in 1914 just before WWI and married 1917. They lived in Melbourne and at Toolangi, in the Victorian Dandenongs.

FICTION *My Dear*, Sydney, Cornstalk, 1928; *Seed and Stubble*, Sydney, A & R 1936.
NON-FICTION *Down the Years, the Life Story of C. J. Dennis*, Melbourne, Hallcraft Publ. Co., 1953; *Random Verse: A Collection of Verse and Prose by C. J. Dennis*, selected by Margaret Herron, Melbourne, Hallcraft Publ. Co., 1952.

Hewett, Dorothy (1923–)
Playwright, poet. Born in Perth, WA. Educated at Perth College and the University of WA. Published her first poetry in *Meanjin* at the age of 17 and early in her career won poetry and drama competitions. Left for Sydney 1948 where she worked for some time in factories (which provided material for the novel *Bobbin Up*). Was an active member of the CPA which she joined when 19; both her husbands were also members of the CPA. Returned to WA and tutored at the University of WA before settling again in Sydney, where she still lives. Has received a number of Senior Writers' Fellowships from the Literature Board and had six writer-in-residencies at various Australian universities. Has won many awards including the ABC National Poetry Prize 1945 and 1965, two AWGIE awards, 1974 and 1981, and the *Australian* Poetry Prize 1986. Was awarded the AO 1986 for services to literature.

DRAMA *The Chapel Perilous*, Sydney, Currency Press, 1972; *This Old Man Comes Rolling Home*, Sydney, Currency Press, 1976; *Bons Bons and Roses for Dolly; The Tatty Hollow Story*, Sydney, Currency Press, 1976; *The Beautiful Mrs Portland*, in *Theatre Australia*, Nov-Dec, 1976; *Pandora's Cross*, in *Theatre Australia*, Sept-Oct, 1978; *The Man from Mukinupin*, Fremantle, Fremantle Arts Centre Press, 1979; *Susannah's Dreaming; The Golden Oldies*, Sydney, Currency Press, 1981; *Joan*, Melbourne, Yackandandah Playscripts, 1984; *Golden Valley; Song of the Seals*, Sydney, Currency Press, 1985.
POETRY *What about the People* (with M. Lilley), Qld, National Council of Realist Writers, 1961; *Hidden Journey*, Newnham, Tas., Wattle Grove Press, 1967; *Windmill Country*, Melbourne, Overland, 1968; *Rapunzel in Suburbia*, Sydney, Prism, 1975; *Greenhouse*, Sydney, Big Smoke Books, 1979; *Journeys* (with others, ed. F. Zwicky), Melbourne, Sisters, 1982.
FICTION *Bobbin Up*, Melbourne, Australasian Book Society, 1959.
OTHER Plays produced include: *Mrs Porter and the Angel* (1969), *Catspaw* (1974) (unpublished mss held in the Hanger Collection), *Time Flits Away, Lady* (1941) and *Miss Hewett's Shenanigans* (1975). Also edited the WA

anthology, *Sandgropers*, for the FAW (1973). Poems, stories and radio plays have appeared in many journals and magazines.
MANUSCRIPTS NL, Canberra: Dorothy Hewett Mss Notes & Letters; Fisher Library, The University of Sydney: Mss.
SEE ALSO J. Barbour in *Southerly*, Vol. 37, No. 1 (1977), P. Porter (interview) in *Hecate*, Vol. 3, No. 1 (1977), C. Ferrier in *Lip*, Vol. 11 (1977), A. Sykes in *World Literature Written in English*, Vol. 17, No. 1 (1978), B. Kiernan in *Contemporary Australian Drama* (ed. P. Holloway, Currency Press, 1981) and M. Akerholt in *Westerly*, Vol. 29, No. 1 (1984).

Hill, Deirdre (1925–)
Children's author. Born and educated in Sydney. Served in the WAAAF 1944–6 and married 1946. After raising four children, first published for children in 1969. Became Executive Secretary of the ASA 1971–81. Her first book was commended in the Children's Book Council Awards 1970.

FICTION *Over the Bridge*, London, Hutchinson, 1969; *Mario Visits Australia*, Sydney, Methuen, 1978; *A Bridge of Dreams*, Sydney, Hodder & Stoughton, 1982.
NON-FICTION *A Writer's Rights, The Story of the Australian Society of Authors 1963–1983*, Australia and New Zealand Book Co., 1983.

Hill, Ernestine (1900–1972)
Travel writer. Born in Rockhampton, Queensland. Developed a love of travel which she took up in earnest after the death of her husband 1933. All her books record her adventures and are highly descriptive of the Australian landscape. Is best known for *The Territory*, although her only novel, *My Love Must Wait*, the fictionalised biography of navigator Matthew Flinders, had enormous sales and great popularity overseas as well as in Australia. Hill claimed to be mostly responsible for the authorship of Daisy Bates's (q.v.) book, *The Passing of the Aborigines*. Over the years she contributed numerous articles to newspapers and journals such as *Walkabout*, and also worked briefly for the ABC.

NON-FICTION *The Great Australian Loneliness*, London, Jarrolds, 1937; *Water into Gold*, Melbourne, Robertson & Mullens, 1937; *Australian Frontier* (US edn of *The Great Australian Loneliness*), New York, Doubleday, Horan, 1942; *Australia, Land of Contrasts* (ed. Sydney Ure Smith), Sydney, Sands, 1943; *Flying Doctor Calling*, Sydney, A & R, 1947; *The Territory*, Sydney, A & R, 1951; *Kabbarli: A Personal Memoir of Daisy Bates*, Sydney, A & R, 1973.
FICTION *My Love Must Wait, the Story of Matthew Flinders*, Sydney, A & R, 1941.

OTHER Also published: *Peter Pan Land and Other Poems* (with four others, Hibernian Newspaper Co., 1916) and a play, *Santa Claus of Christmas Creek*, in *Australian Radio Plays* (A & R, 1946).
MANUSCRIPTS John Oxley Library, Brisbane: Letters 1917–22.
SEE ALSO J. McKellar in *Victorian Historical Magazine*, Vol. 26, No. 2 (1954).

Hill, Fidelia (c. 1790–1854)
Poet. Born Fidelia Munkhouse in Yorkshire, England and came to Australia with her husband R. K. Hill in the *Buffalo* and settled in Adelaide. Was the first woman to publish a book of poetry in Australia and to write about South Australia. Left Adelaide after the death of her husband, remarried, and settled in Launceston, Tasmania where she died.

POETRY *Poems and Recollections of the Past*, Sydney, T. Trood, 1840.
SEE ALSO Elsie B. Todd in *A Book of South Australian Women in the First 100 Years* (Rigby, 1936).

Hodgman, Helen (1945–)
Novelist, screenwriter. Born in England, and brought up in Tasmania. After leaving school at 15 worked in a variety of jobs and is now a full-time writer. Won the Somerset Maugham Award 1979 for *Jack and Jill*, and was shortlisted for the Faber Memorial Prize 1978 for *Blue Skies*.

FICTION *Blue Skies*, London, Duckworth, 1976; *Jack and Jill*, London, Duckworth, 1978; *Broken Words*, Melbourne, Penguin, 1987.
OTHER Drama produced includes: *Oh Mother, Is It Worth It?* (Vancouver, Waterfront Theatre, 1982); *The Right Hand Men* (screenplay, Australia, UAA Films 1984/5) and *The Silence of Dean Maitland* (mini-series, Australia, Zarwot P/L, 1986).

Holman, Ada (1869–1949)
Journalist, novelist, children's author. Born Ada Kidgell in Ballarat, Victoria. Worked for the *Sydney Morning Herald*, the *Sydney Mail* and the *Melbourne Punch*. Married 1901 to politician William Holman, Premier of NSW 1913–1920. Although her activities were restricted after her husband's entry into State Parliament, she continued to publish short stories and articles in the *Daily Telegraph* and other papers, and also wrote on behalf of her husband. Was a republican and a feminist, advocating women's rights in her stories and articles; *Sport of the Gods*, an unusual romance, has a strong political interest.

NON-FICTION *My Wander Year*, Sydney, William Brooks & Co., 1913; *Memoirs of a Premier's Wife*, Sydney, A & R, 1947.
FICTION *Little Miss Anzac* (children's), London, Jack, 1917; *Sport of the*

Gods, Melbourne, De Garis, 1921; *The Adventures of Woodeny* (children's), London, T. Nelson, 1923; *Elka Reva-Ree* (children's), 1928; *Eve in the Desert*, serialised in the *Sydney Morning Herald*, 1934; *Good Courage*, serialised in the *Sydney Morning Herald*, 1936.
OTHER Various unpublished plays including *Annabel Goes to a Party*, *Mrs Milligan Seeks her Ideal*, *The Premier's Wife* (1936), *The Six Queens*, and *The Three Little Dears*.
MANUSCRIPTS ML, Sydney: Ada Holman Papers c.1911–46 ML MSS 1909.
SEE ALSO S. Encel in *Historical Studies*, Vol. 7 (1965).

Hope, Emily (1940–1979)
Fiction writer, artist. Born in Sydney, the daughter of poet A. D. Hope. Trained as a sculptor and silversmith at the Royal Melbourne Institute of Technology, graduating 1967, followed by 10 years' work as a sculptor and metal worker. Held exhibitions in most of the capital cities in Australia and travelled widely in the 1970s. Visited Nepal 1975 and there studied bronze sculpture. Spent many years researching *The Legend of Pope Joan*, an unusual work combining fact and imagination.

FICTION *The Queen of the Nagas*, Melbourne, Nomad Press, 1979; *The Legend of Pope Joan*, Melbourne, Sisters, 1983.

Hospital, Janette Turner (1942–)
Novelist, short story writer. Born in Melbourne. Educated in Brisbane at the University of Queensland. Graduated MA from Queen's University, Ontario, Canada. Has lived in the USA and Canada since 1971, but still considers herself an Australian writer. Taught high school in Queensland 1963–7 before moving to the USA with her husband. Worked as a librarian at Harvard University for 4 years before returning to graduate studies followed by a lectureship in English at Queen's University. After a 3–year return to schoolteaching in Ontario, became a full-time writer since receiving the prestigious Seal Award for her first novel 1982. During 1985–6 was writer-in-residence at Massachusetts Institute of Technology, Boston and returned to Australia 1985 on a Senior Writer's Fellowship for 3 months. Has twice been nominated for Britain's Booker Prize.

FICTION *The Ivory Swing*, Toronto, McClelland & Stewart, 1982; *The Tiger in the Tiger Pit*, Toronto, McClelland & Stewart, 1983; *Borderline*, London & Sydney, Hodder & Stoughton, 1985; *Dislocations*, St Lucia, UQP, 1987.
OTHER Short stories have appeared in several North American magazines including the *Atlantic Monthly* (1978); *North American Review* (1980,

1985); *Dalhousie Review* (1980); *Queen's Quarterly* (1981, 1982, 1983); *Toronto Life* (1983) and *Canadian Forum* (1980, 1983).
SEE ALSO Interview in the *Australian Author* (Sept. 1985), and C. Baker (interview) in *Yacker 2* (Pan/Picador, 1987).

Houbein, Lolo (1934–)
Bibliographer, short story writer, poet. Born in the Netherlands. Educated at the Universities of Adelaide and Papua New Guinea. Has held a number of positions in social services, schools and tertiary institutions. Is presently a freelance writer and teacher of English as a second language. Compiled the first bibliography of migrant writing in Australia. Her fiction has only appeared in magazines and anthologies but has won a number of awards including the Rolf Boldrewood Short Story Award 1978 and the SPACLALS Short Story Award 1980.

NON-FICTION *Ethnic Writings in English from Australia: A Bibliography*, University of Adelaide, *ALS*, 1976; *Proposal for an Alternative Total Education Project on a Bush Campus in South Australia*, Adelaide, the author, 1977.
OTHER Short stories have appeared in *Inprint* (1978, 1979, 1980) and *South Pacific Stories* (1980).

I, J

Ingram, Anne Bower (1937–)
Children's author, editor. Born in Manilla, NSW, and educated in Queensland. Became an editor with publisher William Collins in Sydney 1971 and since 1980 has worked as a freelance book editor and writer. Worked in bookshops in Brisbane and in London at the Children's Book Centre 1964–6. Edited *Reading Time* (1970–78), the journal of the Children's Book Council, fostering its development into a reputable critical review journal.

FICTION *Shudders and Shakes* (ed.), Sydney, Collins, 1972; *Too True* (ed.), Sydney, Collins, 1974; *The Pickled Boeing* (ed), Sydney, Children's Medical Research Foundation, 1982.
NON-FICTION *It's Reading Time*, Sydney, Hodder & Stoughton, 1971; *Reflections* (ed.), Children's Book Council of Australia, 1977; *The Book of Sydney* (with L. Scott & P. O'Donnell), Melbourne, OUP, 1984.

'Iota' *See:* **Caffyn, Kathleen**

James, Florence (1902–)
Novelist. Born in New Zealand and educated at the University of Sydney. Is best known for her long association with Dymphna Cusack (q.v.) and the book they co-authored, *Come in Spinner.* Not so well known for her work in publishing and editing. Went to England 1947 and worked as an independent literary agent and reader for Constable in London. Was responsible for several Australian authors being published in London including Mary Durack and Nene Gare (q.q.v.). Reviewed regularly for the *Times Literary Supplement*, forsaking creative writing for critical because of the necessity of supporting two children. Was a close friend of Christina Stead (q.v.) and generally a focus for Australian writers in London in the post-war years. Returned to Australia 1963 and now lives in Manly, Sydney.

FICTION *Four Winds and a Family* (children's), Sydney, Shakespeare Head, 1947; *Come in Spinner* (with Dymphna Cusack), London, Heinemann, 1951.

James, Winifred (1876–1941)
Journalist, novelist, travel writer. Born in Melbourne. Worked there as a journalist and left for London 1905. Married an American and lived in South America, the USA and England, returning to Australia 1940, a year before her death. Australia features in at least three of her books.

Enjoyed her greatest success with *Letters to My Son*, which went into twelve editions in less than 12 years.

FICTION *Bachelor Betty*, London, Constable, 1907; *Patricia Baring*, London, Constable, 1908; *Letters to My Son* (anon.), London, Hodder & Stoughton, 1910; *Saturday's Children* (for girls), London, Blackie & Son, 1910; *Letters of a Spinster*, London, G. Bell & Sons, 1911; *More Letters to My Son*, London, Chapman & Hall, 1911; *A Sweeping*, London, Unwin, 1911; *Three Births in the Hemingway Family*, London, Hutchinson, 1929; *The Gods Arrive*, Melbourne, Popular Publications, 1941.
NON-FICTION *The Mulberry Tree*, London, G. Bell, 1913; *A Woman in the Wilderness*, London, Chapman & Hall, 1915; *Out of the Shadows*, 1924; *London is My Lute*, London, Chapman & Hall, 1930; *A Man For England*, London, Chapman & Hall, 1930; *Gangways and Corridors*, 1936.

'Jay, Charlotte' *See:* **Halls, Geraldine**

Jefferis, Barbara (1917–)
Novelist, journalist. Born in Adelaide. Moved to Sydney when in her 20s and worked as a journalist. Has written radio scripts for the ABC as well as book criticism and reviews. Was the first woman president of the ASA 1973–6, and has been active in that society for many years.

FICTION *Contango Day*, London, Dent, 1953; *Beloved Lady*, London, Dent, 1955; *Half Angel*, London, Dent, 1959; *Solo for Several Players*, London, Dent, 1961; *The Wild Grapes*, London, Michael Joseph, 1963; *One Black Summer*, London, Rupert Hart-Davis, 1967; *Time of the Unicorn*, London, Gollancz, 1974; *First Flight*, Sydney, Cassell, 1976; *The Tall One*, London, Gollancz, 1977.
NON-FICTION *Three of a Kind*, Melbourne, Sisters, 1982; *Australian Book Contracts*, Sydney, ASA, 1983.
SEE ALSO N. Keesing in *Southerly*, Vol. 22 (1962).

Jennings, Kate (1948–)
Poet. Born near Griffith, NSW, and now lives in the USA. Was editor of a milestone in Australian women's writing, the feminist anthology of poetry, *Mother, I'm Rooted*, which collected the works of many known and unknown writers.

POETRY *Come to Me My Melancholy Baby*, Melbourne, Outback Press, 1975; *Mother, I'm Rooted* (ed.), Melbourne, Outback Press, 1975.

Jerome, Helen
Poet, playwright, non-fiction writer. Born Helen Bruton in England. Was a catering and cookery teacher at the North Polytechnic in London before coming to Australia.

POETRY *Petals in the Wind: Verses of a Persifleuse*, Melbourne, Lothian, 1910.
DRAMA *Charlotte Corday: A Play in Three Acts*, London, Hamish Hamilton, 1937.
OTHER Also published *The Japan of Today* (Bookstall, 1904) and *The Secret of Woman* (1923) as well as six books on the subjects of cooking and catering.

Johnson, Patricia (1945–)
Playwright, scriptwriter. Born in Sydney. After leaving school worked in secretarial and editing jobs and at 18 edited a small film news magazine. After entering journalism went overseas where she worked on the *London Evening News*, the *Los Angeles Times* and the *Hollywood Reporter*. Completed a screenwriting course at the Australian Film and Television School 1980 and since then has written for television and had plays produced. Was writer-in-residence at the Sydney Theatre Company 1981.

DRAMA *Gladbags*, Melbourne, Yackandandah Playscripts, 1984; *And the Bestman Makes Three*, in *Shorts at the Wharf Vol. 1*, Sydney, Currency Press, 1985.
OTHER Plays produced include *The Cocky on the Lawn* (National Theatre of WA) and *Kindred Spirits* (ABC TV 1984).

Johnston, Dorothy (1948–)
Novelist. Born in Geelong, Victoria and educated at the University of Melbourne, graduating BA and Diploma of Education 1969. Worked as a teacher and in educational research before turning to writing fiction. Now lives in Canberra where she is a full-time writer.

FICTION *Tunnel Vision*, Sydney, Hale & Iremonger, 1984; *Ruth*, Sydney, Hale & Iremonger, 1987.
OTHER Short stories have appeared in *Frictions* (Sybylla 1982) and *The State of the Art* (Penguin, 1983).

Jolley, Elizabeth (1923–)
Novelist, short story writer. Born in Birmingham, England into a partly European family. Educated in England, Strasbourg, Paris and Hamburg. Trained as a nurse in London and Birmingham. Came to Australia with her husband and children in 1959, settling in Perth. Has been a salesperson and a nurse as well as a teacher of creative writing and literature at the Fremantle Arts Centre, at the University of WA, and at WAIT, where she is presently a part-time tutor. Has been writer-in-residence at Scarborough High School, at the WAIT School of English, and at the WA CAE. Produced an impressive series of novels in the early 1980s,

for which she has received a number of awards including the *Age* Book of the Year Award 1982 for *Mr Scobie's Riddle*, the NSW Premier's Award for Fiction 1985 for *Milk and Honey* and most lately the Miles Franklin Award 1987 for *The Well*. In her spare time Jolley also runs a small orchard and goose farm.

FICTION *Five Acre Virgin and Other Stories*, Fremantle, Fremantle Arts Centre Press, 1976; *The Travelling Entertainer*, Fremantle, Fremantle Arts Centre Press, 1979; *Palomino*, Melbourne, Outback Press, 1980; *The Newspaper of Claremont Street*, Fremantle, Fremantle Arts Centre Press, 1981; *Mr Scobie's Riddle*, Melbourne, Penguin, 1983; *Woman in a Lampshade*, Melbourne, Penguin, 1983; *Miss Peabody's Inheritance*, St Lucia, UQP, 1983; *Milk and Honey*, Fremantle, Fremantle Arts Centre Press, 1984; *Foxybaby*, St Lucia, UQP, 1985; *The Well*, Melbourne, Viking, 1986.
OTHER Short stories have appeared in over 20 anthologies and collections and in as many literary journals and magazines. Has contributed many book reviews and articles to papers and between 1975–81 had six plays produced on ABC radio.
SEE ALSO H. Garner in *Meanjin*, Vol. 42, No. 2 (1983); J. Kirby in *Meanjin*, Vol. 43, No. 4 (1984); J. Ellison (interview) in *Rooms of their Own* (Penguin, 1986) and S. Trigg (interview) in *Scripsi*, Vol. 4, No. 1 (1986).

Jones, Doris Egerton (1889–1973)
Novelist, playwright. Born in Adelaide and educated at the University of Adelaide, graduating in arts and law. Did not practise law due to ill health, and subsequently took up writing. Married Reginald Callaghan 1918. Her novels are mostly romantic tales with some psychological interest; the first, *Peter Piper*, attracted some noteworthy critical praise.

FICTION *Peter Piper*, London, Cassell, 1913; *Time o'Day*, London, Cassell, 1915; *Green Eyes*, London, Hodder & Stoughton, 1915; *The Coconut Planter*, London, Cassell, 1916; *The Year Between*, London, Cassell, 1918.
DRAMA *Governor Bligh*, Sydney, 1930.

Jones, Margaret
Journalist, novelist. Worked as a foreign correspondent for Australian newspapers in Britain, America and Asia. Lived and worked in Peking 1973–5 after diplomatic relations with China were reopened by the Labor government 1972. Has been the Foreign Editor of the *Sydney Morning Herald* and is presently its Literary Editor. Both her novels are political thrillers set in Asian countries.

FICTION *The Confucius Enigma*, Sydney, McGraw-Hill, 1979; *The Smiling Buddha*, London, Hamish Hamilton, 1985.
NON-FICTION *Pressures on the Press*, Sydney, Journalists' Club, 1986; *Thatcher's Kingdom*.

Jones, Suzanne Holly (1945–)
Novelist. Born in Melbourne. Published her first novel when 19. Concerned with an adolescent girl's relationship with her foster father, it was well received by critics. Judith Wright called Jones a 'born writer'.

FICTION *Harry's Child*, Brisbane, Jacaranda, 1964; *Crying in the Garden*, Melbourne, Outback Press, 1974.
SEE ALSO S. Higgins in *Meanjin*, Vol. 34, No. 4 (1975).

K

Kalamaras, Vasso

Poet, playwright, short story writer. Born in Athens, Greece, and came to Western Australia with her husband 1951. Settled in the Manjimup district and worked on a tobacco farm. Studied fine arts, language and drama in Greece, and completed diplomas in fine arts at Claremont Technical College and at WAIT. Taught sculpture at Claremont Technical College and Perth Technical College; has exhibited her work in five shows and won prizes for her paintings. In 1951 began writing in Greek and publishing poems in Greek and Australian magazines, and has since then published in a wide range of newspapers and journals in both countries. Has won several awards for her work including two prizes for the play *Breadtrap* and the Perth Play of the Year Award two years running. Five of her plays have been produced, although none has been published, and her work has been broadcast on radio in Australia and Greece.

FICTION *Alla Homata, Stories in Greek*, Estia, Athens, 1961; *Pikres, Stories in Greek*, Estia, Athens, 1977; *Impressions of a Journey*, Athens, 1977; *Other Earth, Four Greek-Australian Stories* (trans. Reg. Durack & Vasso Kalamaras), Freemantle, Fremantle Arts Centre Press, 1977; *Bitterness, Stories in Greek and English* (trans. Reg Durack & Vasso Kalamaras), Perth, Artlook, 1983.
POETRY *Stalagmaties*, Greek Poems, Athens, 1960; *Twenty-two Poems*, Greek and English Poems (trans. Durack & Vasso Kalamaras), Perth, 1977; *The Hammer of the Sculptor*, Greek Poems, Athens, 1979; *Landscape and Soul*, Greek and English Poems (trans. June Kingdon & Vasso Kalamaras), Perth, 1980.
DRAMA Plays produced are: *The Breadtrap* (in Greek, Melbourne, 1981; in English, Perth, 1982–3) and all the following by the Patch Theatre, Perth: *Holiday in Greece* (1983/4), *Little Eros* (1984), *Olympos in the Porongorups* (1984) and *Phryne* (1984).

Kan, Diana (1934–)

Poet. Born and educated in Melbourne. Studied at the Art School of the Royal Melbourne Institute of Technology. Began writing poetry in the early 1970s. Has had work published in newspapers and journals and broadcast on the radio. Has a particular interest in the use of verbal and visual imagery to convey religious meaning. A series of poems, *The Hill of the Cross*, was published as a special feature in *On the Move*, by the Joint Board of Religious Education of Australia and New Zealand.

Was joint winner of the Patricia Hackett prize for poetry 1983. Also continues to work as a graphic artist.

POETRY *Happy Families and Other Poems* (illust. by the author), South Australia, Austaprint, 1973; *The Bird-man* (illust. by the author), Victoria, Pariah Press, 1984.
OTHER Work is included in the following anthologies: *Australian Voices* (ANU Press, 1975), *Mother I'm Rooted* (Outback Press, 1975), *Walk a Different Way* (FAW, 1979), *Poetry South East 4* (South-East Arts, 1979) and *Network* (Fringe Arts Festival, 1983).

Kata, Elizabeth
Novelist. Born in Sydney of Scottish parents. Lived in Japan and was married in Tokyo 1937. Continued to live there during WWII where her son was born, and later returned to Australia. Taught English at the university in Tokyo. Her first novel became popular when published in the USA as *A Patch of Blue* and filmed, starring Sidney Poitier; *Child of the Holocaust* was serialised by ABC television.

FICTION *Be Ready with Bells and Drums*, London, Michael Joseph, 1961; *Someone Will Conquer Them*, London, Michael Joseph, 1962; *Child of the Holocaust*, London, Fontana Collins, 1979; *Tilda*, Hong Kong, Horwitz, 1979; *The Death of Ruth*, Sydney, Pan Books, 1981; *With Kisses on Both Cheeks*, Sydney, Child & Henry, 1982.

Keesing, Nancy (1923–)
Poet, freelance writer, editor. Born in Sydney. Educated at the University of Sydney. Worked as a clerk in the Navy during WWII, and then as a social worker until 1951. Afterwards embarked upon a career as a writer that has involved her in numerous publications (particularly anthologies and collections) and literary activities. Has been a member and Vice President of the English Association, member of the ASA and also edited its journal, the *Australian Author*, 1971–4. Has also been involved with the Literature Board of of the Australia Council and was its chair (1974–7), and has been active in the National Book Council. In 1979 was awarded the AO for services to literature.

POETRY *Imminent Summer*, Sidney, Lyrebird Writers, 1951; *Three Men and Sydney*, Sydney, A & R, 1955; *Showground Sketchbook*, Sydney, A & R, 1968; *Hails and Farewells*, Sydney, Edwards & Shaw, 1977.
FICTION *By Gravel and Gum* (children's), Melbourne, Macmillan, 1963; *The Golden Dream* (children's), Sydney, Collins, 1974.
NON-FICTION *Elsie Carew: Australian Primitive Poet*, Sydney, Wentworth Press, 1965; *Douglas Stewart*, Melbourne, Lansdowne Press, 1965; *Garden Island People*, Sydney, Wentworth Press, 1975; *John Lang and*

'The Forger's Wife', Sydney, John Ferguson, 1979; *Lily on the Dustbin, Slang of Australian Women and Families*, Melbourne, Penguin, 1982; *Just Look Out the Window*, Melbourne, Penguin, 1985.
EDITED *Australian Bush Ballads* (with Douglas Stewart), Sydney, A & R, 1955; *Old Bush Songs* (with Douglas Stewart), Sydney, A & R, 1957; *Pacific Book of Bush Ballads* (with Douglas Stewart), Sydney, A & R, 1967; *Gold Fever*, Sydney, A & R, 1967; *Transition, an Australian Society of Authors Anthology*, Sydney, A & R, 1970; *The Kelly Gang*, Sydney, Ure Smith, 1975; *Australian Post-War Novelists*, Brisbane, Jacaranda, 1975; *The White Chrysanthemum*, Sydney, A & R, 1977; *Henry Lawson: Favourite Verse*, Melbourne, Nelson, 1978; *Shalom: Australian Jewish Short Stories*, Sydney, Collins, 1978.
OTHER Short stories have also appeared in the *Bulletin* (since 1952), *Quadrant, Southerly*, etc.
MANUSCRIPTS ML. Sydney: Nancy Keesing Papers and Mss 1959–74.

Kefala, Antigone (1935–)
Poet, prose writer. Born in Romania of Greek parents. Lived in Greece following WWII and migrated with her family to New Zealand 1951. Studied at Victoria University, Wellington, graduating MA, and came to Australia in the 1960s. Her first story was published in a university magazine 1959 and her first poem appeared in *Australian Letters* 1962. Since then her work has appeared in numerous magazines and collections and has also been broadcast on radio. Has been a teacher of English and a member of the Literature Board of the Australia Council.

POETRY *The Alien*, St Lucia, Makar Press, 1973; *Thirsty Weather*, Melbourne, Outback Press, 1978.
FICTION *The First Journey*, Sydney, Wild & Woolley, 1975; *The Island*, Sydney, Hale & Iremonger, 1984; *Alexia*, Sydney, John Ferguson, 1984.
OTHER Also translated *Men for the Rights of Men, Rise*, by John Koutsoleras (Alpha Books, 1974). Poems have been published in the *Bulletin, Poetry Australia, Westerly, Luna, Aspect, Makar, Hemisphere*, and in the collections: *Australian Poetry* (A & R, 1970, 1972, 1973), *Mother, I'm Rooted* (Outback Press, 1975), *Australian Voices, Poetry and Prose of the 1970s* (ANU Press, 1975), *The Tabloid Story Pocket Book* (Wild & Woolley, 1978), *The Penguin Book of Modern Australian Verse* (Penguin, 1981), *The Collins Book of Australian Poetry* (Collins, 1981), *Mrs Noah and the Minoan Queen* (Sisters, 1983) and *Joseph's Coat* (Hale & Iremonger, 1985).
SEE ALSO S. Gunew in *Meanjin*, Vol. 42, No. 1 (1983) and *A. Fremd* (interview) in *Outrider* (Dec. 1984).

Kelly, Carmel
Short story writer. Born in Melbourne. Has a BA and a Diploma of Education and has been a teacher. Lived and worked in England where

she received recognition for her stories. Received third prize 1970 in the Nottingham Scribe Award, an international short story competition administered by the British Arts Council. Was awarded a commonwealth literary grant 1973, and has since published stories in several magazines.

FICTION *The Waters of Vanuatu*, Sydney, Sea Cruise Books, 1985.
OTHER Fiction has appeared in the following: *Westerly* (June 1971), *Thor* (1972), *Nation Review* (April, May 1973), *Outback Reader* (1973), *Tabloid Story* (Nos 11 & 12, 1974) and *No Regrets* (Nos 2 & 3, 1981/2).

Kelly, Gwen (1922–)
Novelist, short story writer, poet. Born in Sydney and educated at Fort Street Girls' High and the University of Sydney. Graduated with first-class honours in English and philosophy and the University Medal 1944. Held a position with the public service for some years but has mainly been a schoolteacher, university and college lecturer, and writer. Has published stories and articles in journals and magazines since the mid-1950s. Her work has attracted several awards including the Henry Lawson Prose Award, which she has won four times, and the inaugural Hilarie Lindsay Award 1981 from the Society of Women Writers.

FICTION *There is No Refuge*, London, Heinemann, 1961; *The Red Boat*, Sydney, Alpha Books, 1968; *The Middle-Aged Maidens*, Melbourne, Nelson, 1976; *Always Afternoon*, Sydney, Collins, 1981.
POETRY *Fossils and Stray Cats* (with A. J. Bennet), Armidale, Kardoorair Press, 1980.
OTHER Has also published *What is Right? Case Studies in the Ethics of Education* (with M. Mackie, A & R, 1970). Short stories have appeared in over 15 anthologies, including *Coast to Coast* (1961–70), *Transition* (A & R, 1970), *Australian New Writing* (1973) and *Room to Move* (Redress/Unwin, 1985), and in numerous magazines and journals including the *Bulletin, Hemisphere, Inprint, Overland, Quadrant, Phoenix*, the *National Times* and *Southerly*.

Kerr, Doris Boake, 'Capel Boake' (1899–1945)
Novelist, poet. Born in Sydney into an Anglo-Irish family, and was the niece of poet Barcroft Boake. Moved when a child with her family to Melbourne, remaining there for the rest of her life. Worked in shops and offices as a typist, drawing upon her experiences for the novel *Painted Clay*. Published her first story 1916 in the *Australasian*, but continued to work as a book-keeper to support herself whilst writing. Her final novel and a selection of her poems were published posthumously.

FICTION *Painted Clay*, Melbourne, Australasian Authors' Agency, 1917; *The Romany Mark*, Sydney, Bookstall, 1923; *The Dark Thread*, London, Hutchinson, 1936; *The Twig is Bent*, Sydney, A & R, 1946.

POETRY *The Little Track and Other Verses* (with others), 1922; *Kangaroo Rhymes* (with Bernard Cronin), 1922; *Selected Poems of Capel Boake*, introd. by Myra Morris, Victoria, Kirtley Press, 1949.

Kiddle, Margaret Loch (1914–1958)
Historian. Born in Melbourne. Educated at the University of Melbourne, graduating 1947. Later lectured there in history. Made history broadcasts for schools 1947–54. *Men of Yesterday*, published after her death, was researched from letters and other records of early Victorian pioneers. Also wrote a biography of Caroline Chisholm and some children's books.

NON-FICTION *Caroline Chisholm*, Melbourne, MUP, 1950; *Men of Yesterday: A Social History of the Western District of Victoria 1834–1890*, Melbourne, MUP, 1961.
FICTION *Moonbeam Stairs*, Sydney, Australasian Publ. Co., 1945; *West of Sunset*, Sydney, Australasian Publ. Co., 1949.
MANUSCRIPTS La Trobe Library, Melbourne: Margaret Loch Kiddle Papers MS 8637.

King, Katharine
Novelist. Born in England and later came to Australia, at one stage living in Toowong, Queensland. Published at least two novels anonymously, probably before her arrival in Australia. *Lost for Gold* is a mystery romance set in Australia; it went into several editions.

FICTION *Petite's Romance*, by M.J.M., 1869; *Ethel Mildmay's Follies* (anon.), 1872; *Queen of the Regiment*, London, Ward Lock, 1872; *Cruel Constancy*, London, Ward Lock, 1873; *Lost for Gold*, London, Ward Lock, 1873; *Off the Roll*, London, Ward Lock, 1875; *Our Detachment*, London, Ward Lock, 1875; *Bubble Reputation*, 1878; *Fallen Foe*, 1883; *The Law Forbids*, 1885; *Sweet is True Love*, 1887.

Kingston, Beverley (1941–)
Historian. Born in Sydney. Brought up and educated in Queensland, completing a BA honours at the University of Queensland 1964. Graduated as PhD from Monash University 1969. Held positions as researcher, tutor and editor until 1968. Was lecturer and senior lecturer 1968–80 in the School of History, University of New South Wales until appointed Associate Professor 1980. Is currently preparing the 1860–1900 volume of the *Oxford History of Australia*, 'Glad Confident Morning.'

NON-FICTION *My Wife, My Daughter and Poor Mary Ann; Women and Work in Australia*, Melbourne, Nelson, 1975; *The World Moves Slowly, A Documentary History of Women in Australia* (ed.), Sydney, Cassell, 1977.

Kirwan, Valerie Grierson (1943–)
Fiction writer, playwright. Born in Victoria and has worked in a variety of jobs. Since 1974 has written, directed and performed in plays for La Mama Theatre in Carlton, Melbourne. Has also been playwright-in-residence there (1979) as well as at Rusden State College (1981).

FICTION *Wandering*, Melbourne, Neptune Press, 1984; *Will to Fall*, Melbourne, Penguin, 1984.
OTHER Plays produced include: *The Art of Lobster Whistling* (Melbourne, 1979).

Klein, Colleen (1921–)
Novelist, playwright. Born in Blacktown, NSW. Educated at Sydney Teachers' College and the University of Sydney where she won three prizes for English literature including the Wentworth Medal 1956. In 1957 was a runner-up to Hal Porter in the *Sydney Morning Herald* literary competition. Was encouraged to write by poet A. D. Hope and began as a writer of poetry. Writes novels which owe much to the compression, richness, and symbolic qualities of poetry. *Deirdre Kincaid* has for some years been set for study at Stockholm University. Is currently working on three more novels.

FICTION *The Heart in the Casket*, Sydney, Reardon Press, 1977; *The Pomegranate Tree*, Sydney, Reardon Press, 1977; *Deirdre Kincaid*, Sydney, Reardon Press, 1978; *Women of a Certain Age*, Sydney, Reardon Press, 1979.
DRAMA *From Blacktown to St Ives, Two Plays*, Sydney, Reardon Press, 1978.
OTHER Plays produced include: *Seven Players in Search of a Locksmith* (Sydney, The Rocks Players, 1980).

Klein, Robin (1936–)
Children's author. Born in Kempsey, NSW, into a large family. Left school at 15 and had a series of jobs ranging from telephonist, nurse, library assistant and teacher, to wife and mother of four children. Began writing seriously in the mid–1970s to make money following her divorce. Had some early publications in Victorian and NSW education department magazines. Since 1981 has been a full-time writer and become one of Australia's most popular children's authors with several best-selling books. Won the Australian Junior Book of the Year Award 1983 for *Thing*.

FICTION *The Giraffe in Pepperell Street*, Sydney, Hodder & Stoughton, 1978; *Honoured Guest*, Melbourne, Macmillan, 1979; *Thing*, Melbourne, OUP, 1982; *Sprung*, Adelaide, Rigby, 1982; *Junk Castle*, Melbourne,

OUP, 1983; *Ooodoolay*, Melbourne, Era Publs, 1983; *People Might Hear You*, Melbourne, Puffin, 1983; *Hating Alison Ashley*, Melbourne, Puffin, 1984; *Penny Pollard's Diary*, Melbourne, OUP, 1984; *Penny Pollard's Letters*, Melbourne, OUP, 1984; *Thalia the Failure*, Sydney, Ashton Scholastic, 1984; *Thingnapped*, Melbourne, OUP, 1984; *Brock and the Dragon*, Sydney, Hodder & Stoughton, 1984; *The Tomb Comb*, Adelaide, Rigby, 1984; *Halfway Across the Galaxy and Turn Left*, Melbourne, Viking Kestrel, 1985; *Ratbags and Rascals*, Melbourne, J. M. Dent, 1985; *The Enemies*, Sydney, A & R, 1985; *Annabel's Ghost, and Don't Tell Lucy*, Melbourne, OUP, 1985; *Separate Places*, Kenthurst, NSW, Kangaroo Press, 1985; *Boss of the Pool*, Adelaide, Omnibus Books, 1986; *The Princess Who Hated It*, Adelaide, Omnibus Books, 1986; *Games*, Melbourne, Viking Kestrel, 1986; *Penny Pollard in Print*, Melbourne, OUP, 1986; *The Lonely Hearts Club* (with Max Dann), Melbourne, OUP, 1987.
POETRY *Snakes and Ladders*, Melbourne, J. M. Dent, 1985.

Knowles, Marion Miller (1865–1949)
Novelist, poet. Born in Victoria and became a schoolteacher. Had a prolific output of fiction and poetry, most of it connected with bush life and also reflecting her Roman Catholic ideals. Also contributed to various journals and magazines such as the *Australasian*, some of her work appearing under the pseudonym 'John Desmond'.

FICTION *Country Tales and Sketches*, Melbourne, Edgerton & Moore, 1896; *Barbara Halliday: A Story of the Hill Country of Victoria*, Melbourne, G. Robertson, 1896; *Shamrock and Wattle Bloom: A Series of Short Tales and Sketches*, Melbourne, Edgerton & Moore, 1900; *Corinne of Corall'a Bluff: A Seashore Tale*, Melbourne, Linehan, 1912; *The Little Doctor: An Australian Story*, Melbourne, Varley, 1919; *The House of the Garden of Roses*, Melbourne, J. F. Bracken, 1923; *Meg of Minadong: An Irish-Australian Romance*, Melbourne, Vidler, 1926; *Pierce O'Grady's Daughter*, Sydney & Melbourne, Pellegrini, 1928; *Pretty Nan Hartigan*, Sydney & Melbourne, Pellegrini, 1928; *The Wonder Find at Power's Luck: A Mining Tale of the Seventies*, Sydney & Melbourne, Pellegrini, 1929.

POETRY *Songs from the Hills*, Melbourne, Melville, Mullen & Slade, 1898; *Fronds from the Blacks' Spur*, Melbourne, G. Robertson, 1911; *Roses on the Window Sill*, Melbourne, Varleys, 1913; *A Christmas Bouquet*, Melbourne, H. Mullin, 1914; *Shamrock Sprays*, Melbourne, Advocate Press, 1916; *Songs from the Land of Wattle*, Melbourne, H. Mullin, 1916; *Songs from the Heart: Christmas Flowers and Verse*, Melbourne, W. H. Bennett, 1917; *Christmas Bells*, Melbourne, H. Mullin, 1919; *Love, Luck and Lavender*, Melbourne, H. Mullin, 1919; *Ferns and Fancies*, Melbourne, H. Mullin, 1923; *Selected Poems*, Preface by James McRae, Melbourne, Arrow Printery, 1935.

OTHER Also had novels serialised (see: J. R. Stevens, *Adam Lindsay Gordon and Other Australian Writers* 1937, pp. 44–50).
MANUSCRIPTS La Trobe Library, Melbourne: Papers & Correspondence 1939–31 MS 5705–7.

Kroll, Jeri (1946–)
Poet, short story writer, academic. Born in New York. Educated at Smith College, the University of Warwick, England, and Columbia University, New York where she completed a PhD in English. Has taught literature and writing at many tertiary institutions in England and the USA. Came to Australia 1978 and taught at the University of Adelaide and at Croydon Park CAE. Is presently a tutor at Flinders University. Has had wide experience as a literary producer for radio, conducting interviews with writers and working on material for the ABC. Has also edited poetry anthologies and conducted several talks and workshops in writing. Won the Artlook National Poetry Contest 1981 and the Anne Elder Award 1982 for the collection *Death as Mr Right*.

POETRY *Death as Mr Right*, Adelaide, Friendly St, 1982; *Indian Movies*, Melbourne, Hyland House, 1984.
FICTION *The Electrolux Man*, Melbourne, Hyland House, 1987.
OTHER Also edited *No 8 Friendly St Reader* (with R. Clarke, Friendly St, 1984) and *Montage* (with V. Dreisner & A. Mykyta, Country & City Women Writers, 1985). Poetry has appeared in many anthologies including *Pearls: Writing by SA Women* (Women's Art Movement, 1980), *Dots Over Lines: Recent Poetry in SA* (AUUP Press, 1980) and *The Orange Tree* (Wakefield Press, 1986). Poems and fiction have been published in over 25 journals and papers including *Aspect*, the *Bulletin*, *Helix*, *Luna*, *Quadrant*, and *Southern Review*.

L

Ladds, Isabel
Short story writer, playwright. Born Isabel Dulcie Dunlop; later became Mrs Samuel Charles. Published in the *New Idea*, the *Sunday Mail* and the *Adelaide Mail*. Wrote stories about domestic problems and the relations between the sexes which invariably come down on the side of convention.

FICTION *The Lighted Window and Other Stories*, Brisbane, Bunyip Press, 1944; *Marriage is Monotonous and Other Stories*, Brisbane, Bunyip Press, 1944.
DRAMA *We Have Our Dreams*, Brisbane, Jacaranda Press, 1957.

Lambert, Elisabeth (1918–)
Poet. Born in England, went to Jamaica as a teenager before coming to Australia. Worked as a journalist and feature writer for many Sydney newspapers and magazines and also as a court reporter and theatre critic. Had verse plays broadcast on the ABC and poems published in various journals. Returned to England to become a feature writer and film editor of *Woman's Own* magazine and then went to New York 1951 where she worked as a scriptwriter at the United Nations.

POETRY *Insurgence*, Sydney, Viking Press, 1939; *The Map*, Sydney, Viking Press, 1940; *Poems*, Sydney, Viking Press, 1943.
FICTION *The Sleeping House Party*, London, M. Joseph, 1951.
OTHER Poems were published in *Angry Penguins, Meanjin, Southerly*, etc. Also edited (wtih H. Roskolenko) *Voices*, No. 118 (Summer 1944).

'Lancaster, G. B.' *See:* **Lyttleton, Edith**

Lang, Mary (1914–)
Poet. Born in Sydney. Educated at convent schools before being sent to London at 13 where she stayed 5 years and finished her education. The lyric poetry from her first volume was written before she turned 17; the verses struck critics with their intense dramatic feeling and emotional authenticity.

POETRY *Strange Battalion and Other Poems*, London, Dent, 1933; *Tom Groggin and Other Poems*, London, Dent, 1936.

Langley, Eve (1908–1974)
Novelist, poet. Born in Forbes, NSW. Her family moved to Molong, then to Gippsland, Victoria, the Dandenongs, and finally New Zealand,

where she joined them in 1930. Married Hilary Clark and had three children, eventually returning to Australia. In later years lived in seclusion in the Blue Mountains of NSW. *The Pea Pickers* is a fanciful, autobiographical, first-person narrative of the adventures of two young women, 'Steve' and 'Blue' who seek excitement, love and 'poetry' in rural Gippsland. Highly original both in style and content, it won the S. H. Prior Memorial Prize 1941; *White Topee* is its sequel.

FICTION *The Pea Pickers*, Sydney, A & R, 1942; *White Topee*, Sydney, A & R, 1954.
OTHER Also published poetry in the *Bulletin, Poetry Magazine*, etc.
MANUSCRIPTS ML, Sydney: Papers 1928–72 ML MSS 4188 (Includes diaries, misc. papers, unpublished mss, poems, etc).
SEE ALSO N. Lindsay in the *Bulletin*, 3 June (1942), D. Stewart in *The Flesh and the Spirit* (A & R, 1948), H. Porter in *London Magazine*, Vol. 5, No. 6 (1965), M. Arkin in *Modern Fiction Studies*, Vol. 27, No. 1 (1981) and J. Thwaite in *Gender, Politics and Fiction* (ed. C. Ferrier, UQP, 1985).

Langsford, Dorothy (1896–?)
Novelist. Born in South Australia; educated in Adelaide. Published fairy stories at the age of 11 in a weekly newspaper; these were later collected in *The Water Babies* 1913.

FICTION *The Water Babies and Other Stories*, Adelaide, Hussey & Gillingham, 1913; *Cooee of Glenowie: An Australian Story*, Adelaide, Gillingham, 1922; *The Outlaw, or The Dawning of the Morning: An Australian Story*, London, Epworth, 1925; *Sun-chased Shadows: An Australian Story*, London, Epworth, 1927; *Dean of the Ridge*, London, Epworth, 1928.

Lansbury, Coral (1935–)
Novelist, academic. Born in Melbourne. Educated at the University of Sydney and Auckland University graduating with a doctorate in English and history 1969. A cousin of actor Angela Lansbury, has herself acted for ABC radio and has written plays for the ABC, the BBC and for television. Has taught for over 10 years in the USA and currently lives in Pennsylvania where she is Professor of English and Dean of Graduate Studies at Rutgers University. Has published widely in scholarly journals on Victorian literature and history and is best known in her native country for her book on the perceptions of Australia found in English nineteenth-century literature, *Arcady in Australia*. Won the Henry Lawson Prize 1949 for the play *Krubi of the Illawarra*.

FICTION *Ringarra*, London, Pan Books, 1985; *Sweet Alice*, London, Pan Books, 1986; *Felicity, or A Life of Art*, London, Pan Books, 1987.

NON-FICTION *Arcady in Australia*, Melbourne, MUP, 1970; *Elizabeth Gaskell*, New York, Harper & Row, 1972; *The Reasonable Man, Trollope's Legal Fiction*, Princeton, Princeton University Press, 1982; *The Old Brown Dog – Women, Workers and Vivisection in Edwardian England*, Wisconsin, University of Wisconsin Press, 1985.
OTHER *Krubi of the Illawarra*, in *Hermes* (Sydney, 1949). Plays produced on ABC radio include: *The Gate of the Sea, The Bronze Plain* (during the 1940s), *The Living Rock, Mockery Bend, The Bombora*, and *Court of Angels* (during the 1950s–1960s).

Lawson, Bertha (1876–1957)
Memoir writer. Born Bertha Bredt in Bairnsdale, Victoria; married writer Henry Lawson 1896 and had two children. Endured a difficult marriage which resulted in separation in 1903 followed by years of bitterness due to financial problems. Writer Will Lawson (no relation) assisted in her reminiscences of her husband.

NON-FICTION *Henry Lawson by His Mates* (ed. with John le Gay Brereton), Sydney, A & R, 1931; *My Henry Lawson*, Sydney, Frank Johnson, 1943.

Lawson, Louisa (1848–1920)
Publisher, editor, journalist, poet. Born Louisa Albury in Mudgee, NSW. Married 1866 to Norwegian sailor Peter Larsen and had five children including writer Henry Lawson. Spent some years moving from Mudgee to Grenfell and Gulgong before moving to Sydney 1883. Became a leading figure in the feminist movement, editing the *Republican* 1887 and in 1888 founding the *Dawn*, Australia's first feminist journal. Edited and wrote for the *Dawn* until 1905 when it was forced to close down. Arranged the publication of her son's first book 1894 and of her own work. Contributed numerous articles for the *Dawn* either anonymously or under pseudonyms. Even invented a mailbag fastener used by the NSW Post Office; their refusal to acknowledge this as her invention led to the legal action and overall strain which resulted in the *Dawn*'s closure.

FICTION *Dert and Do*, Sydney, Dawn, 189–?.
POETRY *The Lonely Crossing and Other Poems*, Sydney, Dawn, 1905.
MANUSCRIPTS ML, Sydney: Louisa Lawson Newscuttings QA 920.7L, and the *Dawn* May 1888–July 1905, QO59/D.
SEE ALSO S. Lawson in *Nation*, No. 3 (Oct. 25, 1958), L. Ollif, *Louisa Lawson, Henry Lawson's Crusading Mother* (Rigby, 1978) and B. Matthews in *ALS*, Vol. 9, No.3 (1980).

Lawson, Sylvia (1932–)
Historian, journalist, critic. Born in Sydney, a great-granddaughter of Louisa Lawson (q.v.). Attended state schools and the University of

Sydney. Wrote daily journalism in Sydney 1954–7, and in 1957 helped to establish and produce the independent fortnightly paper, *Nation*, for which she wrote until 1972. In 1966 began teaching in adult education groups on film, the media, etc, and between 1971–5 taught part-time at various universities and colleges. Was appointed to a lectureship at Griffith University, Brisbane 1976, and continues to teach there. Her biography of publisher J. F. Archibald 1983 is noted for its penetrating examination of the social and cultural issues of his day.

NON FICTION *Mary Gilmore* (for children), Melbourne, OUP, 1966; *J. F. Archibald*, Great Australians Series, Melbourne, OUP, 1971; *The Archibald Paradox: A Strange Case of Authorship*, London, Allen Lane, 1983.
OTHER Critical journalism appeared in *Nation* 1958–72, the *Australian* 1969–72, and *Filmnews* 1980–84. Articles have been published in various journals and collections including a chapter in *Nellie Melba, Ginger Meggs and Friends* (Kibble Books, 1982). A short story, *Brisbane in October*, appeared in *Meanjin* (September 1985).

Leakey, Caroline Woolmer (1827–1881)
Novelist, poet. Born in Exeter, England and lived in Tasmania with her sister 1848–53 where she gathered material for *The Broad Arrow*, published under the pseudonym Oline Keese. This was the first significant novel about convict life in Australia, and an undoubted influence upon Marcus Clarke's later convict novel, originally entitled *His Natural Life* (1873). Her life was plagued by ill-health but enhanced by strong religious beliefs. *The Broad Arrow* was written partly to demonstrate by example the dangers of immorality. Also wrote for the Religious Tract Society and the *Girls' Own Paper*.

FICTION *The Broad Arrow: Being Passages from the History of Maida Gwynnham, a Lifer*, by Oline Keese, London, Bentley, 1859.
POETRY *Lyra Australis, or Attempts to Sing in a Strange Land*, London, Bickers, 1854.
SEE ALSO E. P. Leakey, *Clear Shining Light, a Memoir of Caroline Leakey* (J. F. Shaw, 1883), J. E. Poole in *Southerly*, Vol. 26, No. 2 (1966), L. Hergenhan in *Southerly*, Vol. 36, No. 2 (1976) and J. Raggio in *ALS Working Papers*, Vol. 3, No. 1 (1979).

Lee, Ida (c. 1875–1943)
Historian, poet. Born in Kelso, NSW, of an early pioneering family. Was married to Charles Marriot. Apart from her six historical works listed, also published articles in historical journals.

NON-FICTION *The Coming of the British to Australia 1788–1829*, London,

Longmans Green, 1906; *Commodore Sir John Hayes: His Voyage and Life*, London, Longmans Green, 1912; *The Logbooks of the 'Lady Nelson'*, London, Grafton & Co., 1915; *Captain Bligh's Second Voyage to the South Sea*, London, Longmans Green, 1920; *Early Explorers of Australia*, London, Methuen, 1925; *The Voyage of the 'Caroline' from England to Van Diemen's Land and Batavia* by R. Hare (ed.), London, Longmans Green, 1927.
POETRY *Songs and Verses*, Walton, Suffolk, the author, 189–?; *The Bush Fire and Other Verses*, London, Sampson Low, 1897.

Lee, Joyce (1913–)
Poet. Born in Murtoa, Victoria; educated at the Methodist Ladies' College, Melbourne. Qualified as a pharmacist in 1934, and has also worked as a lecturer and tutor in poetry at the Victoria College, Melbourne. Won the Grenfell Henry Lawson Award 1978 and the McGregor Prize for poetry 1982. Has received two Literature Board Grants and is a member of the Pariah Press cooperative. Her poems have been widely published in journals and magazines.

POETRY *Sisters Poets I, Four Women Poets*, Melbourne, Sisters, 1979; *Abruptly from the Flatlands*, Melbourne, Pariah Press, 1984.

Le Plastrier, Constance (1864–1938)
Fiction, non-fiction writer. Born in Australia of a pioneer family who settled in 1848. Became a teacher of Latin, English and botany in Sydney and was Secretary of the Teachers' Guild. Was in favour of the advancement of women although held mixed views upon the subject of girls' education. Active in the council of the Shakespearian Society, she also published and introduced editions of Shakespeare's plays for schools.

FICTION *Heirs in Exile*, Melbourne, Lineham, 1910; *The Cloudy Porch*, Sydney, Sands, 1929.
NON-FICTION *Botany for Australian Students* (with A. A. Brewer), Sydney, Dymocks, 1916; *The Story of Our Plants: First Steps in Australian Botany*, Sydney, Shakespeare Head, 1933.
OTHER Also published *Willoughby's 50 Years 1865–1915*, and an edition of Milton's *Paradise Lost.*

'Levy, Esther' *See:* **Newton, Ellen**

Levy, Julia Ethel, 'Juliet'
Playwright, novelist, poet. A prolific and popular writer of the 1920s who sometimes published under the pseudonym 'Juliet'; today her works seem sentimental and lightweight.

DRAMA *The Way Out*, Melbourne, Vidler, 1925; *The Snob*, Melbourne, Vidler, 1925; *The Proposal*, Melbourne, Vidler, 1926; *A Woman Disposes* Melbourne, Vidler, 1927; *The Choice: In Three Acts*, Melbourne, Vidler, 1928.
FICTION *A Soul of Sincerity*, Melbourne, Vidler, 1923; *God's Good Woman*, Melbourne, Vidler, 1926; *Devotion: A Tale of Australian Life*, Melbourne, Vidler, 1927; *The Snob and the Lady*, Melbourne, Vidler, 1929.
POETRY *Songs of Solace*, Melbourne, Keating Piace, 1922; *Sign Posts on Life's Highway*, Melbourne, 1926.

Lindsay, Hilarie (1922–)
Children's author, non-fiction writer, poet. Born Hilarie Dyson in Sydney. Educated at North Sydney Girls' High, then business college, later studying arts through Deakin University, Victoria. Married Philip Lindsay 1944 and had three children. Has worked as a secretary and telegraphist, but mostly in literary circles, and is presently curator of the Children's Treasure House Book and Toy Museum in Sydney. Over the years has been active in several literary organisations including the FAW (President 1981–3) and the Society of Women Writers (President 1970–73). The Hilarie Lindsay Award was established by the Society of Women Writers NSW for achievement in writing. Has herself won awards for her poems and stories including the Grenfell Henry Lawson Prose Award 1966 and 1967, the Realist Writers' Short Story Award 1967, and the Rotary International Poetry Award 1974. Was awarded the MBE 1974 for services to literature and the Queen's Silver Jubilee Medal 1977.
FICTION *Midget Mouse Finds a House*, Sydney, Ansay, 1978; *One for the Road*, Sydney, Ansay, 1978; *The Gravy Train*, Sydney, Ansay, 1981; *Murder at the Bellevue*, Sydney, Ansay, 1982; *Mr Poppleberry and the Dog's Own Daily*, Sydney, Ansay, 1983; *Mr Poppleberry and Fred the White Cockatoo*, Sydney, Ansay, 1983; *Mr Poppleberry and the Milk Thieves*, Sydney, Ansay, 1983.
NON-FICTION *101 Toys to Make*, Sydney, Ansay, 1972; *You're on Your Own*, Sydney, Ansay, 1976; *Grenfell Sketchbook*, Adelaide, Rigby, 1977; *Ink No. 2* (ed.) Sydney, Society of Women Writers, 1977; *So You Want to be a Writer*, (ed.), Sydney, Society of Women Writers, 1977; *Culinary Capers*, Sydney, Society of Women Writers, 1979; *Society of Women Writers Handbook*, Sydney, Society of Women Writers, 1980; *Echoes of Henry Lawson* (ed.), Sydney, Ansay, 1981; *Paul Delprat Etchings* (ed.), Sydney, Ansay, 1981; *New Life with a Colostomy* (ed.), Sydney, Ansay, 1982.
DRAMA *The Withered Tree*, Sydney, Ansay, 1980.
POETRY *One Woman's World*, Sydney, Ansay, 1980.

Lindsay, Jane (1920–)
Novelist, biographer. Born in Sydney, daughter of writer Rose Lindsay (q.v.) and artist Norman Lindsay. Left school at the age of 15. Had two early stories published in *Smith's Weekly*. *Portrait of Pa* describes her father's later years at Springwood in the Blue Mountains.

FICTION *Kurrajong*, Sydney, A & R, 1945.
NON-FICTION *Portrait of Pa*, Sydney, A & R, 1973.

Lindsay, Joan A'Beckett, Lady (1896–1984)
Novelist. Born in Melbourne, a member of the Boyd family. Educated at a private school upon which the famous Appleyard College in *Picnic at Hanging Rock* was based. Studied art at the National Gallery School and married Sir Daryl Lindsay 1922. Her first book was a humorous parody of British exploration accounts. *Picnic at Hanging Rock* was her most successful book and was filmed 1975; its final chapter was only recently published (according to her wishes) but despite this the book still remains ambiguous and intriguing.

FICTION *Through Darkest Pondelayo*, by S. Livingstone-Stanley, London, Chatto & Windus, 1936; *Picnic at Hanging Rock*, Melbourne, Cheshire, 1967; *Syd Sixpence* (children's) 1982; *The Secret of Hanging Rock*, Sydney, A & R, 1987.
NON-FICTION *Time Without Clocks*, Melbourne, Cheshire, 1962; *Facts Soft and Hard*, Melbourne, Cheshire, 1964; *A Company of Carols* (with M. Bassett, M. Casey and R. Dobson) Melbourne, 1967.
SEE ALSO A. Crittenden in *Meanjin*, Vol. 35, No. 2 (1976), J. Kirkby in *ALS*, Vol. 8, No. 3 (1978) and D. Barrett in *Southerly*, Vol. 42, No. 3 (1982).

Lindsay, Rose (1885–1978)
Biographer. Born Rose Soady in Sydney, and became the second wife of artist Norman Lindsay. Was an artists' model before she met Lindsay and later modelled for him. *Ma and Pa* is the story of her childhood in a large family, while *Model Wife* provides descriptions of life with her husband and his friends at Springwood in the Blue Mountains of NSW. Her memoirs were first published in the *Bulletin*, Feb.-May 1953.

NON-FICTION *Ma and Pa: My Childhood Memories*, Sydney, Ure Smith, 1963; *Model Wife*, Sydney, Ure Smith, 1967.
SEE ALSO J. Hetherington, *Norman Lindsay, The Embattled Olympian* (OUP, 1973, passim).

Lisle, Mary (1879–1973)
Poet. Born and grew up in the NSW country. After marriage to D. M. Cornish lived in the outback for 26 years, returning to Sydney in later

life. Published her first poetry in the *Australasian* and contributed to many other papers and literary magazines. Won a prize in the *Sydney Morning Herald* poetry competition 1946.

POETRY *The Secret Fire*, Melbourne, Meanjin Press, 1947; *The Inlander and Other Poems*, Sydney, Writers' Press, 1968.
OTHER Published poetry in the *Australasian*, the *Bulletin, Country Life, Poetry Magazine, Southerly*, the *Sydney Morning Herald*, the *Australian Woman's Mirror*, etc.

Litchfield, Jessie Sinclair (1883–1956)
Poet, non-fiction writer, editor. Born Jessie Phillips in Sydney; educated at one stage by Mary Gilmore (q.v.). Married Valentine Litchfield in Darwin 1908, travelled with him in and around the Northern Territory, and had seven children. Edited the *Northern Territory Times*, Darwin, 1930–42 and also contributed poems and stories to the *Age*, the *Bulletin* and the *Australian Woman's Mirror*. From 1946 ran her own library, the Roberta Library, in Darwin. In 1951 tried to enter politics, but her bid to win a seat in Federal parliament as an independent was unsuccessful. Received the Coronation Medal 1953 for outstanding service to the Territory. The Jessie Litchfield Award was established 1964 and is presented annually to new writers.

NON-FICTION *Far North Memories*, Sydney, A & R, 1930.
SEE ALSO Janet Dickinson, *Jessie Litchfield: Grand Old Lady of the Territory*, (Qld, 1982).

Littlejohn, Agnes
Poet, short story writer, novelist, children's author. Born in Australia and travelled widely as a girl; was handicapped by deafness as a child. Had a prolific output of work and was commended in her day for the romanticism, charm and simple beauty of her lyrics, although today her poetry seems flowery and conventional rather than inspired. Was also a regular contributor to Sydney newspapers and journals.

POETRY *Verses*, Sydney, H. Gorton, 1914; *Poems*, Sydney, H. Gorton, 1915; *Patriotic Poems*, Sydney, H. Gorton, 1915; *War Poems*, Sydney, Vale & Pearson, 1916; *Lyrics and Lyrical Prose*, Sydney, Edwards Dunlop & Co., 1927; *Lyrics and Mystic Sketches*, Sydney, Edwards Dunlop & Co., 1928; *The Lady of Doves and Other Poems*, Sydney, Edwards Dunlop & Co., 1929; *The Guardian of the Gate and Other Poems*, Sydney, Edwards Dunlop & Co., 1933; *The Unforgotten Watch and Other Poems*, Sydney, Edwards Dunlop & Co., 1935; *Drowsy Hours and Other Poems*, Sydney, Edwards Dunlop & Co., 1936; *Lighthouse Keepers and Other Poems*, Sydney, Edwards Dunlop & Co., 1938.

FICTION *The Daughter of a Sailor and Other Stories*, Sydney, J. A. Packer, 1907; *A Lapse of Memory and Other Stories*, Sydney, J. A. Packer, 1909; *Mirage of the Desert*, Sydney, J. A. Packer, 1910; *The Breath of India*, Sydney, H. Gorton, 1914; *The Silver Road: Fairy and Other Stories*, Sydney, H. Gorton, 1915; *Star Dust and Sea Spray: Imaginative Tales and Fairy Lore for the Young*, Sydney, Edwards Dunlop & Co., 1918; *Rainbow Dreams*, Sydney, Edwards Dunlop & Co., 1919; *The Sleeping Sea-Nymph*, Sydney, Edwards Dunlop & Co., 1921; *The Lost Emerald and Other Stories*, Sydney, Edwards Dunlop & Co., 1924; *The Pipes o'Pan and Other Short Stories*, Sydney, Edwards Dunlop & Co., 1939.
SEE ALSO James Devaney, 'Agnes Littlejohn, a Poet of Quiet Charm', *The Catholic Leader* (Dec. 22, 1938).

Liverani, Mary Rose (1939–)
Biographer, journalist. Born Mary Rose Lavery in Glasgow, Scotland. Migrated to Australia when aged 13 with her family, settling in Wollongong, NSW. Educated at the universities of NSW and Sydney graduating BA 1968. Has worked as a teacher, librarian and journalist in Wollongong. *The Winter Sparrows* describes her early life in the slums of her home town, and her family's experiences as migrants in Australia. Presently works as a freelance writer and journalist, contributing regularly to papers such as the *Sydney Morning Herald*.

NON-FICTION *The Winter Sparrows: Growing Up in Scotland and Australia*, Melbourne, Nelson, 1975.
SEE ALSO J. Strauss in *Luna*, Vol. 2, No. 1 (1979).

Llewellyn, Kate (1940–)
Poet. Born in SA. Educated at the University of Adelaide. Won the Anne Elder award for the collection *Trader Kate and the Elephants* 1982, and has received two Literature Board grants. Her poems have appeared in numerous magazines and she is represented in many anthologies. Recently researched, with poet Susan Hampton (q.v.) the poetry of Australian women, which culminated in the *Penguin Book of Australian Women Poets*, 1986.

POETRY *Trader Kate and the Elephants*, Adelaide, Friendy St, 1982; *Luxury*, Sydney, Redress, 1985; *The Penguin Book of Australian Women Poets* (with S. Hampton), Melbourne, Penguin, 1986.
NON-FICTION *The Waterlily, A Blue Mountains Journal*, Melbourne, Hudson, 1987.
OTHER Poems have appeared in over 18 journals and magazines including *Meanjin, Island, Compass, Refractory Girl* and *Poetry Australia*. Is represented in the following anthologies: *Sisters Poets I* (Sisters, 1979), *Dots Over Lines* (Griffin, 1982), *Frictions* (Sybylla, 1982), *The Heritage of*

Australian Poetry (Curry O'Neil, 1983), *After the Rage* (Tutu, 1984), *Off the Record* (Penguin, 1985), *Room to Move* (Redress/Unwin, 1985) and *The Orange Tree* (Wakefield, 1986).

Lloyd, Anne (1954–)
Poet. Born in Manly, NSW. Took her BA honours at Macquarie University in 1976 majoring in German and linguistics. Lectured in linguistics at Capricornia Institute of Advanced Education, Rockhampton 1977–81. Since 1982 has been a journalist with the *Rockhampton Morning Bulletin*. Was awarded a Literature Board fellowship 1987. Poetry has appeared in journals and newspapers in Australia and overseas. Is married to the poet R. G. Hay and lives on a property west of Rockhampton, Queensland.

POETRY *The Hips Slither*, Wentworth Falls, NSW, Black Lightning Press, 1983.
OTHER Is included in *Sisters Poets I* (Sisters, 1979; and *Place and Perspective: Contemporary Queensland Poetry* (Jacaranda, 1984).

Lloyd, Jessie Georgiana, 'Silverleaf' (1843–1885)
Novelist, essayist, short story writer. Born near Launceston, Tasmania and married George Lloyd who later entered politics. Lived on a station in NSW and contributed articles under her pseudonym to the *Illustrated Sydney News;* also wrote for the *Sydney Mail* and the *Echo*. Her regular work as a writer enabled her to provide a formal education for her children.

FICTION *All Aboard*, serialised in the Sydney *Echo* 1897; *The Wheel of Life: A Domestic Tale of Life in Australia*, by Silverleaf, Sydney, G. Robertson, 1880; *Retribution*, by Silverleaf, serialised in the *Illustrated Sydney News* June 7, 1884–June 6, 1885.

Locke, Sumner (1881–1917)
Novelist, playwright. Born Helena Sumner Locke in Brisbane and became popular as a writer with the successful 'Mum Dawson' series, humorous sketches of a set of rustic selectors not unlike Steel Rudd's 'Dad and Dave' characters. Travelled and wrote in England, where she won prizes for her stories, and America. Upon her return to Australia married and shortly after died from giving birth to her son, writer Sumner Locke Elliot; she is recalled in his novel *Careful, He Might Hear You* 1963.

FICTION *Mum Dawson, 'Boss'*, Sydney, Bookstall, 1911; *The Dawsons' Uncle George*, Sydney, Bookstall, 1912; *Skeeter Farm Takes a Spell*, Sydney, Bookstall, 1915; *Samaritan Mary*, New York, Holt, 1916.

OTHER A play, *The Vicissitudes of Vivienne* was produced in Melbourne, 1908.
SEE ALSO *In Memoriam Sumner Locke* (various authors, S. J. Endacott, 1921).

Lord, Gabrielle (1946–)
Novelist. Born in Sydney. Educated at the Sacre Coeur Convent, Rose Bay, and the University of New England. Has been a teacher and was an employment officer with the Commonwealth Employment Service for 8 years, but has been writing full-time for the last 6 years. Has reviewed occasionally for the *National Times* and the *Sydney Morning Herald*, and contributes irregular pieces to the former (now the *Times on Sunday*). Some short stories have appeared in *Inprint*, but Lord is essentially a writer of 'thrillers', and is currently preparing a futuristic novel. *Fortress*, based on the real life drama of teacher Mary Gibb and her pupils, has been made into a film; *Jumbo* is presently being scripted for film.

FICTION *Fortress*, London, Bodley Head, 1980; *Tooth and Claw*, London, Bodley Head, 1983; *Jumbo*, London, Bodley Head, 1986.
OTHER *Growing up Catholic* (with others, Ellsyd Press, 1986).
SEE ALSO F. McInherney in *ABR* (Nov. 1983), J. Palmer (interview) in the *Weekend Australian Literary Magazine* (Sept. 28–9, 1985) and J. Ellison (interview) in *Rooms of their Own* (Penguin, 1986).

Luffman, Laura Bogue (1846–1929)
Novelist, journalist. Born Lauretta Maria Lane in Bedford, England and educated in France. Travelled widely through Europe before arriving in Australia where she married Carl Bogue Luffman. Wrote under the name Laura M. Lane in England and afterwards Laura Bogue Luffman in Australia. Was active in the women's movement and as journalist contributed to various papers both in Australia and overseas. Edited the *Women's Voice* and, as 'Una', contributed to the *Daily Telegraph*, Sydney; also edited the journal *At Home* 1905. A literary competition was established in her memory.

FICTION *Will Aylmer: A Tale of the Australian Bush* (children's), London, Religious Tract Society, 1907; *A Question of Latitude*, London, Lane, 1912.
OTHER Published the following, mostly religio-moral books for children, as Laura M. Lane in England: *Gentleman Perschayle* (1875), *Mrs Roberts, or No Time to be Religious* (1877), *A Character: A Story for Girls* (1879), *My Sister's Keeper: A Story for Girls* (1879), *Harry's Discipline* (1881), *Ella's Mistake* (1882), *Dresden Romance* (1884), *A Nineteenth-Century Hero* (1885), *Teresa's Secret* (1885), *Dr Maynard's Daughter* (1886), *Living it Down* (1886), *Hawkbrook Farm, or Esther Gaunt's Wooing* (1891), *Violet*

Maitland, or By Thorny Ways (1894), and *The Life and Writings of Alexander Vine* (1890).

Lyons, Enid, Dame (1897–1981)
Biographer, politician. Born in Tasmania; educated at state schools and the Hobart Teachers' College. Married 1915 J. A. Lyons (who later became Prime Minister of Australia) and bore twelve children. Became the first woman member of the House of Representatives, and was member for Darwin, Tasmania 1943–51. Was commissioner of the ABC 1951–62, and after her retirement wrote autobiographical accounts of her political career.

NON-FICTION *So We Take Comfort*, London, Heinemann, 1965; *The Old Haggis*, Melbourne, Heinemann, 1969; *Among the Carrion Crows*, Adelaide, Rigby, 1972.
MANUSCRIPTS NL, Canberra: Papers 1931–74, MS 4852 (guide available).
SEE ALSO K. White, *A Political Love Story: Joe and Enid Lyons*, (Penguin 1987).

Lyttleton, Edith, 'G. B. Lancaster' (1873–1945)
Novelist. Born Edith Joan Lyttleton in Tasmania, but mostly published under the pseudonym 'G. B. Lancaster'. Went to New Zealand as a child, visiting Australia until 1908 when her family moved to England. Continued to travel, visiting Canada and returning to Australia and New Zealand, but died in England 1945. The countries she lived and travelled in are represented in her novels; the best of these is said to be *Pageant* 1933 which won the Australian Literary Society's Gold Medal. Also contributed short stories to the *Lone Hand* and the *Bulletin*.

FICTION *Sons o'Men*, London, Melrose, 1904; *The Spur to Smite*, London, Melrose, 1905; *The Tracks We Tread*, London, Hodder & Stoughton, 1907; *The Altar Stairs*, London, Hodder & Stoughton, 1908; *Jim of the Ranges*, London, Constable, 1910; *The Honourable Peggy*, London, Constable, 1911; *The Law-Bringers*, London, Hodder & Stoughton, 1913; *Fool Divine*, London, Hodder & Stoughton, 1917; *The Savignys*, London, Hodder & Stoughton, 1919; *Pageant*, London, Unwin; Sydney, Endeavour Press, 1933; *The World is Yours*, London, Unwin; Sydney, Endeavour Press, 1934; *Promenade*, Sydney, A & R, 1938; *Grand Parade*, London, Lane, 1943.
SEE ALSO Miles Franklin, 'G. B. Lancaster' in *Talk* (April, 1946).

M

Macadam, Constance, 'Constance Clyde', 'Clyde Wright' (1872–?)
Poet, novelist. Born in Glasgow and emigrated when a young girl with her family to New Zealand. Published poems and stories in many magazines, especially in London where she went to work for the suffragist cause after living and writing in Australia. Returned to New Zealand where during WWI she worked in mental institutions and prisons, before coming back to Australia. In England her work appeared in the *Strand Magazine*, *London Opinion*, *Grand Magazine* and the *Idler*. In Australia she published poems in the *Australasian*, the *Bulletin* and the *Sydney Mail*.

FICTION *A Pagan's Love*, London, Fisher Unwin, 1905; *Will They Never Come*, Melbourne, Australian Catholic Truth Society, n.d.

McAuliffe, Nora
Poet, journalist. Born in New Zealand of Irish parents. Came to Australia and worked for the *Bulletin* as a cadet. Edited that magazine's weekly Woman's Letter in the late 1920s. Also contributed to the *Lone Hand*.

POETRY *The Song-maker and Other Verses*, Sydney, Bulletin Co., 1937; *1940–1942, A Poem*, Sydney, A & R, 1944.

McCrae, Dorothy Frances
Poet. Granddaughter of Georgiana Huntly McCrae (q.v.) and sister of poet Hugh McCrae. Also known as Mrs C. E. Perry and later Mrs C. Elliot. Published lyrical poetry about Melbourne and Sydney, love and nature.

POETRY *Lyrics in Leisure*, Melbourne, Lothian, 1909; *Some Children's Songs*, Melbourne, G. Robertson, 1910; *Soldier, My Soldier!*, Melbourne, G. Robertson, 1914; *The Clear Call*, Melbourne, G. Robertson, 1915; *Caedmon's Gift*, Melbourne, Vidler, 1926.
OTHER Poems were also published in the *Australasian*, the *Bookfellow*, the *Bulletin*, *Steele Rudd's Magazine*, etc.

McCrae, Georgiana Huntly (1804–1890)
Diarist. Born and educated in London, an illegitimate daughter of the Duke of Gordon. Learnt languages, music and painting and was particularly skilled in portraiture, from which she tried to make her living before her marriage in 1830 to Andrew McCrae. Came to Australia in 1841 to join her husband and lived in Victoria where she made friends within the political and cultural world of her day. Her journals reveal a witty

and lively personality and vividly recreate the Melbourne of the late 1840s.

NON-FICTION *Georgiana's Journal: Melbourne a Hundred Years Ago* (ed. Hugh McCrae), Sydney, A & R, 1934.
SEE ALSO Extracts from English journals published in *Southerly* (1946–7) and H. F. Chaplin, *A McCrae Miscellany* (Wentworth Press, 1969).

McCullough, Colleen (1937–)
Novelist. Born in Wellington, NSW into an Irish-Catholic family. Educated at a convent school and later the University of Sydney. Qualified as a neurophysiologist and practised in Australia, England and at Yale University. Has also worked as a teacher, librarian and journalist. Her novels have always enjoyed great popular appeal and are generally characterised by sensationalism. *The Thorn Birds* in particular was distinguished by the combination of spectacular commercial success and facetious or hostile critical treatment that has more or less greeted all her novels. *Tim* and *An Indecent Obsession* have been made into films and *The Thorn Birds* was serialised for television in the USA 1983. Colleen McCullough now lives on Norfolk Island with her husband Ric Robinson.

FICTION *Tim*, New York, Harper & Row, 1974; *The Thorn Birds*, New York, Harper & Row, 1977; *An Indecent Obsession* New York, Harper & Row, 1981; *A Creed for the Third Millenium*, New York, Harper & Row, 1985; *The Ladies of Missalonghi*, Melbourne, Hutchinson, 1987.
OTHER *Cooking with Colleen McCullough and Jean Easthope* (Harper & Row, 1982).
SEE ALSO D. Green in *Quadrant*, Vol. 21 (1977) and C. Simpson in *The Australian Author*, Vol. 9, No. 2 (1977).

McDonald, Nan (Nancy) (1921–1974)
Poet, editor. Born in Sydney and educated at the University of Sydney. Worked as an editor for Angus & Robertson and greatly promoted the publication of Australian authors in the 1950s and 1960s. Her first volume of poetry won the inaugural Grace Leven Prize for Poetry.

POETRY *Pacific Sea*, Sydney, A & R, 1947; *Australian Poetry* (ed.), Sydney, A & R, 1953; *The Lonely Fire*. Sydney, A & R, 1954; *The Lighthouse and Other Poems*, Sydney, A & R, 1959; *Selected Poems*, Sydney, A & R, 1969.

McFadyen, Ella May (1891?-)
Poet, journalist, children's author. Born in NSW, and as a journalist worked for the *Sydney Mail* 1918–38. Published poetry in a number of papers such as the *Lone Hand* and the *Sydney Morning Herald*, as well as her two collections, but was mainly a writer of children's stories and poems. The well-known *Pegmen* books were begun as a radio serial.

POETRY *Outland Born and Other Verses*, Melbourne, Australasian Authors' Agency, 1911; *Songs of the Last Crusade*, Sydney, Winn & Co., 1917; *Here's Fun for You*, Sydney, Dymocks, 1938.
FICTION *Pegmen Tales*, Sydney, A & R, 1946; *Pegmen go Walkabout*, Sydney, A & R, 1947; *Little Dragons of the Never-never*, Sydney, Australasian Publ., Col., 1949; *The Wishing Star*, Sydney, A & R, 1956; *The Big Book of Pegmen Tales*, Sydney, A & R, 1957.
OTHER Also published drama: *Kookaburra Comedies: Junior Plays* (Sydney, n.d.).

McGuire, Frances Margaret (1900–)
Journalist, novelist. Born in Glenelg, SA, and educated at the University of Adelaide, training, and later working, in biochemistry. After marrying Paul McGuire 1927 she lived in Asia, Europe and the USA. Has written a variety of books demonstrating a wide range of interests. Spent several years in Italy (where her husband was Australia's first ambassador) where she developed an interest in Italian literature and received awards for her work. After her travels returned to Adelaide where she ran a bookshop.

FICTION *Twelve Tales of the Life and Adventures of Saint Imaginus*, London, Sheed & Ward, 1946; *September Comes In*, London, Heinemann, 1961; *Time in the End*, London, Heinemann, 1963; *Three and Ma Kelpie* (children's), London, Longman, 1964.
NON-FICTION *The Price of Admiralty, the Story of Captain J. H. Walker, the RAN, and HMAS Parramatta* (with P. McGuire), Melbourne, OUP, 1944; *The Royal Australian Navy*, Melbourne, OUP, 1948; *The Australian Theatre* (with P. McGuire & B. Arnott), Melbourne, OUP, 1948; *The Flight of the Falcon*, by John Gerard (translated), 1954; *Bright Morning: The Story of an Australian Family Before 1914*, Adelaide, Rigby, 1975.

Macintyre, Elisabeth (1916–)
Children's author. Born in Sydney and grew up in the NSW country. Has worked as a commercial artist, designing and cartoon-drawing, as well as writing for the *Age* and the *Sunday Telegraph*. Is best known as the creator and illustrator of the *Ambrose Kangaroo* series of books for children. Won the Australian Children's Book Council Book of the Year Award 1965 for the *Affable Amiable Bulldozer Man*.

FICTION *Ambrose Kangaroo*, Sydney, Consolidated Press, 1941; *Ambrose Kangaroo Has a Busy Day*, Sydney, Consolidated Press, 1944; *The Black Lamb*, Sydney, Dawfox Productions, 1944; *The Forgetful Elephant*, Sydney, Dawfox Productions, 1944; *The Willing Donkey*, Sydney, Dawfox Productions, 1944; *The Handsome Duckling*, Sydney, Jons Productions, 194–?; *Katherine*, Sydney, Australasian Publ. Co., 1946; *Willie's Woollie's*, Melbourne, Georgian House, 1951; *Mr Koala Bear*, New York, Scribner's, 1954; *Jane Likes Pictures*, London, Collins, 1959; *Hugh's Zoo*, London, Constable Young, 1964; *Ambrose Kangaroo Goes to Town*, Sydney, A & R, 1964; *The Affable Amiable Bulldozer Man*, New York, Alfred A. Knopf, 1965; *Ninji's Magic*, New York, Alfred A. Knopf, 1966; *The Purple Mouse*, Nashville, T. Nelson, 1975; *It Looks Different When You Get There*, Sydney, Hodder & Stoughton, 1978; *Ambrose Kangaroo Delivers the Goods*, Sydney, A & R, 1978; *A Wonderful Way to Learn the Language*, Sydney, Hodder & Stoughton, 1982.

Mack, Amy (1876–1939)
Children's author. Born in Port Adelaide, SA, and educated at Sydney Girls' High along with sister Louise Mack (q.v.). Married Professor Launcelot Harrison 1908. Was editor of the Women's Page of the *Sydney Morning Herald* 1907–14 before going to London where she worked in the ministry of munitions for two years. Also published in English and American journals. All her books for children were illustrated.

FICTION *A Bush Calendar*, Sydney, A & R, 1909; *Bushland Stories for Children*, Sydney, A & R, 1910; *Birdland Stories*, Sydney, A & R, 1910; *Waterside Stories*, Sydney, A & R, 1910; *Bush Days*, Sydney, A & R, 1911; *Scribbling Sue and Other Stories*, Sydney, A & R, 1914; *The Tomtit's Nest and Other Stories*, Sydney, A & R, 1914; *The Wilderness*, Sydney, A & R, 1922; *The Fantail's House and Other Australian Nature Stories*, Sydney, Cornstalk, 1928; *The Birds' Concert and Other Stories of Australian Bush Birds*, Sydney, Cornstalk, 1928; *The Little Black Duck and Other Stories of Bushland and Seas*, Sydney, Cornstalk, 1928; *The Flower Fairies and Other Stories of the Australian Bush*, Sydney, Cornstalk, 1928; *The Gum Leaf that Flew and Other Stories of Australian Bushland*, Sydney, Cornstalk, 1928; *Why the Spinebill's Beak is Long and Other Stories of Australia's Bushland*, Sydney, Cornstalk, 1928.

Mack, Louise (1874–1935)
Children's author, novelist, journalist. Born Marie Louisa Mack in Hobart and educated at Sydney Girls' High where she met and collaborated with Ethel Turner (q.v.) on the girls' magazine, the *Parthenon*. Worked on the *Bulletin* 1896–1901 before leaving for London. Lived also in Italy and was in Belgium at the outbreak of WWI. Was married twice and survived both her husbands. Eventually returned to Sydney where she died 1935. The three *Teens* books for girls demonstrate her writing skills at their lively and realistic best.

FICTION *In an Australian City*, serialised in *Cosmos* Oct. 31, 1895–April 30, 1896; *The World is Round*, London, Fisher Unwin, 1896; *Teens: A Story of Australian School Girls*, Sydney, A & R, 1897; *Girls Together*, Sydney, A & R, 1898; *Children of the Sun*, London, Melrose, 1904; *The*

Red Rose of Summer, London, Alston Rivers, 1909; *Theodora's Husband*, London, Alston Rivers, 1909; *In a White Place*, London, Alston Rivers, 1910; *The Romance of a Woman of Thirty*, London, Alston Rivers, 1911; *Wife to Peter*, London, Alston Rivers, 1911; *The Marriage of Edward*, London, Mills & Boon, 1913; *Attraction*, London, Mills & Boon, 1913; *The Music Makers*, London, Mills & Boon, 1914; *The House of Daffodils*, London, Mills & Boon, 1915; *Teens Triumphant*, Sydney, Stephenson, 1933; *The Maiden's Prayer*, Sydney, Bookstall, 1934.
POETRY *Dreams in a Flower*, Sydney, Bulletin, 1901.
NON-FICTION *An Australian Girl in London*, London, Fisher Unwin, 1902; *A Woman's Experiences in the Great War*, London, Fisher Unwin, 1915.
OTHER Also published short stories in magazines, e.g. the *Bulletin*.
MANUSCRIPTS ML, Sydney: Papers 1880–1915 QA821/M1534/1A1.

Mackellar, Dorothea (1885–1968)
Poet, novelist. Born Isobel Marion Dorothea Mackellar in Sydney; educated at the University of Sydney. Travelled abroad after her education and her verse included translations from European poems. Is mostly remembered for the nationalistic poem *My Country* which she wrote when 19 and which was first published in the *Spectator*, London 1908. It is one of the best-known Australian poems and has been set to music. Gave up writing about half-way through her life due to ill health but remained active in the literary world. Was awarded the OBE 1968.

POETRY *The Closed Door and Other Verses*, Melbourne, Australasian Authors' Agency, 1911; *The Witch Maid and Other Verses*, London, Dent, 1914; *Australia's Men*, Sydney, 191–?; *Dreamharbour and Other Verses*, London, Longmans, 1923; *Fancy Dress and Other Verses* Sydney, A & R, 1926; *My Country and Other Poems*, Sydney, Honey, 1945.
FICTION *The Little Blue Devil* (with Ruth Bedford), London, Alston Rivers, 1912; *Outlaw's Luck*, London, Mills & Boon, 1913; *Two's Company* (with Ruth Bedford), London, Alston Rivers, 1914.
OTHER *My Country* was also published in *The Art of J. J. Hilder* (ed. Sydney Ure Smith and B. Stevens, 1918). *The Poems of Dorothea Mackellar* was published 1971 (Rigby).
MANUSCRIPTS ML, Sydney: Dorothea Mackellar Papers 1902–27 ML MSS 1959.
SEE ALSO T. Inglis Moore, D. Green & J. Lynrave in the *Canberra Times* (Jan.16, 1969), and V. Hankel in *South Australiana*, Vol. 8 (1969).

McKemmish, Jan (1950–)
Prose writer. Born in Tongala, Victoria and educated in country schools. Studied social sciences at La Trobe University and taught high school

1973–7. Afterwards worked in many jobs full and part-time while writing. Taught writing at the NSW Institute of Technology, and for the WEA 1986. Received a New Writers Fellowship 1985 to work on second novel entitled *It Wasn't Like That.* Her first novel was not without its critics but also attracted considerable praise for its experimental feminist style and for extending the frontiers of realist fiction.

FICTION *A Gap In The Records*, Melbourne, Sybylla, 1985.
OTHER Short stories have appeared in *Frictions* (Sybylla, 1982) and *Meanjin* (July 1983).
SEE ALSO K. Goldsworthy in *Meanjin*, Vol. 44, No. 4 (1985).

Macken, Linda
Novelist. Born and brought up in NSW. Travelled widely in Europe and South America. Began writing in 1981, and is author of one of the few fantasy novels by a woman in Australia.

FICTION *And Brothers All*, Sydney, Fontana Collins, 1984.

McLeod, Marjorie (1893–)
Playwright, poet. Born in Victoria; was a speech and drama teacher, actor, and ABC radio script writer before founding the Swan Hill National Theatre 1956 where she directed and produced plays. Some of her plays are historical, such as *Within These Walls*. *A Shillingsworth* (in *Four Period Plays*), set in Melbourne during the Depression, won the Australian Literary Society drama competition 1931.

DRAMA *Travail*, in *Eight Plays by Australians*, Melbourne, Dramatists' Club, 1934; *Moonshine*, in *Five Plays by Australians*, Melbourne, Dramatists' Club, 1936; *Within These Walls: A Period Play in Four Acts*, Swan Hill National Theatre Movement, 1948; *Four Period Plays*, Swan Hill, Vic., the author, 1958.
POETRY *Verses from Swan Hill*, including *The Enchanted Tryst*, Swan Hill, Vic., the author, 1946.
OTHER Autobiography, *All the World's A Stage* (1980).

McMaster, Rhyll (1947–)
Poet. Born in Brisbane, and educated at Somerville House. First published in the *Bulletin* 1962, and has been publishing regularly in Australian magazines and papers since then. Was awarded the Harri Jones Memorial Prize for Poetry 1971 from the University of Newcastle, and the Victorian Premier's Literary Prize 1986 (co-winner). Is married to writer Roger McDonald and has three children.

POETRY *The Brineshrimp*, St Lucia, UQP, 1972; *Washing the Money*, Sydney, A & R, 1986.

OTHER Poems and short stories have appeared in the *Australian, Quadrant, Southerly*, the *Sydney Morning Herald*, etc.
MANUSCRIPTS Mss of all works are lodged with the NL, Canberra.

McNamara, Barbara, 'Elizabeth O'Conner', 'Anne Willard' (1913–)
Novelist. Born at Dunedoo, NSW, the daughter of writer Eric Lowe. Educated in Sydney and Adelaide, studied art at the Julian Ashton Art School, Sydney, and became a teacher in Brisbane. Married Phillip McNamara 1942 and moved to the northern Australian outback where he managed a cattle station. Was encouraged to write by friend Eleanor Dark (q.v.) and wrote two books based upon station life, *Steak for Breakfast* and *A Second Helping*. Her three novels are set in northern Queensland. *The Irishman* won the Miles Franklin Award 1960 and was made into a film 1978.

FICTION *Steak for Breakfast*, Sydney, A & R, 1958; *The Irishman*, Sydney, A & R, 1960; *Find a Woman*, Sydney, A & R, 1963; *The Chinese Bird*, Sydney, Ure Smith, 1966; *A Second Helping*, Sydney, A & R, 1969; *Spirit Man*, 1980.

Maiden, Jennifer (1949–)
Poet. Born in Penrith, NSW. Left school in her early teens but later returned to study for matriculation and tertiary education, graduating BA 1974 from Macquarie University. Married David Toohey 1984 and has one daughter. Has written professionally since her graduation and tutored in creative writing in numerous workshops and seminars. Has won several awards for her work including the Harri Jones Memorial Prize and the Henry Lawson Festival Award. As well as listed work, has also published articles, reviews, plays and short stories in various literary journals. Her poetry is especially noted for its subtle and ambiguous use of language.

POETRY *Tactics*, St Lucia, UQP, 1974; *The Problem of Evil*, Sydney, Prism Poets, 1975; *The Occupying Forces*, St Lucia, Makar Press, 1975; *Birthstones*, Sydney, A & R, 1978; *The Border Loss*, Sydney, A & R, 1979; *For the Left Hand, Poetry Australia*, Berrima, South Head Press, 1981; *The Trust*, Wentworth Falls, NSW, Black Lightning Press, 1987.
FICTION *Mortal Details* (poetry & prose), Melbourne, Rigmarole, 1977; *The Terms*, Sydney, Hale & Iremonger, 1982.
OTHER Also edited the anthologies *Dark City* 1979–80, 1984, 1986 (Blacktown Council).

Maltby, Agnes Newberry, 'Peg' (1899–1981?)
Children's author and illustrator. Born Agnes Newberry Orchard in England and studied at engineering college in England and later at the

National Gallery Art School in Melbourne. Married Major George Maltby 1916, and worked as an engineering designer of battleships and aeroplanes during the 1920s. Is best known for her distinctively Australian fairy stories and illustrations of the bush. Also illustrated the work of several other authors, and retold classic fairy tales such as *Goldilocks, Red Riding Hood*, etc.

FICTION *Peg's Fairy Book*, Melbourne, Murfett, 1944; *Pepita's Party*, Melbourne, Murfett, 1945; *Pip and Pepita in Goblinland*, Melbourne, Murfett, 1945; *Pip and Pepita's New Home*, Melbourne, Murfett, 1945; *Nursery Rhymes*, Melbourne, Murfett, 1945; *Nutchen of the Forest*, Melbourne, Murfett, 1945; *Ben and Bella*, Melbourne, Murfett, 1947; *Ben and Bella in the Hills*, Melbourne, Murfett, 1947; *Ben and Bella in the Clouds*, Melbourne, Murfett, 1947; *Ben and Bella Down on the Farm*, Melbourne, Murfett, 1947; *Nutchen and the Golden King*, Melbourne, Murfett, 1948; *Meet Mr Cobbledick*, Melbourne, Murfett, 1948; *Ben and Bella at the Beach*, Melbourne, Murfett, 1949; *Ben and Bella in the Apple Tree*, Melbourne, Murfett, 1949; *Forever Cuckoo*, Melbourne, Murfett, 1950; *Ben and Bella in the Garden*, Melbourne, Murfett, 1951; *Peg Maltby's Birthday Book*, London, A & R, 1978.

Manners-Sutton, Doris (1895–1972)

Novelist, journalist. Born Doris Dinham in Sydney, and adopted an old family name under which she wrote for Melbourne newspapers and magazines. Left for Europe and Africa in the 1920s. Was extremely advanced and well-educated, spoke five languages and gained a PhD. Also took up travelling with a great vigour, travelling 2,000 miles into the African interior. Married Italian Salvatore Gentile and had two children. Returned to North Africa during WWII but later she and her children became political prisoners in Italy. She had been involved in the underground movement, assisting in the escape of Allied airmen and playing a part in the capture of Mussolini. Her marriage broke down during the war, after which she lived in England and Canada. Returned to Australia 1970 where she lived in the Blue Mountains of NSW until her death in 1972. Wrote adventure novels, as well as various unproduced film scripts and an unpublished book on wartime Italy.

FICTION *A Marked Soul*, Melbourne, A. McCubbin, 1923; *Black God: A Story of the Congo*, London, Longmans, 1935; *The Last Secret*, London, Longmans, 1939.

SEE ALSO Ian Moffit, 'Mother Courage', the *Australian* (Oct. 13, 1973, p.15).

Manning, Emilie, 'Australie' (1845–1890)
Poet, journalist. Born Emilie Matilda Australie Manning in Sydney, daughter of Sir W. M. Manning, Judge of the Supreme Court. Contributed articles on the arts and current affairs to the *Sydney Morning Herald*, the *Australian Town and Country Journal*, the *Illustrated Sydney News* and the *Sydney Mail*, usually under her third name only. Also wrote for London papers whilst visiting England. Was married to solicitor Hubert Heron and became a well-known figure in the cultural life of Sydney in her day. Was appointed Assistant Editor of the *Illustrated Sydney News* earlier in the year of her death.

POETRY *The King's Highway*, words by E. M. A. Heron, Sydney, J. Reading, 1872; *The Balance of Pain and Other Poems*, by E. M. A. Heron, London, Bell, 1877; *The Emigrants: A Dramatic Cantata*, lyrics by E. M. A. Heron, Sydney, R. Bone printers, 1880.
SEE ALSO W. L. Curnow in *Centennial Magazine* (Sept. 1890).

Mansell, Chris (1953–)
Poet. Born in Sydney; graduated from the University of Sydney with a Bachelor of Economics and has a Diploma of Education. Was the founder of *Compass*, the poetry and prose magazine, and has been its editor from 1978. Has also been active in the NSW Poets' Union and the Australian Copyright Council. Was a participant in the NSW Poets in Schools programme 1983–4, and writer-in-residence at WAIT 1985.

POETRY *Delta*, Sydney, Compass, 1979; *Heart, Head & Stone*, Melbourne, Fling, 1982.

Marlowe, Mary, 'Puck' (1892–1958)
Novelist, journalist. Born Mary O'Shannassy in Melbourne, of a political family. Began her career as an actor and left for England 1910. Toured (with Bert Bailey) the English-speaking world playing leading parts and enjoying considerable success. Began to write while in the USA and published two novels in England before returning to Australia 1920. Here she worked as a Red Cross nurse before embarking upon a career as a journalist. Worked on the Sydney *Sun* where she published a theatre column under the name 'Puck'. Began radio broadcasting during the 1930s and achieved popularity with her interviews and talks upon varied topics. Some of her novels were serialised in *All Story Magazine* (New York) and the *Australian Woman's Mirror;* most of them enjoyed the status of popular romance. *Kangaroos in King's Land* was based upon her own experiences in London as a young woman.

FICTION *Kangaroos in King's Land: The Adventures of Four Australian Girls in England*, London, Simpkin, 1917; *The Toll Gate of Mars*, serialised in

All Story Magazine, New York, 1917; *The Women Who Wait*, London, Simpkin, 1918; *The Ghost Girl*, London, Collins, 1921; *Gypsy Royal, Adventuress*, London, Collins, 1923; *A Child by Proxy*, serialised in the *Australian Woman's Mirror*, Sydney, 1925; *An Unofficial Rose*, London, Collins, 1927; *Said the Spider: A Romance of Papua and New York*, London, Collins, 1929; *Psalmist of the Dawn*, Sydney, Endeavour Press, 1934; *Island Calm*, serialised in the *Australian Woman's Mirror*, Sydney, 1940.
SEE ALSO D. Campbell in *Australian Popular Culture* (Allen & Unwin, 1979).

Marrington, Pauline (1921–)
Historical novelist. Born Pauline Stephens in Montreal, Canada and educated in England. Came to Australia as a teenager and attended art school. Later taught at a Sydney Girls' High School and also worked as a freelance artist and copywriter. Married John Marrington 1944 and had two children. Took up serious writing in the late 1950s and has become a writer of carefully researched historical novels. Received the Con Weichart Award for local history 1981 for *In the Sweet Bye and Bye*.

FICTION *The October Horse*, Sydney, Hodder & Stoughton, 1975; *A House Full of Men*, Melbourne, Nelson, 1979; *In the Sweet Bye and Bye*, Sydney, Reed, 1981.
OTHER Short stories have appeared in *Ink No. 2* (Society of Women Writers, 1977), and in *Vogue* and *Reader's Digest*.

Martin, Catherine (1847–1937)
Novelist, journalist. Born Catherine Edith Macauley Mackay on the Isle of Skye and brought to SA 1855. Worked as a journalist in Adelaide, then as a clerk in the Education Department. Was married to Frederick Martin. Apparently a very private person, she published anonymously or under pseudonyms and has left little trace of her life and work. *An Australian Girl* was noted at the time of publication for its depiction of a complex heroine with cultivated tastes and intellect and for its concern with philosophical and religious issues. *The Incredible Journey*, an early example in Australian literature of fiction sympathetic to the Aborigines, was reprinted by Pandora Press 1987.

FICTION *The Moated Grange*, serialised in the *SA Chronicle and Weekly Mail*, Feb.-Oct. 1877; *An Australian Girl*, (anon.), London, Bentley, 1890; *The Silent Sea*, by Mrs Alick Mcleod, London, Bentley, 1892; *At a Crisis*, serialised in the *Adelaide Observer*, April-June 1900; *The Old Roof-Tree: Letters of Ishbel to her Half-Brother Mark Latimer* (anon.), London, Longmans, 1906; *The Incredible Journey*, London, Jonathan Cape, 1923.
POETRY *The Explorers and Other Poems*, by M. C. Melbourne, G. Robertston, 1874.

OTHER Also published poetry in the *SA Chronicle* and the *Mt Gambier Standard;* articles and reviews appeared in the *Victorian Review* 1881–5 and the *Melbourne Review* 1884; a series of travel vignettes was published in the *Age* 1895–6 while short stories appeared in the Melbourne *Leader* 1890–5 and the *Observer Miscellany* 1878–9.
SEE ALSO J. V. Byrnes in *Australian Letters*, Vol. 3, No. 4 (1962) and G. Dutton in *Quadrant*, No. 9 (Jan.-Feb. 1965). A full bibliography is being prepared by Margaret Allen at the SA CAE.

Martin, Harriet Patchett
Editor, short story writer. Born Harriet Cookesley in Queensland, and married writer Arthur Patchett Martin. Gathered together the stories of various expatriate authors in London and anthologised their work. Her contributors included Rosa Praed, Jessie Couvreur (q.q.v.), Hume Nisbet, Kathleen Caffyn (q.v.) and Victor Daly.

FICTION *Over the Sea: Stories of Two Worlds*, London, Griffith Farran, 1889?; *Volcanic Gold and Other Tales*, Melbourne, 1890; *Under the Gum Tree: Australian Bush Stories*, London, Trischler, 1890; *Coo-ee: Tales of Australian Life by Australian Ladies*, London, Griffith Farran, 1891.

Mas, Joan (1926–1974)
Poet. Born Joan Morgan in Sydney, of Welsh and German parents. Contributed to various Australian and overseas journals and anthologies. Also wrote for the ABC and edited *Poetry Magazine*. Lived as a recluse after her husband's death in 1957, but began publishing again in the 1960s.

POETRY *Isis in Search*, Sydney, Allan Press, 1966; *The Fear and the Flowering*, Sydney, Edwards & Shaw, 1975.

Mass, Nuri (1918–)
Children's author, novelist. Born in Melbourne of Spanish and English parents and partly brought up in Argentina. Educated at the University of Sydney, receiving an MA and the University Medal. Worked as an editor with a number of firms including Angus & Robertson. Established the Writers' Press and founded and edited *Australian Children's World* 1945–6, a monthly magazine for children.

FICTION *Australian Wildflower Fairies*, Sydney, Shakespeare Head Press, 1937; *The Little Grammar People*, Sydney, A & R, 1942; *Magic Australia*, Sydney, A & R, 1943; *The Wizard of Jenolan*, Sydney, A & R, 1946; *Randy Blair*, Sydney, Writers' Press, 1955; *The Silver Candlestick*, Sydney, Writers' Press, 1956; *The Gift*, Sydney, Writers' Press, 1969; *Donna Roon*, Sydney, Alpha Books, 1970; *As Much Right to Live*, Sydney, Alpha Books, 1971; *Don't Kill It – It's Me*, Sydney, Alpha Books, 1972.

NON-FICTION *Where the Incas Trod*, Sydney, Writers' Press, 1956; *The Wonderland of Nature*, Sydney, Writers' Press, 1964; *Many Paths, One Heaven*, Sydney, Writers' Press, 1965; *China – the Walking Giant*, Sydney, Writers' Press, 1966; *Australian Wildflower Magic*, Sydney, Writers' Press, 1967.

Masters, Olga (1919–1986)
Novelist, short story writer, journalist. Born in Pambula on the NSW south coast. Worked for many years on suburban and country newspapers. Lived in Manly for much of her life and moved back to the south coast in later years. Raised seven children and thus did not begin publishing fiction until her late 50s. Won nine prizes for her short stories 1979–80 and an award in the National Book Council Awards 1983 for *The Home Girls*. Her brief but highly successful career as a fiction writer was ended by her unexpected death 1986 and she left much unpublished material. Her last novel appeared posthumously and a collection of short stories is also being prepared for publication.

FICTION *The Home Girls*, St Lucia, UQP, 1982; *Loving Daughters*, St Lucia, UQP, 1984; *A Long Time Dying*, St Lucia, UQP, 1985; *Amy's Children*, St Lucia, UQP, 1987.
SEE ALSO E. Webby in *Meanjin*, Vol. 42, No. 1 (1983) and J Ellison (interview) in *Rooms of Their Own* (Penguin, 1986).

Mattingly, Christobel (1931–)
Children's author. Born in Brighton, SA; educated in SA and at the Presbyterian Ladies' College, Sydney. Trained and worked as a teacher in Adelaide. Has written stories, film scripts, articles, papers and bibliographies of children's literature. Was one of the first professional librarians appointed to a school in SA 1955. Is a member of the Children's Book Council and various other literary organisations.

FICTION *The Picnic Dog*, London, Hamish Hamilton, 1970; *Windmill at Magpie Creek*, London, Hamish Hamilton, 1971; *Worm Weather*, London, Hamish Hamilton, 1971; *Emu Kite*, London, Hamish Hamilton, 1972; *Queen of the Wheat Castles*, Leicester, Brockhampton, 1973; *The Surprise Mouse*, London, Hamish Hamilton, 1974; *Tiger's Milk*, Sydney, A & R, 1974; *The Battle of the Galah Trees*, Leicester, Brockhampton, 1974; *Show and Tell*, Sydney, Hodder & Stoughton, 1974; *Lizard Log*, Sydney, Hodder & Stoughton, 1975; *The Great Ballagurdi Damper Bake*, Sydney, A & R, 1975; *The Long Walk*, Melbourne, Nelson, 1976; *New Patches for Old*, Sydney, Hodder & Stoughton, 1977; *The Special Present and Other Stories*, Sydney, Collins, 1977; *The Big Swim*, Melbourne, Nelson, 1977; *Budgerigar Blue*, Sydney, Hodder & Stoughton, 1978; *The Jetty*, Sydney, Hodder & Stoughton, 1978; *Black Dog*, Sydney, Collins, 1979; *Rummage*,

Sydney, A & R, 1981; *Lexl and the Lion Party*, Sydney, Hodder & Stoughton, 1982; *Brave with Ben*, London, Hamish Hamilton, 1983; *Duck Boy*, Sydney, A & R, 1983; *The Magic Saddle*, Sydney, Hodder & Stoughton, 1983; *Southerly Buster*, Sydney, Hodder & Stoughton, 1983; *Ghost Sitter*, London, Patrick Hardy, 1984; *The Miracle Tree*, Sydney, Hodder & Stoughton, 1985.

Meranda, Wolla
Novelist. Born in Provence and lived in New Caledonia before coming to Australia. Wrote in both French and English. *Pavots de la Nuit* was written in English but first published in a French translation. It was included by A. G. Stephens in his list of *100 Best Australian Books*. Also wrote books on the occult, and contributed to the *Bookfellow*. Lived at one stage at Sunny Corner, near Bathurst, NSW.

FICTION *In Mulga Town*, serialised in the *Bookfellow*, 15 March 1921 – 28 Feb. 1922; *Pavots de la Nuit: Roman de Meours Australiennes*, Paris, S. R. Chiberre, 1922; *Poppies of the Night* (trans. of above), Sydney, W. Brooks, 1930; *Vila of the Isles*, Sydney, W. Brooks, 1930; *The Red River of Life*, Sydney, W. Brooks, 1931.
OTHER Also published the following novels: *The Summer Seas*, *Big Jack of Mittewa Creek*, *The Perfidy of Jane Forster*, and *Gold Dust of Mittewa Creek*. Occult books included: *Light and Outer Darkness* (1935), *The World Tongue*, and *What is Truth*. Also edited *Poesies*, by Julian de Sanary (Sydney, 1931).

Meredith, Gwen (1907–)
Playwright, novelist. Born in Orange, NSW, and educated at the University of Sydney where she began to write plays. Wrote an early radio serial for the ABC, *The Lawsons*, which ran 1943–49, but is best remembered for the enormously popular serial *Blue Hills* which ran for 27 years. Both serials had bush settings and owed their appeal to dramatisation of the lives of ordinary people. Was contracted to the ABC for over 30 years and wrote other plays for stage and radio. In 1967 was created MBE.

DRAMA *The Lawsons*, ABC Radio, 1943–9; *Great Inheritance*, in *Australian Radio Plays*, Sydney, A & R, 1946; *Wives Have Their Uses*, Sydney, Mulga Press, 1949; *Blue Hills*, ABC Radio, 1949–76.
FICTION *The Lawsons*, Sydney, A & R, 1948; *Blue Hills*, Sydney, A & R, 1950; *Beyond Blue Hills*, Sydney, A & R, 1953; *Into the Sun*, Sydney, A & R, 1961.
NON-FICTION *Inns and Outs* (with A. Harrison), Sydney, A & R, 1955.
MANUSCRIPTS NL, Canberra: Gwen Meredith Papers & Mss; ABC Archives.
SEE ALSO A. Ashbolt in *Focus*, Vol. 1, No. 2 (1946–7)

Meredith, Louisa (1812–1895)
Non-fiction writer, poet, novelist, artist. Born Louisa Anne Twamley in Birmingham, England. Achieved a considerable reputation as a poet, artist and critic in her own land before marrying her cousin Charles Meredith and emigrating to Tasmania 1839. They intended staying only a few years, however a series of financial failures and family disappointments led to their permanent 'exile' in Tasmania. Moved from home to home as their fortunes dictated, and Louisa only visited England years later, after her husband's death. She earned praise from within and without Australia for her descriptive writings and exquisite paintings and sketches of the native flora and fauna; her descriptions of life in Tasmania in the 1840s still remain some of the best. Also wrote for children, and one of her volumes was used as a school primer. Remained active in literary, dramatic and social life until her death. Was also a naturalist, botanist and possibly Tasmania's first conservationist. Was the only literary figure ever to have been voted a pension by the Tasmanian government. *Notes and Sketches* went into many editions, and was reprinted by Penguin 1973.

NON-FICTION *The Romance of Nature, or The Flower Seasons Illustrated*, London, Charles Tilt, 1836; *Flora's Gems, or The Treasures of the Parterre*, London, Charles Tilt, 1837; *Our Wild Flowers Familiarly Described and Illustrated*, London, Charles Tilt, 1839; *An Autumn Ramble by the Wye*, London, Charles Tilt, 1839; *Notes and Sketches of New South Wales During a Residence in that Colony from 1839 to 1844*, London, John Murray, 1844; *The Bouquet, Containing the Poetry and Language of Flowers*, Boston, O. L. Perkins, 1845; *My Home in Tasmania, or Nine Years in Australia*, New York, Bunce & Brother, 1853; *Some of My Bush Friends in Tasmania*, London, Day & Son, 1860; *Over the Straits: A Visit to Victoria*, London, Chapman & Hall, 1861; *Souvenir of the Masques of Christmas and of the Old and New Year*, Hobart, *Tasmanian Morning Herald*, 1866; *Our Island Home, A Tasmanian Sketch Book*, Hobart, J. Walch & Sons, 1879; *Tasmanian Friends and Foes, Feathered, Furred and Finned*, London, Marcus Ward & Co., 1880.
POETRY *Poems*, London, Charles Tilt, 1835; *Grandmamma's Verse Book for Young Australia*, Hobart, J. Walch & Sons, 1878; *Waratah Rhymes for Young Australia*, London, Vincent Brooks Day, 1896.
FICTION *Loved and Lost! The True Story of a Short Life*, London, Day & Son, 1860; *A Tasmanian Memory of 1834. In Five Scenes*, Hobart, J. Walch & Sons, 1869; *Phoebe's Mother*, London, Tinsley Brothers, 1869; *Nellie, or Seeking Goodly Pearls*, London, J. Nisbet, 1882.
OTHER Also published pamphlets, lyrics to songs, and contributed to journals such as *Chambers's Edinburgh Journal*, and the *Australasian*.

MANUSCRIPTS State Library of Tasmania: Meredith Family Papers; Allport Library, Tasmania: Ms novel; ML, Sydney: Letters 1875–95.
SEE ALSO M. Swann in *Proceedings of the J.R.A.H.*, Vol. 15, PT.1 (1929); E. Pownall in *Mary of Maranoa* (F. H. Johnston, 1959); V. R. Ellis, *Louisa Anne Meredith, a Tigress in Exile* (Blubber Head Press, 1979) and J. Gillison in *Victorian Historical Journal*, Vol. 51, No. 2 (May 1980).

Mitchell, Elyne (1913–)
Children's author, novelist, non-fiction writer. Born in Melbourne but spent the years 1914–19 in England when her father served in the army. Developed a love of the Australian countryside and particularly the Snowy Mountains country from an early age. Eventually combined her love of adventure and the bush with the writing of stories and novels about the Australian Alps, originally writing for her own four children. *Light Horse to Damascus* is based upon her father's experiences in the Middle East during WWI.

FICTION *Flow River, Blow Wind*, London, Harrap, 1953; *Black Cockatoos Mean Snow*, London, Hodder & Stoughton, 1956; *Silver Brumby*, London, Hutchinson, 1958; *Silver Brumby's Daughter*, London, Hutchinson, 1960; *Kingfisher Feather*, London, Hutchinson, 1962; *Winged Skies*, London, Hutchinson, 1964; *Silver Brumbies of the South*, London, Hutchinson, 1965; *Silver Brumby Kingdom*, London, Hutchinson, 1966; *Moon Filly*, London, Hutchinson, 1968; *Jinki, Dingo of the Snow* London, Hutchinson, 1970; *Light Horse to Damascus*, London, Hutchinson, 1971; *Silver Brumby Whirlwind*, London, Hutchinson, 1973; *The Colt at Taparoo*, Melbourne, Hutchinson, 1975; *Son of the Whirlwind*, Melbourne, Hutchinson, 1976; *The Colt from Snowy River*, Melbourne, Hutchinson, 1979; *Snowy River Brumby*, Melbourne, Hutchinson, 1980; *Brumby Racer*, Melbourne, Hutchinson, 1981; *The Man from Snowy River*, Sydney, A & R, 1982.
NON-FICTION *Australia's Alps*, Sydney, A & R, 1942; *Speak to the Earth*, Sydney, A & R, 1945; *Soil and Civilization*, Sydney, A & R, 1946; *Images in the Water*, Sydney, A & R, 1946; *Light Horse, The Story of Australia's Mounted Troops*, Melbourne, Macmillan, 1978; *Snowy Mountains* (with Mike James), Adelaide, Rigby, 1980; *Chauvel Country*, Melbourne, Macmillan, 1983; *Discoverers of the Snowy Mountains*, Melbourne, Macmillan, 1985.
OTHER Short stories have also appeared in *Meanjin* (1948), *Coast to Coast* (A & R, 1949, 1952) and *Modern Australian Short Stories* (1965).

Mitchell, Mary (1892–1973)
Novelist. Born in Melbourne and educated privately and in Europe. Trained as a secretary at the Women's Institute, London, returning to

Australia 1923 to work for the Red Cross Society where she stayed until 1932. Achieved popularity with her first novel, *A Warning to Wantons*, which was translated into several other languages and filmed 1949. Lost her sight around 1947, and later wrote *Unchartered Country* 1963 to describe her experience and understanding of the blind. Australia features only slightly in her fiction.

FICTION *A Warning to Wantons*, London, Heinemann, 1934; *Pendulum Swing*, London, Heinemann, 1935; *Maidens Beware*, London, Heinemann, 1936; *The Decline and Fall of a British Matron: A Caustic Comedy*, London, Heinemann, 1937; *Meat for Mammon*, London, Heinemann, 1938; *Who Pays?*, London, Methuen, 1939; *Viper's Progress*, London, Methuen, 1939; *Stupidity's Harvest*, London, Methuen, 1941; *Dark Tapestry*, London, Methuen, 1942; *One More Flame*, London, Methuen, 1942; *The Wood and the Trees*, London, Methuen, 1944; *Simon Learns to Live*, London, Methuen, 1945; *Servants of the Future*, London, Methuen, 1946; *The Pilgrimage of Mrs Destinn*, London, Methuen, 1948; *Black Crusade*, London, Methuen, 1949; *Prelude to Jesting*, London, Methuen, 1950; *Prisoner's Base*, London, Methuen, 1951; *Simple Simon*, London, Methuen, 1952; *Proof of a Victory*, London, Methuen, 1954; *Birth of a Legend*, London, Methuen, 1956.
OTHER *Unchartered Country: Aspects of Life in Blindness* (Cheshire, 1963).
SEE ALSO J. Hetherington in *Forty-Two Faces* (F. W. Cheshire, 1963).

Modjeska, Drusilla (1946–)
Historian, critic. Born in London and educated in England. Came to Australia 1971 after spending 3 years in New Guinea. Her doctoral thesis at the University of NSW on women writers of the earlier twentieth century was published as *Exiles at Home;* it is the only thorough examination of Australian women writers of the period between the wars. Has also published numerous reviews for magazines such as *Refractory Girl*, and for radio. Currently works at the NSW Institute of Technology lecturing in writing and textual studies.

NON-FICTION *Exiles at Home, Australian Women Writers 1925–1945*, Sydney, Sirius, 1981; *Nellie Melba, Ginger Meggs and Friends, Essays in Australian Cultural History* (ed. with S. Dermody & J. Docker), Malmsbury, Kibble Books, 1982; *The Poems of Lesbia Harford* (ed. with M. Pizer), Sydney, Sirius, 1985.
OTHER Contributed a chapter to *Women, Class and History* (ed. E. Windschuttle, Fontana, 1980) and published introductions to: Dorothy Green, *The Music of Love* (Penguin, 1984), Katharine Susannah Prichard, *The Roaring Nineties, Golden Miles, Winged Seeds* (Virago, 1983, 1984, 1984) and Eleanor Dark, *The Little Company* (Virago, 1985).

Montefiore, Dora (1852–1927?)
Poet. Born in England and came to Australia where she married and had two children; was widowed c. 1889. Became involved in the feminist cause and founded the Womanhood Suffrage League of NSW 1891. Returned to England 1892 and worked with the Women's Social and Political Union. In 1911 returned to Australia where she remained, editing the *International Socialist*.

POETRY *Singings Through the Dark*, London, Sampson Low, 1898.
OTHER Autobiography, *From a Victorian to a Modern* (E. Archer, 1927).

Moorhead, Finola (1947–)
Fiction writer. Born in Melbourne. Educated at Catholic schools and at the University of Tasmania graduating BA 1968. Has worked in a number of occupations including teaching, and for 3 years was editorial assistant for *Meanjin*. Several of her plays have been produced. Was writer-in-residence at Monash University, Melbourne 1980.

FICTION *Quilt, A Collection of Prose*, Melbourne, Sybylla, 1985; *A Handwritten Modern Classic*, Melbourne, Post-Neo Publs, 1985.
OTHER Plays produced include *Horses* (La Boite, Brisbane, 1973) and *Curtain Raiser* (Women's Theatre Group, 1975). Is represented in the following collections: *The True Life Story Of* (UQP, 1980); *Frictions* (Sybylla, 1983); *Minute to Midnight* (Red Spark, 1985); *Difference* (Waterloo, 1985); *The Best of the Ear* (Rigmarole, 1985) and *Room to Move* (Redress/Unwin, 1985).

Mordaunt, Elinor (c. 1872–1942)
Novelist. Born Evelyn Mary Clowes in Nottinghamshire, England. Published as Elinor, and sometimes Eleanor, Mordaunt, her married name. Lived in Mauritius, where she was briefly married, returned to England 1900 and came to Australia 1902 where she settled in Melbourne. In 1910 returned to England once more and remained there until her death in Oxford 1942. Whilst in Australia she worked on newspapers and journals and published some stories (e.g. in the *Lone Hand*) but did not flourish as a novelist until after her return to England. However about ten of her novels are connected with Australia.

FICTION *The Garden of Contentment*, London, Heinemann, 1904; *A Ship of Solace*, London, Heinemann, 1911; *Tropic Heat*, London, Hutchinson, 1911; *The Kid and the Captain* (for boys), London, Hutchinson, 1912; *The Cost of It*, London, Heinemann, 1912; *Lu of the Ranges*, London, Heinemann, 1913; *Simpson*, London, Heinemann, 1913; *The Island*, London, Heinemann, 1913; *Bellamy*, London, Methuen, 1914; *The Family*, London, Methuen, 1915; *The Rose of Youth*, London, Cassell &

Co., 1915; *The Park Wall*, London, Cassell & Co., 1916; *Before Midnight*, London, Cassell & Co., 1917; *The Pendulum*, London, Cassell & Co., 1918; *The Processionals*, London, Cassell & Co., 1918; *Old Wine in New Bottles*, London, Hutchinson, 1919; *The Little Soul*, London, Hutchinson, 1920; *Laura Creighton*, London, Hutchinson, 1921; *Short Shipments*, London, Hutchinson, 1922; *Reputation*, London, Hutchinson, 1923; *Peoples, Houses and Ships*, London, Hutchinson, 1924; *The Real Sally*, London, Hutchinson, 1925; *The Dark Fire*, London, Hutchinson, 1926; *And Then – ? Tales of Land and Sea*, London, Hutchinson, 1927; *Father and Daughter*, London, Hutchinson, 1928; *These Generations*, London, Hutchinson, 1930; *Full Circle*, London, Secker & Warburg, 1931; *Cross Winds*, London, Secker & Warburg, 1932; *Mrs Van Kleek*, London, Secker & Warburg, 1933; *Traveller's Pack*, London, Secker & Warburg, 1933; *The Tales of Elinor Mordaunt*, London, Secker & Warburg, 1934; *Prelude to Death*, London, Secker & Warburg, 1936; *Royals Free*, London, Michael Joseph, 1937; *Pity of the World*, London, Michael Joseph, 1938; *Roses in December*, London, Michael Joseph, 1939; *Death It Is*, London, Hutchinson, 1939; *Judge Not*, London, Hutchinson, 1940; *Blitz Kids*, London, OUP, 1941; *This Was Our Life*, London, Hutchinson, 1942; *To Sea, To Sea*, London, Muller, 1943.

NON-FICTION *Rosemary, That's For Remembrance*, Melbourne, Lothian, 1909; *On the Wallaby Through Victoria*, London, Heinemann, 1911; *The Venture Book*, London, J. Lane, 1926; *The Further Venture Book*, London, J. Lane, 1926; *Purely for Pleasure*, 1932; *Sinabada* (autobiography), London, Michael Joseph, 1937; *Here Too is Valour* (autobiography), London, Muller, 1941.

Morell, Musette (1898–1950)

Playwright, children's author. Born Moyra Martin. Was a writer of mainly radio plays and of popular children's serials. Two of the plays in *Three Radio Plays* are verse-dramas while the third is Irish in setting.

DRAMA *The Quick and the Dead*, in *Australian Writers' Annual* (1936); *Plays for Children* (ed.), Sydney, Currawong, 1947; *Presented Without Courtesy*, in *Australian Youth Plays No. 2*, Sydney, A & R, 1948; *Three Radio Plays*, Sydney, Australasian Publ. Co., 1948; *Ten Puppet Plays*, Sydney, Currawong, 1950.

FICTION *The Antics of Algy*, Sydney, A & R, 1946; *Bush Cobbers*, Sydney, Australasian Publ. Co., 1948.

OTHER Unpublished plays include *Brolgah the Beautiful*, *His Gentle Art of Making Enemies* and *The World His Oyster*.

SEE ALSO L. Rees in *Australian Quarterly*, Vol. 20, No. 3 (1948).

Morgan, Sally (1951–)
Writer, artist. Born Sally Milroy in Perth, the eldest of five children. Educated at the University of WA and WAIT, majoring in psychology. Married Paul Morgan 1972 and has three children. Began to write when questions concerning her family's Aboriginal history led to research into her mother's and grandmother's past, and scrutiny of her own life. The resulting *My Place* is a remarkable autobiography which discovers the lost story of several generations of Australian women. Sally Morgan's paintings are represented in several collections and hung in the Australian National Gallery.

NON-FICTION *My Place*, Fremantle, Fremantle Arts Centre Press, 1987.

Morris, Meaghan (1950–)
Essayist. Born in Tenterfield, NSW, and educated at the University of Sydney (BA honours 1975) and Paris VIII (M.ès L 1978). Has worked as an editor and freelance writer and was film critic for the *Sydney Morning Herald* 1979–81 and the *Australian Financial Review* 1981–5. Is presently writing full-time and completing a book for publication, *Upward Mobility, an Essay on Myth*. An important contemporary critic and essayist, has published many articles in Australian and overseas journals. The following list represents a selection of her work.

NON-FICTION *Language, Sexuality and Subversion* (ed. with Paul Foss), Sydney, Feral, 1978; *Michel Foucault: Power, Truth, Strategy* (ed. with Paul Patton), Sydney, Feral, 1979; 'Operative Reasoning: Michele Le Douff, Philosophy and Feminism', in *I & C*, Oxford, No. 9 (Winter 1981/2): 'A-Mazing Grace: Notes on Mary Daly's Poetics', in *Intervention*, Sydney, No. 16 (1982); 'Identity Anecdotes', in *Camera Obscura*, Los Angeles, No. 12 (1984); 'Room 101, or A Few Worst Things in the World', in *Seduced and Abandoned, the Baudrillard Scene* (ed. A. Frankouris), Sydney, Stonemoss, 1984; 'Postmodernity and Lyotard's Sublime' in *Art & Text*, New York & Melbourne (Summer, 1984).

Morris, Myra (1893–1966)
Novelist, short story writer, poet. Born in the Mallee district of Victoria, and educated at a convent school. Became a freelance writer of stories, poetry and articles. Wrote with simplicity and clarity of the Victorian landscape and its inhabitants in her poetry; her fiction frequently addresses the problems to be found within marriage.

FICTION *Us Five* (children's), Melbourne Publishing Co., 1922; *The Wind on the Water*, London, T. Butterworth, 1938; *Dark Tumult*, London, T. Butterworth, 1939; *The Township* (stories), Sydney, A & R, 1947.
POETRY *England and Other Verses*, Melbourne, Australasian Authors'

Agency, 1918; *The Little Track* (with others), 1922; *White Magic*, Melbourne, Vidler, 1929.
OTHER *Australian Landscape* (John Sands, 1944). Also contributed to *Coast to Coast* (A & R, 1941, 1942) and *Tales by Australians* (ed. E. M. Fry, 1939).

Murdoch, Nina (1890–1976)
Children's author, travel writer. Born in Melbourne and brought up in NSW. Educated at Sydney Girls' High School. Qualified and worked as a school teacher, afterwards working for the Sydney and Melbourne *Sun* newspapers. Turned to radio work 1930 and concentrated upon broadcasting for children. Founded the 'Argonauts' Club' after the popular programme of the same name. Earlier contributed poetry to the *Bulletin* and won a prize for poems, but later turned to fiction and travel books.

FICTION *Miss Emily in Black Lace*, Sydney, A & R, 1930; *Portrait of Miss Emily*, Sydney, A & R, 1931; *Exit Miss Emily*, Sydney, A & R, 1937.
NON-FICTION *Seventh-Heaven*, Sydney, A & R, 1930; *She Travelled Alone in Spain*, London, Harrap, 1935; *Tyrolean June*, London, Harrap, 1936; *Vagrant in Summer*, London, Harrap, 1937; *Portrait in Youth of Sir John Longstaff*, Sydney, A & R, 1948.
POETRY *Songs of the Open Air*, Sydney, W. Brooks, 1915; *More Songs of the Open Air*, Melbourne, Robertson & Mullens, 1922.
MANUSCRIPTS NL, Canberra: Papers MS 634.

Murray, Elizabeth Alicia (1820–1877)
Novelist. Born Elizabeth Poitier in Jamaica and after the death of both parents moved to Ireland at the age of 18. Married Captain Virginius Murray 1844 who came to Melbourne 1852; she and their five sons followed 1855 and lived in Melbourne while her husband worked around the goldfields. Returned with four of her sons 1859, her husband dying in Melbourne 2 years after. Wrote other successful novels before *Ella Norman*, which was inspired by her dismay at the plight of young women sent out to the colony.

FICTION *Ella Norman, or A Woman's Perils*, London, Hurst & Blackett, 1864, (reprinted Melbourne, Hill cf Content, 1985).

N

Nankivell, Joice
Prose writer. Born in Queensland and brought up in Victoria. Married to writer Frederick Sydney Loch and with him visited and wrote about Ireland, Poland and Greece. Worked for Polish refugees during the war 1939–44, after which they returned to Greece.

FICTION *The Cobweb Ladder* (poetry and prose for children), Melbourne, Lothian, 1916; *The Solitary Pedestrian*, Melbourne, Australasian Authors' Agency, 1918; *The Fourteen Thumbs of St Peter*, London, Murray, 1926.
NON-FICTION With Sydney Loch: *Ireland in Travail: Personal Experience of Two Independent Visitors in 1920–21*, London, Murray, 1922; *The River of a Hundred Ways: Life in the War-Devastated Areas of Eastern Poland*, London, Unwin, 1924; *A Fringe of Blue*, by Joice Loch, London, Murray, 1968.

Nayman, Michele (1956–)
Poet, fiction writer. Born in London. Educated in Australia and the USA, graduating with honours in town planning from the University of Melbourne, and as MSc in journalism from Columbia University, New York. Has worked as a journalist for the *Age* and the *Asian Business Press* (in Hong Kong), and as a marketing manager in various international locations. Currently works as a freelance writer.

POETRY *Where You Love You Are*, Victoria, Neptune Press, 1977.
FICTION *Faces You Can't Find Again*, Victoria, Neptune Press, 1980.
OTHER Is represented in the following anthologies: *The State of the Art* (Penguin, 1983), *Jewish Writing from Down Under* (Micah, 1984) and *Poet's Choice* (Island, 1977, 1978). Work has also appeared in *Quadrant, Westerly, Tabloid Story, Inprint, Ash* and the *Canberra Times*.
SEE ALSO S. Sayers in the *Age* (7 Jan. 1978).

Neville, Anne *See:* **'Neville, Margot'**

Neville, Jill (1932–)
Novelist, journalist, critic. Born in Sydney. Left for England in the 1950s where, apart from spending time in Paris, she has lived since. Has worked as a teacher, journalist and social worker. Her literary criticism and reviews have appeared in the *Times Literary Supplement* and in the *Sydney Morning Herald*. Has also published in London newspapers and presently writes a column for the *Sunday Times*.

FICTION *Fall-Girl*, London, Weidenfeld & Nicolson, 1966; *The Girl Who*

Played Gooseberry, London, Weidenfeld & Nicolson, 1968; *The Love Germ*, London, Weidenfeld & Nicolson, 1969; *The Living Daylights*, London, Weidenfeld & Nicolson, 1974; *Last Ferry To Manly*, Melbourne, Penguin, 1984.

'Neville, Margot'

Novelists. Collaborative pseudonym of sisters Margot Goyder and Anne Neville. Born in Australia but lived for some time in London, returning 1939 to settle in Melbourne. Belonged to the well-known Goyder family of Melbourne and were the nieces of George Goyder, Surveyor-General of SA. They wrote detective stories and thrillers, some of which have been translated into other languages. Margot Goyder also published *The Book of Beauty* 1932 as 'Lili Van Heems'.

FICTION *Mariette is Stolen*, London, Parsons, 1922; *This Can't Be I*, London, Parsons, 1923; *Safety First*, London, Hodder & Stoughton, 1924; *Kiss Proof*, London, Chapman & Hall, 1928; *Giving the Bride Away*, London, Chapman & Hall, 1930; *Jennifer's Husband*, serialised in the *Australian Women's Weekly*, Sydney, 1936–7; *Murder in Rockwater*, London, Bles, 1944; *Murder and Gardenias*, London, Bles, 1946; *Murder in a Blue Moon*, London, Bles, 1948; *Murder of a Nymph*, New York, Doubleday, 1950; *Murder Before Marriage*, New York, Doubleday, 1951; *Come, Thick Night*, New York, Doubleday, 1951; *Murder of the Well-beloved*, London, Bles, 1953; *Murder and Poor Jenny*, New York, Doubleday, 1954; *The Hateful Voyage*, New York, Doubleday, 1956; *Murder of Olympia*, London, Bles, 1956; *Murder to Welcome Her*, London, Bles, 1957; *Confession of Murder*, New York, Doubleday, 1960; *Murder Beyond the Pale*, London, Bles, 1961; *Drop Dead*, London, Bles, 1962; *Come See Me Die*, London, Bles, 1963; *My Bad Boy*, London, Bles, 1964; *Ladies in the Dark*, London, Bles, 1965; *Head on the Sill*, London, Bles, 1966.

Newton, Ellen, 'Esther Levy' (1896–)

Journalist, critic, short story writer. Born in Melbourne. Educated at boarding school in NSW, later the University of Melbourne. Worked as a freelance journalist for various papers including the *Bulletin* and *Meanjin*, publishing under her pseudonym. Also broadcast literary talks on radio, worked as a librarian, and was a friend and correspondent of Nettie Palmer (q.v.).

NON-FICTION *This Bed My Centre*, Melbourne, McPhee Gribble, 1979.
OTHER Literary articles appeared in the Red Page of the *Bulletin*, in *Table Talk*, *Stead's Review* and *Meanjin*.
MANUSCRIPTS NL, Canberra: Esther Levy Papers 1923–64 MS 2035.

Nicholson, Joyce (1919–)
Children's author, feminist writer, publisher. Born in Melbourne, the daughter of publisher D. W. Thorpe. Educated at the Methodist Ladies' College and the University of Melbourne, graduating MA. Is now managing director and proprietor of her father's firm which publishes (inter alia) *Australian Books in Print* annually. Was co-founder of Sisters Publishing Limited in Melbourne, and is an active member of the WEL. Many of her children's books are based upon actual persons or events from Australian history. Is currently working on writer Dora Birtles (q.v.) and upon her own autobiography for Virago.

FICTION *The Little Blue Car*, Melbourne, Little Books Publishing House, 1952; *The Little Green Tractor*, Melbourne, Little Books Publishing House, 1952; *The Little Red Helicopter*, Melbourne, Little Books Publishing House, 1954; *ABC of Ships and the Sea*, Melbourne, Little Books Publishing House, 1954; *Adventure at Gulls Point*, London, Epworth Press, 1956; *Gulls Point and Pineapple*, London, Epworth Press, 1958; *Man Against Mutiny*, London, Lutterworth Press, 1960; *Kerri and Honey*, Melbourne, Lansdowne Press, 1962; *A Mortarboard for Priscilla*, Melbourne, Cheshire, 1963; *Andy's Kangaroo*, Melbourne, Lansdowne Press, 1963; *Cranky, The Baby Australian Camel*, Melbourne, Lansdowne Press, 1964; *Ringtail The Possum*, Melbourne, Lansdowne Press, 1965; *Sir Charles and the Lyrebird*, Melbourne, Lansdowne Press, 1966; *The Goldseeker*, Melbourne, OUP, 1966; *Yap, The Penguin*, Melbourne, Lansdowne Press, 1967; *Woop The Wombat*, Melbourne, Lansdowne Press, 1968; *The Convict's Daughter*, Melbourne, Nelson, 1976.
NON-FICTION *How To Play Solo*, Melbourne, Gordon & Gotch, 1955; *Successful Parties and Social Evenings*, London, Epworth Press, 1956; *Games, Competitions and Quizzes*, London, Epworth Press, 1956; *The Children's Party and Games Book*, London, Epworth Press, 1956; *What Society Does To Girls*, London, Virago, 1975; *The Half Open Door*, Sydney, Hale & Iremonger, 1983; *The Heartache of Motherhood*, London, Sheldon Press, 1982; *Why Women Lose At Bridge*, London, Gollancz, 1985.

Nolan, Cynthia (?1913–1976)
Novelist, travel writer. Born Cynthia Reed in Tasmania and was educated at home then boarding school. Trained as a nurse at St Thomas's Hospital, London and worked in hospitals in London, Paris and New York; underwent post-graduate training at the New York Medical Center. Early had connections with writers and artists especially in the 1940s when her brother John Reed edited *Angry Penguins*. Published two novels as Cynthia Reed, but is probably only now remembered for being the wife of artist Sidney Nolan whom she married 1948. Spent years as an expatriate with Nolan; *Open Negative* 1967 describes their time in the

USA and her experience as a patient in New York being treated for tuberculosis, the disease which tormented her for many years. Committed suicide in London 1976. Is fondly recollected by Patrick White (in his autobiography *Flaws in the Glass* 1981), who claims she was a great influence upon her husband's work.

FICTION *Lucky Alphonse*, Melbourne, Reed & Harris, 1944; *Daddy Sowed a Wind!*, Sydney, Shakespeare Head, 1947; *A Bride for St Thomas*, London, Constable, 1970.
NON-FICTION *Outback*, London, Methuen, 1962; *One Traveller's Africa*, London, Methuen, 1965; *Open Negative*, London, Macmillan, 1967; *A Sight of China*, London, Macmillan, 1969; *Paradise and Yet*, London, Macmillan, 1971.

Norman, Lilith (1927–)
Children's author. Born and raised in Sydney; attended business college in Auckland, New Zealand. Has worked as a typist, clerk, sales assistant, nurse, librarian, research officer, and, until recently, as editor of *School Magazine*, for the NSW Department of Education. Has been closely involved with children's literature, being active in the Children's Book Council of Australia and having taught on the subject in a number of institutions. Was awarded the Queen's Silver Jubilee Medal 1977. Some of her novels have been translated into other languages.

FICTION *Climb a Lonely Hill*, Sydney, Collins, 1970; *The Shape of Three*, Sydney, Collins, 1971; *The Flame Takers*, Sydney, Collins, 1973; *Mocking-Bird Man*, Sydney, Hodder & Stoughton, 1977; *A Dream of Seas*, Sydney, Collins, 1978; *My Simple Little Brother*, Collins Young Fiction, 1979.
NON-FICTION *The Brown and Yellow: Sydney Girls' High 1883–1983*, Melbourne, OUP, 1983.
OTHER Has published local histories of Sydney; stories have appeared in the anthologies *Beneath the Sun* (Collins, 1972), *Too True* (Collins, 1974) and *Stories of the City* (Evans Bros, 1977). Hundreds of articles, stories, poems, plays, etc appeared in *School Magazine*, 1971–9. Has also contributed to the *Encyclopaedia Britannica*, and to biographical and critical works.

O

'O'Conner, Elizabeth' *See:* **McNamara, Barbara**

O'Doherty, Eva (1826–1910)
Poet. Born Mary Eva Kelly in Ireland, and published partriotic verse there in the paper the *Nation* before joining Kevin O'Doherty (transported for political crimes 1848) in Australia. They married after his pardon 1854 and travelled overseas before returning to settle in Brisbane in the 1860s. He practised medicine and entered politics and she published poetry under her old pseudonym 'Eva'. Her poems were after the style of her earlier Irish verse, and she remained a popular writer both in Ireland and Queensland.

POETRY *Poems*, by Eva of the *Nation*, San Francisco, P. J. Thomas, 1877; *Poems*, Dublin, 1880.
SEE ALSO H. A. Kellow, *Queensland Poets* (Harrap, 1930, ch. 5).

O'Harris, Pixie (1903–)
Children's author and illustrator. Born Rhona Harris in Wales, and nicknamed 'Pixie'. Attended the Royal Art Society of South Wales at the age of 14. Arrived in Australia with her family 1920, settling initially in WA. She quickly acquired a reputation as an illustrator of children's books, and is now best known for her fairy-tale books. Also illustrated about 20 books by other authors including Frank Dalby Davison, C. J. Dennis and Ruth Bedford. Over a period of about 40 years has also decorated more than 50 children's hospital walls, schools and clinics. Also occupies a place in the adult art world and has exhibited widely. O'Harris has been awarded the Coronation Medal, the Jubilee Medal and the MBE. Is married to Bruce Pratt and lives in Sydney.

FICTION *Pixie O'Harris Fairy Book*, Adelaide, Rigby, 1925; *Pearl Pinkie and Sea Greenie*, Sydney, A & R, 1935; *The Story of Our Baby*, New Century Press, 1940; *The Pixie O'Harris Story Book*, Sydney, A & R, 1940; *The Fortunes of Poppy Treloar*, Sydney, A & R, 1941; *Marmaduke the Possum*, Sydney, A & R, 1943; *The Fairy Who Wouldn't Fly*, Sydney, Marchant, 1945; *Poppy and the Gems*, Sydney, Currawong, 1945; *Poppy Faces the World*, Sydney, A & R, 1947; *The Pixie O'Harris Gift Book*, Sydney, Dymocks, 1950; *Marmaduke and Margaret*, Sydney, A & R, 1953; *The Town of Flowers*, Cornwall, Stockwell, 1957; *Pixie O'Harris Birthday Book*, Sydney, A & R, 1977; *The Teddy Bears' Picnic*, Sydney, Golden Press, 1978; *The Bunny Who Lost His Tail*, Sydney, Golden Press, 1978; *The Kangaroo Who Couldn't Hop*, Sydney, Golden Press, 1979; *The Pixie*

O'Harris Treasury of Animal Verse, Sydney, Golden Press, 1980; *The Pixie O'Harris Gift Book*, Sydney, Golden Press, 1981; *The Pixie O'Harris Cavalcade of Cats*, Sydney, Golden Press, 1981; *The Little Grey Mouse*, Sydney, Golden Press, 1982; *Loveleaves the Koala*, Sydney, Methuen, 1985.
NON-FICTION *Was it Yesterday?* (autobiography) Adelaide, Rigby, 1983; *Our Small Safe World: Recollections of a Welsh Childhood*, Sydney, Boobook, 1986.

'O'Rane, Patricia' *See:* **Dark, Eleanor**

Osborn, Beatrice, 'Margaret Fane' (1888–?)
Short story writer, poet. Born in Melbourne of a Spanish-American family and educated privately. Lived most of her life in NSW where she first contributed poetry to the *Bulletin* and the *Lone Hand*. Wrote the regular 'Margaret's Letter' in the *Quarterly Journal* and published stories in the *Sydney Mail;* also published under various other pseudonyms.

FICTION *The Happy Vagabond* (with Hilary Lofting), Sydney, Cornstalk, 1928.

Osmond, Sophie
Novelist. Published five novels of mixed quality. Her first is a fairly trivial romance; but *An Australian Wooing* is an interesting, somewhat cynical, examination of snobbery, colonial gullibility versus old English guile, and the marriage market.

FICTION *Dulgabeena: An Australian Story*, Melbourne, Pater & Knapton, 1894; *Snags: A Story of the Shearing Strike*, Melbourne, Pater & Knapton, 1895; *The Foot of the Rainbow, A Fantasy* and *The Wattle Blossom*, Melbourne, Pater & Knapton, 1896; *An Australian Wooing: A Story of Trade, a Gold Mine and a Ghost*, Letchworth, Garden City Press, 1916; *Ponga Bay: A Story of Old New Zealand*, London, Hutchinson, 1922.

P, Q

Paice, Margaret (1920–)
Children's author. Born in Brisbane and educated at Queensland Primary Correspondence School and Moreton Bay High School. Later studied illustration at the National Art School, Sydney, and painting at the Royal Art Society. Several of her books have been published in Braille and translated into other languages; others have been published in school editions. *Colour in the Creek* was televised as a series 1985. Twice widowed, Paice now lives in the Blue Mountains of NSW.

FICTION *Mirram*, Sydney, A & R, 1955; *Namitja*, Sydney, A & R, 1956; *Valley in the North*, Sydney, A & R, 1958; *The Lucky Fall*, Sydney, A & R, 1959; *A Joey for Christmas*, Sydney, A & R, 1960; *The Secret of Greycliffs*, Sydney, A & R, 1961; *Over the Mountain*, Sydney, A & R, 1964; *The Bensons*, Sydney, Collins, 1966; *They Drowned a Valley*, Sydney, Collins, 1969; *The Morning Glory*, Sydney, Collins, 1971; *Run to the Mountains*, Sydney, Collins, 1972; *Dolan's Roost*, Sydney, Collins, 1974; *Jackey Jackey*, Sydney, Collins, 1976; *Colour in the Creek*, Sydney, Collins, 1976; *Shadow of Wings*, Sydney, Collins, 1978; *Wheels and Wings*, Sydney, Collins, 1979; *Applewood*, Melbourne, Penguin, 1986; *Alan's Mate*, Macmillan Australia, 1987.
MANUSCRIPTS CAE, Canberra: Lu Rees Archives (papers, mss, etc.).

Palmer, Helen (1917–1979)
Historical writer, journalist. Born in Melbourne, the daughter of Nettie Palmer (q.v.). Educated at the University of Melbourne and became a high school teacher. During WWII worked in the education section of the WAAAF. Wrote several historical textbooks for children in collaboration with Jessie McLeod, as well as other school texts. Was a committed socialist, a member of the Communist Party until 1957 and founder and editor of *Outlook: An Australian Socialist Review* in which she also published various articles on education.

NON-FICTION *Our Sugar*, London, Longmans Green, 1949; *Australian Teacher in China*, Sydney, Teachers' Sponsoring Committee, 1953; *Beneath the Southern Cross*, Melbourne, Cheshire, 1954; *The First 100 Years of Australia as Seen by the People Who Lived in It*, (with Jessie McLeod), Melbourne, Longmans Green, 1954; *Makers of the First 100 Years*, (with Jessie McLeod), Melbourne, Longmans Green, 1956; *After the First 100 Years*, (with Jessie McLeod), Melbourne, Longmans Green, 1961; *Fencing Australia*, Melbourne, Longmans, 1961; *W. G. Spence and*

the Rise of the Trade Unions (with Jessie McLeod), Melbourne, Longmans, 1964; *'Banjo' Patterson*, Melbourne, Longmans, 1966.
MANUSCRIPTS NL, Canberra: Eileen & Helen Palmer Papers 1920s–60s MS 33044.
SEE ALSO D. Bridges (ed.) *Helen Palmer's Outlook* (Hale & Iremonger, 1982).

Palmer, Nettie (1885–1964)
Literary journalist, critic, poet. Born Janet Gertrude Higgins in Bendigo, Victoria. Educated at the Presbyterian Ladies' College and the University of Melbourne where she graduated MA 1912. Spent some years travelling and studying, before and after her marriage to writer Vance Palmer, and has become known as the woman who invested most in Australian literature (particularly women's) during the first half of this century. Early published poetry but from the 1920s onwards concentrated on literary criticism and journalism, delivering lectures, reviewing books, broadcasting, researching, editing, collecting the works of other writers and generally fostering the development of Australian literature in a unique and invaluable manner. Was the first to publish substantially on Henry Handel Richardson (whom she knew over 25 years) and on other authors such as Miles Franklin, Katherine Susannah Prichard, M. Barnard Eldershaw and Barbara Baynton (q.q.v.) Also worked for the socialist cause, helping migrants and refugees of the Spanish Civil War, helped her husband research his books, and raised two daughters.

POETRY *The South Wind*, London, G. Wilson, 1914; *Shadowy Paths*, London, Euston Press, 1915.
NON-FICTION *Modern Australian Literature 1900–1923*, Melbourne, Lothian, 1924; *An Australian Story Book: A Selection from the Best Australian Short Stories, Written in the 20th Century* (selected), Sydney, A & R, 1928; *Henry Bournes Higgins: A Memoir*, London, George Harrap, 1931; *Talking It Over*, Sydney, A & R, 1932; *Centenary Gift Book* (ed. with Frances Fraser), Melbourne, Robertson & Mullens, 1934; *Spain: The Spanish People Present their Case; Australian Nurses' Response*, Melbourne, Spanish Relief Committee, 1937; *Australians in Spain*, Sydney, Spanish Relief Committee, 1937; *Memoirs of Alice Henry* (edited), Melbourne, no imprint, 1944; *Fourteen Years: Extracts from a Private Journal 1925–1939*, Melbourne, *Meanjin*, 1948; *Coast to Coast* (ed.), Sydney, A & R, 1950; *Henry Handel Richardson*, Sydney, A & R, 1950; *The Dandenongs*, Melbourne, National Press, 1952; *Bernard O'Dowd*, (with Victor Kennedy), Melbourne, MUP, 1954.
OTHER Most of her criticism appeared in journals, e.g. *All About Books* (1928–38), the *Argus*, the *Brisbane Courier*, the *Bulletin*, the *Illustrated Tasmanian Mail* and the *Australian Woman's Mirror*.

MANUSCRIPTS NL, Canberra: Vance & Nettie Palmer Papers MS 1174 (Main collection; guide available). La Trobe Library, Melbourne: Letters 1928–33 in the James Booth Collection 497/4 and Letters 1957–62 at MS 8696.

SEE ALSO V. Smith, *Vance and Nettie Palmer, A Biography* (Twayne, 1975) and (ed.) *The Letters of Vance and Nettie Palmer 1915–1963* (National Library of Australia, 1977), D. Modjeska, *Exiles at Home* (Sirius, 1981), *Meanjin*, Vol. 18, No. 2 (1959, Vance and Nettie Palmer Issue), and D. Jordan in *Gender, Politics and Fiction* (ed. C. Ferrier, UQP, 1985).

Palmer-Archer, Laura, 'Bushwoman' (1864–1929)
Short story writer. Born Laura Maud O'Ferrall of second-generation Irish settlers in Fitzroy, Victoria. Educated in Melbourne, and developed a love of story telling from her Irish mother. Began writing articles and stories at the age of 17. Married Tom Palmer-Archer, 1888, moved to a station in north-east Victoria and had four children. Moved to the far west of Queensland 1893 where she began to write her bush stories, contributing to the *Argus*, the *Australasian* and the *Australian Town and Country Journal*. Her tales described aspects of bush life in a vivid and humorous manner. Later returned to live in Melbourne and died at Belgrave 1929. Her sister Nannie O'Ferrall also published stories in the *Australasian* and other papers under the pseudonym 'Bohemia', while her brother Ernest O'Ferrall was the well-known 'Kodak' of the *Bulletin* and *Smith's Weekly*.

FICTION *Racing in the Never Never*, by Bushwoman, Melbourne, G. Robertson, 1899; *A Bush Honeymoon and Other Stories*, Foreword by Rolf Boldrewood, London, Fisher Unwin, 1904.

Parker, Catherine Langloh (c. 1855–1940)
Fiction writer, Aboriginal folklorist. Born Catherine Somerville at Encounter Bay, SA, and brought up on a cattle station in the Darling Downs region of Queensland. Married K. Langloh Parker, under whose name she published, and lived with him on properties in NSW and Queensland. After his death married Percival Stowe and eventually returned to SA. Collected stories and legends of the Aborigines and became the first to collect and publish Aboriginal tales in any systematic manner. *Australian Legendary Tales* has seen numerous editions; in 1954, edited by Henrietta Drake-Brockman (q.v.) and illustrated by Elizabeth Durack, it received the Children's Book of the Year Award.

FICTION *Australian Legendary Tales: Folk-lore of the Noongahburrahs*, London, Nutt, 1896; *More Australian Legendary Tales*, London, Nutt, 1898; *My Best Boy and My Boy-in-law* and *Bobbity, a Bush Baby*, Sydney, Dymocks, 1901; *The Walkabouts of Wur-Run-Nah, Compiled by Catherine*

Stowe from the Legends Collected by K. Langloh Parker, Adelaide, Hassell 1918; *Woggheeguy: Australian Aboriginal Legends*, Adelaide, Preece, 1930.
NON-FICTION *The Euhlayi Tribe: A Study of Aboriginal Life in Australia*, London, Constable, 1905; *A Gardening Calendar* (with Christina Wright), Adelaide, Hassell, 1917.
OTHER Is represented in *Lady Galway Belgium Book* (1916).
SEE ALSO Marcie Muir, *My Bush Book: K. Langloh Parker's 1890s Story of Outback Station Life*, (Rigby, 1982).

Parratt, Anne Chapman (1926–)
Poet. Born in Melbourne and educated at Sydney Teachers' College. Has taught in schools in NSW, Victoria and in England and has also tutored in creative writing in Victoria. Was an original member of the *Luna* poetry collective, and is active in a number of other literary organisations. Her poetry has attracted several awards including the Ernestine Hill Poetry Competition prize 1976, the Society of Women Writers' Award 1977 and first prize in the Ballarat-Esso Poetry Competition 1983.

POETRY *Tangents*, Wodonga, Vic., the author, 1972; *Paint me a Poem*, Melbourne, the author, 1974; *Faith in Life*, (ed.), Melbourne, Communicating Arts Centre, Toorak Uniting Church, 1982.
OTHER Poems have been published in literary magazines such as: *Expression, Contempa, Endeavour, Luna, Nation Review* and *Westerly* and have also appeared in the anthologies, *Dahlia and Eagle Hawk Anthology* (1976) and *The Bronze Swagman Book of Bush Verse* (1976).

Parry, Anne Spencer (1931–1985)
Fantasy/science fiction writer. Born in Melbourne but lived in Sydney for many years. Completed a BA at the University of NSW. Married 1950 and had three children; divorced in the 1970s and died in Sydney 1985 where she had practised as a psychotherapist for over 20 years. Was one of the few Australian writers of fantasy for children and adults.

FICTION *The Land Behind the World*, Sydney, Pinchgut Press, 1976; *The Lost Souls of the Twilight*, Sydney, Pinchgut Press, 1977; *The Crown of Darkness*, Sydney, Pinchgut Press, 1979; *The Crown of Light*, Sydney, Pinchgut Press, 1980; *Below the Surface*, (with Marjorie Pizer) Sydney, Pinchgut Press, 1982; *Zaddick and the Seafarers*, Sydney, Pinchgut Press, 1983; *Beyond the Outlandish Mountains*, Sydney, Second Back Row Press, 1984.

Partridge, Kate, 'Sydney Partridge' (1871–1953)
Novelist, poet. Born in New Zealand of English descent and came to Australia as a girl, settling in Adelaide. Was married to H. E. Stone,

publisher, editor and proprietor of the Wayside Press. Published short stories in the *Australasian* and the *Bulletin*. In partnership with Cecil Warren (Raworth) wrote several novels, not all published in book form. Won first prize in the novel section at the Commonwealth Women's Exhibition 1909.

FICTION *Rocky Section: An Australian Romance*, Brisbane, Steele Rudd & Co., 1907; *Life's Wallaby*, Adelaide, the author, 1908; *The Education of Clothilde*, serialised in the Melbourne *Leader*, 1908?; *The Mystery of Wall's Hill* (with Cecil Raworth), Sydney, Bookstall, 1921.
POETRY *The Lie and Other Lines*, Adelaide, Koolinda Press, 1913; *The One Life and Other Verses*, by K. M. P. Stone, Sydney, Harmony, 1936.
OTHER *The Rubaiyat of Omar Khayyam* (trans. E. Fitzgerald), Notes by Sydney Partridge (S. P. Press, 1910; Edited (with H. E. Stone) the magazine, *The Wayside Goose* (Melbourne 1905–1906).
SEE ALSO C. Hay Thomson in *Cassell's Magazine* (Jan. 1909).

Patchett, Mary Elwyn (1897–)
Children's author. Born in NSW and brought up on a cattle station in northern NSW. Worked in Sydney as a journalist before leaving for England and Europe 1931, travelling and writing. Began to write adventure stories for children using bush settings and characters and has published nearly 50 books, mostly about the animal world. Several have been translated into German, French and Swedish. Lived in London since the late 1940s.

FICTION *Ajax the Warrior*, London, Lutterworth, 1953; *Evening Star*, London, Liutterworth, 1954; *Tam the Untamed*, London, Lutterworth, 1954; *Wild Brother*, London, Collins, 1954; *The Lee Twins*, London, Bodley Head, 1955; *Treasure of the Reef*, London, Lutterworth, 1955; *Undersea Treasure Hunters*, London, Lutterworth, 1955; *Your Call Miss Gaynor*, London, Lutterworth, 1955; *Cry of the Heart*, London, Collins, 1956; *Return to the Reef*, London, Lutterworth, 1956; *Send for Johnny Danger*, London, Lutterworth, 1956; *Caribbean Adventurers*, London, Lutterworth, 1957; *Outback Adventurers*, London, Lutterworth, 1957; *The Great Barrier Reef*, Indianapolis, Bobbs-Merrill, 1958; *The Mysterious Pool*, London, Hamilton, 1958; *The Saffron Woman*, London, Heinemann, 1958; *Brumby, the Wild White Stallion*, Indianapolis, Bobbs-Merrill, 1959; *The Call of the Bush*, London, Lutterworth, 1959; *The Proud Eagles*, London, Heinemann, 1960; *The Quest of Ati Mann*, London, Lutterworth, 1960; *Brit: A Novel*, London, Hodder & Stoughton, 1961; *Come Home Brumby*, London, Lutterworth, 1961; *The End of the Outlaws*, London, Lutterworth, 1961; *Warrimoo*, Leicester, Brockhampton, 1961; *Circus Brumby*, London, Lutterworth, 1962; *Dangerous Assignment*, Leicester, Brockhampton, 1962; *The Golden Wolf*, London, Lutterworth, 1962; *In a Wilderness*, London, Hodder & Stoughton, 1962; *Ajax and the Haunted Mountain*, London, Lutterworth, 1963; *The Venus Project*, Leicester, Brockhampton, 1963; *Ajax and the Drovers*, London, Lutterworth, 1964; *A Budgie Called Fred*, London, Barker, 1964; *Stranger in the Herd*, London, Lutterworth, 1964; *Tiger in the Dark*, Leicester, Brockhampton, 1964; *Brumby Foal*, London, Lutterworth, 1965; *The Last Warrior*, London, Hodder & Stoughton, 1965; *Summer on Wild Horse Island*, New York, Meredith, 1965; *The White Dingo*, London, Lutterworth, 1965; *The Terror of Manooka*, London, Lutterworth, 1966; *Summer on Boomerang Beach*, Leicester, Brockhampton, 1967; *Festival of Jewels*, Leicester, Brockhampton, 1968; *Farm Beneath the Sea*, London, Harrap, 1969; *The Long Ride*, London, Lutterworth, 1970; *Quarterhorse Boy*, London, Harrap, 1970; *Rebel Brumby*, London, Lutterworth, 1972; *Roar of the Lion*, London, Lutterworth, 1973.

Peacock, Marie Winifred
Novelist. Born and educated in Melbourne. Began writing c. 1932, initially contributing stories and articles to magazines and journals. Was Honorary Secretary of the Victorian branch of the FAW and founder of PEN club in Melbourne.

FICTION *Black Valleys*, Sydney, A & R, 1935; *Dead Puppets Dance*, Melbourne, Georgian House, 1944.

Pedley, Ethel (c. 1860–1898)
Children's author. Born in London, the niece of famous contralto singer Mme Sainton-Dolby. Studied music but was prevented from entering the Royal Academy of Music by her family's shift to Australia due to her father's ill-health. Returned later however and studied the violin, receiving the Academy's Medal 1881. Her literary reputation rests upon the success of one book, *Dot and the Kangaroo*, which describes the adventures of a small girl with her native animal friends. It has seen numerous editions over the years, was adapted for the stage 1924, and made into a film 1977.

FICTION *Dot and the Kangaroo*, Illust. F. P. Mahony, London, Burleigh, 1899.
OTHER Also wrote cantatas e.g.: *The Captive Soul*, music by Emmeline Woolley (1895).

Pender, Lydia (1907–)
Children's author. Born in England and came to Australia as a child. Attended school in Hunters Hill, Sydney. Married Walter Pender 1932 and had four children. Has been active in promoting literature for chil-

dren and several of her books have been recommended by the Children's Book Council.

FICTION *Marbles in My Pocket*, Sydney, Writers' Press, 1957; *Barnaby and the Horses*, London, Abelard-Schumann, 1961; *Dan McDougall and the Bulldozer*, London, Abelard-Schumann, 1963; *Sharpur the Carpet Snake*, London, Abelard-Schumann, 1967; *Brown Paper Leaves*, Sydney, Wentworth Press, 1971; *Barnaby and the Rocket*, Sydney, Collins, 1972; *The Useless Donkeys*, Sydney, Methuen, 1979.
POETRY *Poems to Read to Young Australians* (with M. Gilmore) Middlesex, Hamlyn, 1968; *Morning Magpie*, Sydney, A & R, 1984.

Pepworth, Barbara (1955–)
Writer. Born in Sydney and educated at Macquarie University. Has worked in a wide variety of literary forms from poetry, history and science fiction to drama and short stories. Currently editor of the travel journal *Future Tourist*, is reworking a second novel and writing a play for the ABC. Received the Ford Award for Young Playwrights 1975, and a prize in the FAW short story competition 1975. *Early Marks* was shortlisted in the NSW Premier's Literary Awards 1980.

FICTION *Early Marks*, Sydney, A & R, 1980.
NON-FICTION *People who Help People*, Melbourne, Longman-Cheshire, 1979; *Historic Places of Australia*, Melbourne, Macmillan, 1981.
OTHER Plays produced include: *Happy Families* (1979), *Just Another Day* (1983), *Performing Seals* (Nimrod, 1984) and *Sand Hills* (with Duncan Ball, 1986). Poems have appeared in *Compass*, Image, *LiNQ*, and in the anthology *Neon Signs to the Mutes* (Reed, 1976).

Perry, Grace (1927–87)
Poet, publisher, editor. Born in Melbourne and studied medicine at the University of Sydney. For many years occupied a central position in the Australian poetry world, as the proprietor of South Head Press and founder and editor of *Poetry Australia* which she ran from her home and practice in Berrima, NSW. Received a special Literary Award at the NSW Premier's Literary Awards 1985 for services to literature.

POETRY *I am the Songs You Sing and Other Poems*, Sydney, Consolidated Press, 1944; *Red Scarf*, Sydney, Edwards & Shaw, 1964; *Frozen Section*, Sydney, Edwards & Shaw, 1967; *Two Houses: Poems 66–69*, Sydney, South Head Press, 1969; *Black Swans at Berrima*, Sydney, South Head Press, 1972; *Berrima Winter*, Sydney, South Head Press, 1974; *Journal of a Surgeon's Wife and Other Poems*, Sydney, South Head Press, 1974; *Snow in Summer*, Sydney, South Head Press, 1981; *Be Kind to Animals*, Sydney, South Head Press, 1983.

MANUSCRIPTS ML, Sydney: Papers & Mss to May 1985.
SEE ALSO J. E. Chamberlin in *Hudson Review* (Summer (1973), F. Holzknect in *Makar* (1973) and J. G. Tulip in *Southerly*, No. 2 (1973) and in *Poetry Australia* (July, 1980).

Petrie, Barbara (1942–)
Poet, children's author. Born in New Zealand. Spent her early years on a farm, and was encouraged throughout her childhood to write. After leaving school worked as a cadet reporter for *The Press*, Christchurch. Came to Sydney 1963 and had a variety of jobs before moving to the Blue Mountains NSW 1969 where she has lived since with her three children. An acknowledged influence upon her life and work is the poet William Hart-Smith, whom she met when 17.

POETRY *Tones of Survival*, Vista Poets, Blue Mountains Writers Group, 1976; *Cautionary Tales for Australian Children*, Sydney, Hodder & Stoughton, 1986.
OTHER Poems have appeared in *Poet's Choice* (1976, 1977, 1978), *Landfall* (New Zealand, June, 1976), *Compass* (1981), and have also been broadcast on ABC radio.

Phelan, Nancy (1913–)
Novelist, travel writer. Born in Sydney, the niece of writers Louise and Amy Mack (q.q.v.). Educated at the Conservatorium of music and the University of Sydney. Travelled to England 1938 where she married and lived until the end of WWII. Since then has returned to England many times and travelled widely throughout the world. Joined the South Pacific Commission Social Development Section 1951 as an assistant organiser for Island literature, but resigned 1956 to devote herself to writing full-time. *The Voice Beyond the Trees* won a prize in the *Sydney Morning Herald* novel competition 1950 but was not published until 1985. *The Swift Foot of Time*, an autobiographical book, won the Braille Book of the Year Award 1984. Since 1970 has reviewed regularly for the *Sydney Morning Herald*, and for the Melbourne *Age* since 1972.

FICTION *The River and the Brook*, London, Macmillan, 1962; *Serpents in Paradise*, London, Macmillan, 1967; *The Voice Beyond the Trees*, London, Hyland House, 1985; *Home is the Sailor* (forthcoming).
NON-FICTION *Atoll Holiday*, Sydney, A & R, 1957; *Welcome the Wayfarer*, London, Macmillan, 1965; *Pillow of Grass*, London, Macmillan, 1968; *A Kingdom by the Sea*, Sydney, A & R, 1968; *Some Came Early, Some Came Late*, London, Macmillan, 1970; *The Chilean Way*, London, Macmillan, 1973; *Morocco is a Lion*, Melbourne, Quartet Books, 1982; *The Swift Foot of Time*, Melbourne, Quartet Books, 1983.
OTHER Short stories and articles have appeared in the *Australian Literary*

Supplement, the *Bulletin Literary Supplement*, the *Age*, the *National Times*, *Overland*, the *Sydney Morning Herald*, and in *Coast to Coast* and *Summer's Tales*. Has also in collaboration published several books on yoga and one on Russian cookery.

Phipson, Joan (1912–)
Children's author. Born in Sydney of English parents. Spent time as a child in England, India and Europe. Left school 1929 and completed a correspondence course in journalism. Worked in England and Australia 1934–41 in a variety of jobs before joining the WAAAF. Married whilst in the services and retired after two years to live on a property near Mandurama, NSW, and has remained there since. Her fiction for young adolescents is known for its variety of topics and, lately, its attention to modern social problems of the teenager. Twice won the Children's Book of the Year Award in 1953 and 1962.

FICTION *Good Luck to the Rider*, Sydney, A & R, 1953; *Six and Silver*, Sydney, A & R, 1954; *It Happened One Summer*, Sydney, A & R, 1957; *The Boundary Riders*, Sydney, A & R, 1962; *The Family Conspiracy*, Sydney, A & R, 1962; *Threat to the Barkers*, Sydney, A & R, 1963; *Birkin*, London, Constable, 1965; *The Crew of the Merlin*, Sydney, A & R, 1966; *A Lamb in the Family*, London, Hamish Hamilton, 1966; *Peter and Butch*, Melbourne, Longman, 1969; *The Haunted Night*, Melbourne, Macmillan, 1970; *Bass and Billy Martin*, Melbourne, Macmillan, 1972; *The Way Home*, Melbourne, Macmillan, 1973; *Polly's Tiger*, London, Hamish Hamilton, 1973; *Helping Horse*, Melbourne, Macmillan, 1974; *The Cats*, Melbourne, Macmillan, 1976; *Fly Into Danger*, New York, Atheneum, 1977; *Keep Calm*, Melbourne, Macmillan, 1978; *Ride Till Daytime*, Puffin Books, 1979; *No Escape*, Melbourne, Macmillan, 1979; *Mr Pringle and the Prince*, London, Hamish Hamilton, 1979; *A Tide Flowing*, London, Methuen, 1981; *The Watcher in the Garden*, London, Methuen, 1982; *Beryl the Rainmaker*, London, Hamish Hamilton, 1984; *The Grannie Season*, London, Hamish Hamilton, 1985; *Dinko*, London, Methuen, 1985; *Hit and Run*, New York, Atheneum, 1985.
SEE ALSO W. McVitty in *Innocence and Experience: Essays on Contemporary Australian Children's Writers* (Nelson, 1981).

Pitt, Marie E. J. (1869–1948)
Poet. Born Marie McKeown at Balumwaal in the Gippsland region of Victoria. Married W. H. Pitt 1893 and moved to Tasmania where he worked as a miner. Settled in Melbourne 1902 and remained there until her death. Became deeply interested in the working classes and in the feminist cause. Was a member of the Victorian Socialist Party and editor of its magazine. Her poetry, first published in the *Bulletin*, reflects her

ideological and political commitments. From 1919 she lived with the poet Bernard O'Dowd.

POETRY *The Horses of the Hills and Other Verses*, Melbourne, Lothian, 1911; *Bairnsdale and Other Poems*, Bairnsdale, Vic, 'Back to Bairnsdale' Committee, 1922; *The Poems of Marie E. J. Pitt*, Melbourne, Vidler, 1928; *Selected Poems*, Melbourne, Lothian, 1944.
MANUSCRIPTS NL, Canberra: Papers 1914–44 MS 1657 (mostly letters).
SEE ALSO Colleen Burke, *Doherty's Corner: The Life and Work of Australian Poet Marie E. J. Pitt* (Sirius, 1985).

Pizer, Marjorie (1920–)
Poet. Born in Melbourne; educated at the Church of England Girls, Grammar School and the University of Melbourne, graduating in arts 1942. Now lives in Sydney where she has practised as a psychotherapist for over 20 years. Worked for the public service 1942–6 whilst researching early Australian poetry with poet and journalist Muir Holburn whom she married in 1949. First literary work published was an edited collection of poems by Victor Daly. Since then has edited a number of collections of poetry until the appearance of her own in 1967. Founded (with Holburn) Pinchgut Press 1947, refounded 1975 to publish her own poetry.

POETRY *Thou and I*, Sydney, M. Pizer (limited edition), 1967; *To Life*, Sydney, M. Pizer (limited edition) 1969; *Tides Flow*, Sydney, M. Pizer, 1972; *Seasons of Love*, Sydney, Pinchgut Press, 1975; *Full Summer*, Sydney, Pinchgut Press, 1977; *Gifts and Remembrances*, Sydney, Pinchgut Press, 1979; *To You, the Living*, Sydney, Second Back Row Press, 1981; *The Sixteenth Spring*, Sydney, Pinchgut Press, 1982; *Below the Surface* (with Anne Spencer Parry), Sydney, Pinchgut Press, 1982; *Selected Poems 1963–1983*, Sydney, Pinchgut Press, 1984.
OTHER Edited: *Creeve Roe* (with M. Holburn, Pinchgut, 1947), *Freedom on the Wallaby* (Pinchgut, 1953), *The Men Who Made Australia* (Australasian Book Society, 1957), *Come Listen* (A & R, 1966) and *The Poems of Lesbia Harford* (with Drusilla Modjeska, Sirius, 1985).

Porter, Dorothy Featherstone (1954–)
Poet. Born in Sydney and has published widely in magazines and performed at many poetry readings. Was President of the Sydney University Poetry Society 1974–5.

POETRY *Little Hoodlum*, Sydney, Poetry Society, 1975; *Bison*, Sydney, Poetry Society, 1982; *The Night Parrot*, Wentworth Falls, NSW, Black Lightning Press, 1984.
Other Poems have appeared in *New Poetry, Compass, Overland, Quadrant, Poet's Choice* and the *Sydney Morning Herald*.

'Powell, Elizabeth' *See:* **Sandery, Effie**

Power, Marguerite Helen (1870–1957)
Poet. Born in Tasmania, a descendent of the first Surveyor-General of Tasmania. Lived in Hobart and contributed to the *Australasian*, the *Bulletin* and other journals over about 20 years before publishing her first collection 1934.

POETRY *Poems*, Hobart, The Critic Pty Ltd, 1934; *A Lute with Three Strings*, ed. and introduced by Clive Sansom, London, Hale, 1964.

Power, Muriel Faucett (c. 1875–?)
Poet, children's author. Born Muriel Blain, from a pioneer family. Married Charles Danvers and is sometimes known by his last name. Wrote very alliterative, rather old-fashioned lyrics she described as 'folk art', and some sacred poems.

POETRY *Poems*, Sydney, W. Brooks, 1911; *Hymns*, Sydney, Rhincru Press, 1930; *Little Brothers*, Sydney, Beacon Press, 1932; *The Verse Book of Muriel Faucett Power 1895–1946*, Sydney, Beacon Press, 1948.
NON-FICTION *Mother and Child*, Sydney, F. G. Newton Printer, 1913; *Insect Stories for Little People*, Sydney, R. James Printer, n.d.

Pownall, Eve (?–1982)
Children's author, non-fiction writer. Born and lived in Sydney. Wrote novels and non-fiction for children on aspects of Australian life. Is best known, however, for her book on early Australian women, *Mary of Maranoa* (republished as *Australian Pioneer Women* 1975). Was winner of the Children's Book of the Year Award 1952 for *The Australia Book*.

FICTION *The Story of a Baby*, Sydney, Johnston, 1948; *Squik the Squirrel Possum*, Sydney, John Sands, 1949; *Cousins Come-Lately*, Sydney, Shakespeare Head, 1952; *Bunty the Bandicoot*, Sydney, John Sands, 1957.
NON-FICTION *The Australia Book*, Sydney, John Sands, 1952; *Exploring Australia*, London, Methuen, 1958; *Mary of Maranoa*, Sydney, F. H. Johnston, 1959; *They Live in Australia*, Sydney, Shakespeare Head, 1960; *A Pioneer Daughter*, Melbourne, OUP, 1965; *The Thirsty Land*, Sydney, Hicks Smith, 1967; *The Great South Land*, Sydney, Wentworth, 1967; *A Drover*, Melbourne, OUP, 1970; *The Singing Wire*, Sydney, Collins, 1973; *Elements of Danger*, Sydney, Collins, 1976.

Praed, Rosa (Mrs Campbell Praed) (1851–1935)
Novelist. Born Rosa Caroline Murray-Prior on her father's station in the Lower Logan River, Queensland. Grew up on various stations around Queensland. married Arthur Campbell Mackworth Praed 1872 and lived

for a time on Curtis Island. Went to England 1876, returning only once to Australia about 18 years later. Enjoyed great popularity in London, mixing in literary and artistic circles where her novels (about 20 of which are set in Australia) brought her much success. Her personal life, in contrast, was rather sad; she separated from her husband, and all four of her children died under tragic circumstances. Lived 1899–1927 with spiritual medium Nancy Harward. The psychological aspect of her novels extended in later life to exploration of psychic phenomena and an obsession with reincarnation demonstrated in many of her books.

FICTION *An Australian Heroine*, London, Chapman & Hall, 1880; *Policy and Passion: A Novel of Australian Life*, London, Bentley, 1881; *Nadine: The Study of a Woman*, London, Chapman & Hall, 1882; *Moloch: A Story of Sacrifice*, London, Chapman & Hall, 1883; *Zero; A Story of Monte Carlo*, London, Chapman & Hall, 1884; *The Head Station: A Novel of Australian Life*, London, Chapman & Hall, 1885; *Affinities: A Romance of To-day*, London, Bentley, 1886; *The Brother of the Shadow: A Mystery of To-day*, London, Routledge, 1886; *Miss Jacobsen's Chance: A Story of Australian Life*, London, Bentley, 1886; *The Right Honourable: A Romance of Society and Politics*, (with Justin McCarthy), London, Chatto & Windus, 1886; *The Bond of Wedlock: A Tale of London Life*, London, Chatto & Windus, 1887; *The Rebel Rose* (with Justin McCarthy), London, Chatto & Windus, 1888; *The Ladies' Gallery* (with Justin McCarthy), London, Bentley, 1888; *The Romance of the Station: An Australian Story*, London, Trischler, 1891; *The Soul of Countess Adrian: A Romance*, London, Trischler, 1891; *The Romance of a Chalet*, London, F. V. White, 1891; *Outlaw and Lawmaker*, London, Chatto & Windus, 1894; *December Roses*, London, Simpkin Marshall, 1893; *Christina Chard*, London, Chatto & Windus, 1894; *Mrs Tregaskiss: A Novel of Anglo-Australian Life*, London, Chatto & Windus, 1895; *Nulma: An Anglo-Australian Romance*, London, Chatto & Windus, 1897; *The Scourge Stick*, London, Heinemann, 1898; *Madam Izan: A tourist Story*, London, Chatto & Windus, 1899; *As a Watch in the Night*, London, Chatto & Windus, 1900; *The Insane Root: A Romance of a Strange Country*, London, Unwin, 1902; *Dwellers by the River*, London, J. Long, 1902; *Fugitive Anne: A Romance of the Unexplored Bush*, London, J. Long, 1903; *The Ghost*, London, Everett, 1903; *The Other Mrs Jacobs: A Matrimonial Complication*, London, J. Long, 1903; *Nyria*, London, Unwin, 1904; *Some Loves and a Life: A Study of a Neurotic Woman*, London, F. V. White, 1904; *The Maid of the River: An Australian Girl's Love Story*, London, J. Long, 1905; *The Lost Earl of Ellan: A Story of Australian Life*, London, Chatto & Windus, 1906; *The Luck of the Leura*, London, J. Long, 1907; *Stubble Before the Wind*, London, J. Long, 1908; *By Their Fruits*, London, Cassell, 1908; *A Summer Wreath*, London, J. Long, 1909; *The Romance of Mademoiselle Aisse*, London, J. Long, 1910; *Opal Fire*,

London, Cassell, 1910; *The Body of His Desire: A Romance of the Soul*, London, Cassell, 1912; *The Mystery Woman*, London, Cassell, 1913; *Lady Bridget in the Never-Never Land: A Story of Australian Life*, London, Hutchinson, 1915; *Sister Sorrow: A Story of Australian Life*, London, Hutchinson, 1916; *The Soul of Nyria: The Memory of a Past Life in Ancient Rome*, London, Rider, 1931.
NON-FICTION *Australian Life; Black and White*, London, Chapman & Hall, 1885; *The Grey River* (with Justin McCarthy), London, 1890; *My Australian Girlhood*, London, Unwin, 1902; *Our Book of Memories* (with Justin McCarthy), London, 1912.
OTHER Also wrote plays, one of which, *Ariane* (adapted from the novel *The Bond of Wedlock*) was performed in London, 1888. Contributed to the anthologies *Oakbough and Wattle Blossom: Stories and Sketches by Australians in England* (ed. Arthur Patchett Martin, Scott, 1888), *Under the Gum Tree* (Trischler, 1890) and *Coo-ee: Tales of Australian Life by Australian Ladies* (ed. Mrs Patchett Martin, Griffith, Farran, 1891).
MANUSCRIPTS John Oxley Library, Qld: Rosa Praed Papers c. 1885–1930 (Mss, interviews, unpublished papers, etc).
SEE ALSO D. Byrne in *Australian Writers* (London, 1896), W. Birkett in *The Peaceful Army* (ed. F. Eldershaw, Sydney, 1938), C. Roderick, *In Mortal Bondage: The Strange Life of Rosa Praed* (A & R, 1948), C. Hamer in *ALS*, Vol. 2 (1965) and M. Sharkey in *ALS*, Vol. 10 (1981).

'Praize, Anne' *See:* **Blewett, Dorothy**

Prichard, Katharine Susannah (1883–1969)
Novelist, playwright. Born in Fiji of Australian parents and brought to Australia as a child; grew up in Tasmania and Melbourne. Educated at the South Melbourne College and during her schooldays began the friendship with Nettie Palmer (q.v.) that lasted until the latter's death in 1964. Worked as a freelance journalist in Melbourne before leaving for England 1912 to begin her career as a novelist. Returned a prize-winning author 1916, married Jim Throssell 1919 and settled in Perth, WA. Became a committed Marxist at an early date and a foundation member of the CPA 1920. Remained heavily committed to politics all her life, visiting Russia 1933, and establishing the Unemployed Women and Girls' Association and the Modern Women's Club. Was also active in literary organisations, notably the Australian Writers' League and the WA branch of the FAW. Her books, which reflect her socialist ideals, have been translated into 15 languages.

FICTION *The Pioneers*, London, Hodder & Stoughton, 1915; *Windlestraws*, London, Hodder & Stoughton, 1916; *Black Opal*, London, Heinemann, 1921; *Working Bullocks*, London, Jonathan Cape, 1926; *The Wild*

Oats of Han, Sydney, A & R, 1928; *Coonardoo* (*The Well in the Shadow*), London, Jonathan Cape, 1929; *Haxby's Circus*, London, Jonathan Cape, 1930; *Kiss on the Lips and Other Stories*, London, Jonathan Cape, 1932; *Intimate Strangers*, London, Jonathan Cape, 1937; *Moon of Desire*, London, Jonathan Cape, 1941; *Potch and Colour*, Sydney, A & R, 1944; *The Roaring Nineties*, London, Jonathan Cape, 1946; *Golden Miles*, London, Jonathan Cape, 1948; *Winged Seeds*, Sydney, Australasian Publ. Co., 1950; *N'goola and Other Stories*, Melbourne, Australasian Book Soc., 1959; *On Strenuous Wings* (ed. J. Williams), Berlin, Seven Seas, 1965; *Subtle Flame*, Sydney, Australasian Book Soc., 1967; *Happiness*, Sydney, A & R, 1967.

DRAMA *Pioneers*, in *Best Australian One Act Plays*, Sydney, A & R, 1937; *Brumby Innes*, Perth, Paterson's Printing Press, 1940; *Brumby Innes; Bid Me to Love*, Sydney, Currency Press, 1974.

POETRY *Clovelly Verses*, London, 1913; *The Earth Lover*, Sydney, Sunnybrook Press, 1932.

NON-FICTION *The New Order*, Perth, People's Printing & Publishing Co., 1919; *The Real Russia*, Sydney, Modern Publishers, 1934; *Why I am a Communist*, Sydney, Current Book Distributors, 1957; *Child of the Hurricane: An Autobiography*, Sydney, A & R, 1963; *Straight Left* (ed. R. Throssell), Sydney, Wild & Woolley, 1982.

MANUSCRIPTS NL, Canberra: Katharine Susannah Prichard Papers MSS 1094, 649 & 4708 (Main collection; guide available). Unpublished plays include: *Forward One* (1935), *Woman of Spain* (1937), *Solidarity* (1939–40), *Good Morning* (1955) and *The Burglar*, held in the Campbell Howard Collection, the University of New England, and *Bird with a Medal* (1960–61) in the Hanger Collection, the University of Queensland.

SEE ALSO M. Barnard Eldershaw in *Essays in Australian Fiction* (OUP, 1938), J. Lindsay in *Meanjin*, Vol, 20, No. 4 (1961), J. Beasley, *The Rage for Life* (Current Book Distributors, 1964), H. Drake-Brockman, *Katharine Susannah Prichard* (OUP, 1967), R. Throssell, *Wild Weeds and Wind Flowers* (A & R, 1975), J. A. Hay in *Who is She? Images of Woman in Australian Fiction* (ed. S. Walker, UQP, 1983) and P. Buckridge in *Gender, Politics and Fiction* (ed. C. Ferrier, UQP, 1985).

Purnell, Kathryn

Poet, editor. Born in Vancouver, Canada, and educated there and later the University of Melbourne. Married in Australia and has lived in many parts of the world including the Middle East, Indonesia and Africa. Has been chairman of the Human Rights Committee of the UN Association in Victoria and an active member of various literary organisations including the *Luna* collective, the Society of Women Writers and the Melbourne PEN Centre. Received a number of awards for her work including the Society of Women Writers Poetry Prize 1972, the Maryborough Poetry Prize 1975 and the inaugural Charles Meeking Poetry Award for Women 1979. Gwen Harwood (q.v.) said her poems 'reverberate in the mind and reveal the mature compassion of a woman to whom poetry matters because it is truly part of our being in the world.'

POETRY *Pandora*, Melbourne, Neptune Press, 1979; *Safari*, Melbourne, Neptune Press, 1979; *Trillium* (with Audrey Longbottom and Susan McGowan), Melbourne, Neptune Press, 1982; *Otway Country*, Melbourne, Neptune Press, 1984.
FICTION *Remember* (Adult Education), Melbourne, Neptune Press, 1984; *Journeys*, Safari Press, 1986.
OTHER Edited the poetry anthologies, *A Spin of Pink Heath* (1980) and *A Spin of Gold Wattle* (1984) for the Society of Women Writers. Has also published poetry in the journals, *Southerly, Twentieth Century, Poets of Australia* and *Poetry Magazine*.

Pyke, Lillian Maxwell, 'Erica Maxwell' (c. 1881–1927)
Children's author, novelist. Born Lillian Heath in Victoria. Enjoyed some success as a writer for school age children with her books about school life written in the manner of popular English school writers of the early twentieth century.

FICTION *Max the Sport*, London, Ward Lock, 1916; *Jack of St Virgil's*, London, Ward Lock, 1917; *Phyl of the Camp*, London, Ward Lock, 1918; *A Prince at School*, London, Ward Lock, 1919; *Camp Kiddies*, Melbourne, Speciality Press, 1919; *Bruce at Boonderong Camp*, London, Ward Lock, 1920; *Cole's Happy Time Picture and Nursery Rhyme Book*, 1920; *The Southern Seas Story Book* (ed.), Melbourne, A. McCubbin, 1920; *The Best School of All*, London, Ward Lock, 1921; *Sheila at Happy Hills*, London, Ward Lock, 1922; *The Harp of Life*, Sydney, Bookstall, 1924; *Brothers of the Fleet*, London, Ward Lock, 1924; *The Lone Guide of Merfield*, London, Ward Lock, 1925; *Clem (and others)* by Erica Maxwell, London, Hodder & Stoughton, 1925; *A Wife by Proxy*, London, Hodder & Stoughton, 1926; *The Secret of Wallaby Rock*, London, Ward Lock, 1927.
OTHER *Australian Etiquette* (Speciality Press, 1916).

'Quinn, Harlingham' *See:* **Stonehouse, Patricia**

Quinn, Tarella (1877–1934)
Children's author, novelist. Born near Wilcannia, NSW, and became a popular writer of fairy stories for children. Her imaginative and whimsical stories were accompanied by the illustrations of Ida Rentoul Outhwaite. Also published under her married name of Daskein. *Gum Tree Brownie* was extended and reprinted 1918 with a foreword by Ethel Turner (q.v.).

FICTION *Gum Tree Brownie*, Melbourne, G. Robertson, 1910; *Freckles*,

London, Moring, 1910; *Before the Lamps are Lit*, Melbourne, G. Robertson, 1911; *A Desert Rose*, London, Heinemann, 1912; *Kerno: A Stone*, London, Heinemann, 1914; *Paying Guests*, Melbourne, Lothian, 1917; *Gum Tree Brownie and Other Faerie Folk of the Never Never*, Melbourne, G. Robertson, 1918; *The Other Side of Nowhere*, Melbourne, Robertson & Mullens, 1934; *Chimney Town*, London, Black, 1934.

R

Radic, Therese (1935–)

Playwright, musician. Born and educated in Melbourne, graduating from the University of Melbourne with a doctorate in music. Has written for the *Age* and *Finance Week*, and been a reviewer for *Australian Book Review*.

DRAMA *Some of My Best Friends are Women* (with L. Radic), Melbourne, Yackandandah Playscripts, 1983; *Madame Mao*, Sydney, Currency Press, 1986; *A Whip Round for Percy Grainger*, Melbourne, Yackandandah Playscripts, 1986.
NON-FICTION *Quartet for Two Violins*, Melbourne, Musica Australia Press, 1979; *G. W. L. Marshall-Hall: Portrait of a Lost Crusader*, Perth, University of WA Department of Music, 1982; *A Treasury of Favourite Australian Songs* (ed.), Melbourne, Curry O'Neil, 1983; *Sir Bernard Heinze* (with Barry Jones), Melbourne, Macmillan, 1984; *Melba, the Voice of Australia*, Melbourne, Macmillan, 1986.
OTHER Plays produced include: *40 Watt* (1977) and *Cinders* (1983).

Ramsay-Laye, Elizabeth, 'Isabel Massary'

Novelist, non-fiction writer. Born in England and accompanied her husband to Victoria at the height of the gold fever in the early 1850s. Travelled with him to the gold diggings at Castlereagh and stayed 8 years in Australia before returning to London c. 1860. Published an interesting account of her experiences of travelling, bush and camp life and of the people she met at the diggings. *Memories of Social Life in Australia Thirty Years Ago* (1914) is a later edition of her first novel.

FICTION *Social Life in Sydney, or Colonial Experience: An Australian Tale*, by Isabel Massary, Edinburgh, Grant, 1866; *Our Cousins in Australia, or Reminiscenses of Sarah Norris*, Edinburgh, Nimmo, 1867; *Memories of Social Life in Australia Thirty Years Ago*, London, Grant Richards, 1914; *A Two Years' Folly and Other Stories*, London, Grant Richards, 1916.
NON-FICTION *Social Life and Manners in Australia: Being Notes of Eight Years' Experience by a Resident*, London, Longmans Green, 1861.

Rankin, Jennifer (1941–1979)

Poet, playwright. Born in Sydney and educated at the University of Sydney. Lived in many parts of Australia and England working in a variety of jobs in political science departments, schools, libraries, etc, as well as for the AJA and for the NSW Trades and Labour Council. Her plays were produced on stage and radio both in Australia and England, and her poetry widely published in magazines in both countries as well as in the USA. Her early death in 1979 occurred after a fight against cancer.

POETRY *Ritual Shift*, Brisbane, Makar, 1979; *Earth Hold* (illust. John Olsen), London, Secker & Warburg, 1979.
DRAMA *Bees*, in *Theatre Australia*, Aug.-Oct., 1976.
OTHER Is represented in the anthologies, *Poets' Choice* (1979), *Mrs Noah and the Minoan Queen* (Sisters, 1984) and *The Oxford Anthology of Australian Literature* (OUP, 1985).
SEE ALSO J. Barbour in *Southerly*, Vol. 37, No. 1 (1977) and L. Brett-Lovett (interview) in the *National Times* (Oct. 20, 1979).

Rees, Rosemary
Novelist. Born and educated in Auckland, New Zealand where her father was a Member of Parliament. Left for London at the age of 18 to become an actor, then came to Sydney where she began to write. Published her first few novels while in Sydney where some were also serialised, e.g. in the *Sydney Morning Herald*. Also at this time continued to act, working at one stage for J. C. Williamson's. Returned to London 1926 where she settled. Many of her books went into other editions. Also had plays produced in London and France.

FICTION *April's Sowing*, London, Hubert Jenkins, 1923; *Heather of the South*, London, Hubert Jenkins, 1924; *Lake of Enchantment*, London, Hubert Jenkins, 1925; *Life's What You Make It*, London, Hubert Jenkins, 1927; *Wild, Wild Heart*, London, Chapman & Hall, 1928; *Dear Acquaintance*, London, Chapman & Hall, 1929; *Sane Jane*, London, Chapman & Hall, 1931; *Concealed Turning*, London, Chapman & Hall, 1932; *Local Colour*, London, Chapman & Hall, 1933; *Home's Where the Heart Is*, London, Chapman & Hall, 1935; *Miss Tiverton's Shipwreck*, London, Chapman & Hall, 1936; *Turn the Hour*, London, Chapman & Hall, 1937; *Sing a Song of Sydney*, London, Chapman & Hall, 1938; *I Can Take Care of Myself*, London, Chapman & Hall, 1940; *You'll Never Fail Me*, London, Chapman & Hall, 1940; *Sackcloth for Susan*, London, Chapman & Hall, 1941; *The Mended Citadel*, London, Chapman & Hall, 1943; *Penelope Waits*, London, Chapman & Hall, 1946; *Displaced Person*, London, Chapman & Hall, 1948; *She Who Loves*, London, Chapman & Hall, 1952; *Better to Trust*, London, Chapman & Hall, 1956; *Love in a Lonely Land*, London, Harrap, 1958; *The Proud Diana*, London, Wright & Brown, 1962.
OTHER *New Zealand Holiday* (Chapman & Hall, 1933).

Rentoul, Annie Rattray
Children's novelist and poet. Daughter of poet Annie Isobel Rentoul and sister to artist and book illustrator Ida Rentoul Outhwaite. Several

editions of her fairy stories and poems for children were illustrated by her sister.

FICTION *Mollie's Bunyip*, Melbourne, Jolley, 1904; *The Lady of the Blue Beads, Being an Account of Her First Blue Moon Spent on Sun Island*, Melbourne, G. Robertson, 1908; *The Story of Peter Pan*, Melbourne, S. Day, 1908; *Story of the Pantomime Humpty Dumpty*, Melbourne, S. Day, 1908; *Mollie's Staircase*, Melbourne, Hutchinson, 1911; *At the Sign of the Sword* (with others), 1915; *The Little Green Road to Fairyland*, London, Black, 1925; *Fairyland*, by Ida Rentoul Outhwaite (with others), Melbourne, Ramsay Publ. Co., 1926.
POETRY *Australian Songs for Young and Old*, Melbourne, G. Robertson, n.d.; *Bush Songs of Australia for Young and Old*, Melbourne, G. Robertson, 1910; *More Australian Songs for Young and Old*, Melbourne, G. Robertson, 1914; *Elves and Fairies of Ida Rentoul Outhwaite*, Melbourne, Lothian, 1916; *Australian Bush Songs*, Melbourne, Allan, 1936.

Richardson, Ethel, 'Henry Handel Richardson' (1870–1946)
Novelist. Born Ethel Florence Lindesay Richardson in Melbourne. Educated at the Presbyterian Ladies' College. After leaving school taught as a governess until taken abroad by her mother 1888 to further her musical studies at Leipzig Conservatorium. There she met Scottish student J. G. Robertson whom she married in Ireland 1895. Read widely in European literature, made some translations of European texts and eventually concentrated on writing instead of her music. Lived in Strasbourg 1897–1903 and then settled in London. Apart from a brief visit to Australia while working on the *Mahony* chronicle, she remained in England until her death 1946. Was awarded the Australian Literary Society's Gold Medal 1929 and nominated for the Nobel Prize 1932.

FICTION *Maurice Guest*, London, Heinemann, 1908; *The Getting of Wisdom*, London, Heinemann, 1910; *Australia Felix*, London, Heinemann, 1917; *The Way Home*, London, Heinemann, 1925; *Ultima Thule*, London, J. G. Robertson, 1929; *Two Studies*, London, Simpkin Marshall, 1931; *The Bath: An Aquarelle*, Sydney, P. R. Stephenson, 1933; *The End of a Childhood and Other Stories*, London, Heinemann, 1934; *The Young Cosima*, London, Heinemann, 1939; *The Adventures of Cuffy Mahony*, London, A & R, 1979.
NON-FICTION *Myself When Young*, London, Heinemann, 1948.
MANUSCRIPTS NL, Canberra: Henry Handel Richardson Papers MS 133 (Main collection; detailed guide available).
SEE ALSO N. Palmer, *Henry Handel Richardson, A Study* (A & R, 1950); *The Letters of Henry Handel Richardson to Nettie Palmer* (ed. K. J. Rossing, 1953); *Southerly*, Vol. 23, No. 1 (1963 'Henry Handel Richardson' Issue); L. J. Kramer, *Myself When Laura* (Melbourne, 1966); D. Green, *Ulysses*

Bound (ANU Press, 1973); J. R. Nichols, *Art and Irony, the Tragic Vision of Henry Handel Richardson* (University Press of America, 1982), and K. McLeod, *Henry Handel Richardson, A Critical Study* (CUP, 1985). For a full bibliography see G. Howell, *Henry Handel Richardson 1870–1946* (National Library of Australia, 1970).

'Richardson, Henry Handel' *See:* **Richardson, Ethel**

'Ricketty Kate' *See:* **Filson, Minnie Agnes**

Riddell, Elizabeth, 'Betty Riddell' (1910–)
Poet, critic. Born in New Zealand, educated there until 18. Was invited to work in Sydney as a journalist and over the years has lived and worked in London, Sydney and New York. Was married to E. N. Greatorex and widowed 1964. During a distinguished career has written all types of journalism but her real interest has always been poetry. In 1986 was awarded Critic of the Year by the *Australian Book Review*.

POETRY *The Untrammelled*, by Betty Riddell, Sydney, Viking Press, 1940; *Poems*, Sydney, Ure Smith, 1948; *Forbears*, Sydney, A & R, 1961.
OTHER Two books of songs with music by G. S. English, *Song for a Crowning* (W. H. Paling, 1953) and *Country Tune* (J. Albert, 1973).
SEE ALSO A. D. Moody in *Meanjin*, Vol. 20, No. 4 (1961).

Riley, Elizabeth
Novelist. Author of one of the few examples in Australian literature of lesbian fiction. *All that False Instruction* has been praised for its wide-ranging depiction of sexuality and for its powerful psychological insights, although it has yet to receive sustained critical appreciation. Riley was winner of the first Angus & Robertson Writers' Fellowship 1972.

FICTION *All that False Instruction*, London, A & R, 1975.
SEE ALSO S. Higgins in *Meanjin*, Vol. 34, No. 4 (1975) and M. Smith in *Gender, Politics and Fiction* (ed. C. Ferrier, UQP, 1985).

'Rivers, Georgia' *See:* **Clark, Marjorie**

Rixon, Annie Louisa
Novelist. Also known as Annie Rixon-Studdert or Mrs Richard de Clare. Wrote two novels, the first about nursing in WWI, and a fictionalised account of the bushranger folk hero, Captain Thunderbolt.

FICTION *The Scarlet Cape*, Sydney, G. M. Dash, 1939; *Yesterday and Today*, Sydney, G. M. Dash, 1940; *The Truth about Thunderbolt*, Sydney, G. M. Dash, 1940; *Thunderbolt*, Sydney, F. Johnson, 1945.

Robertson, Marjorie
Short story writer. Published stories in a number of magazines and anthologies, later collected in *In One Town*. Along with Mary Cecil Woods, also wrote a book of brief sketches and facetiae based upon their experiences as lawyers.

FICTION *In One Town: A Selection of Stories*, Sydney, Australasian Publ. Co., 1946; *To Ripen or to Kill*, Sydney, A & R, 1953.
OTHER *Leaves from a Woman Lawyer's Casebook*, by 'Marjorie Woodson' (A & R, 1947). Short stories also appeared in *Southerly*, *Coast to Coast* and *Modern Australian Short Stories*.

Robertson, Mary Ann
Poet. Born in Edinburgh, Scotland. Worked as a clerk and typist in Sydney. Writing sometimes under the initials 'M.A.R.', she first published her rather rapturous poetry in the *Bulletin*.

POETRY *Land of Memory*, Preface by A. G. Stephens, Sydney, Bookfellow, 1919; *Land of Memory and Later Verse*, Sydney, Beacon Press, 1933.

Rodriguez, Judith (1936–)
Poet, story writer, print-maker. Born Judith Green in Perth. Educated in Brisbane graduating BA honours from the University of Queensland; later received an MA honours (Cantab) 1962. Taught and lectured English in several schools and universities including the University of Queensland, Girton College (Cambridge) and La Trobe University, Melbourne, where she was lecturer 1969–85. Presently teaches at the Macarthur Institute, Sydney. Was poetry editor of *Meanjin* 1979–82 and continues to work as a publisher's reader, editor, and poetry reviewer for the *Sydney Morning Herald*. Married academic Fabio Rodriguez 1964, had four children, and divorced 1981; married poet Thomas Shapcott 1982. Received the SA Biennial Prize for Literature for *Water Life* 1978 and the PEN/Peter Stuyvesant Prize for Poetry for *Mudcrab at Gambaro's*.

POETRY *Four Poets* (with David Malouf, Rodney Hall & Donald Maynard), Melbourne, Cheshire, 1962; *Nu-Plastik Fanfare Red*, St Lucia, UQP, 1973; *Waterlife*, St Lucia, UQP, 1976; *Shadow in Glass*, Canberra, Open Door Press, 1978; *Mudcrab at Gambaro's*, St Lucia, UPQ, 1980; *Witch Heart*, Melbourne, Sisters, 1982; *Mrs Noah and the Minoan Queen* (ed.), Melbourne, Sisters, 1983; *The Australian Prize Poems* (ed. with Andrew Taylor), Sydney, A & R, 1985.
OTHER Has also published (with V. Pauli) a book of art criticism: *Noela Hjorth* (Granrott Press, 1984). Stories have appeared in *Southerly* (1976) and *Tabloid Story* (1976). Articles and reviews have appeared in several journals and papers including *ALS*, *Lip* and the *Sydney Morning Herald*.

SEE ALSO D. Kerr and P. Edmonds in the *Bulletin* (Dec. 1984–Jan. 1985).

'Rohan, Criena' *See:* **Cash, Deirdre**

Roland, Betty (1903–)
Playwright, novelist, non-fiction writer. Born Elizabeth Maclean in Kaniva, Victoria; later adopted her father's name as a last name. Left school when 17 to join the staff of *Table Talk* as a social reporter. Later worked for the *Sun News Pictorial* until her marriage 1922. At 16 won a prize for a short story which was published in the *Ballarat Courier*. Her first play, *The Touch of Silk* was first produced 1928 by the Melbourne Repertory Company. She divorced in 1934 and left for Russia where she worked as a journalist. Joined the CPA upon her return to Australia and continued to write political pieces for the stage and for street performance. *Are You Ready Comrade?* won the WA Drama Competition 1948. *Granite Peak* (about central Australia) was televised in England 1952, while the radio serial *A Woman Scorned* formed the basis of the Australian television series *Return to Eden* in 1983. Her biography, *The Eye of the Beholder*, won the Braille Book of the Year Award 1985 and was adapted for ABC radio.

DRAMA *Morning*, in *Best Australian One Act Plays*, Sydney, A & R, 1937; *The Touch of Silk*, Melbourne, MUP, 1942.
FICTION *The Forbidden Bridge*, London, Bodley Head, 1961; *Jamie's Discovery*, London, Bodley Head, 1963; *Jamie's Summer Visitor*, London, Bodley Head, 1964; *Jamie's Other Grandmother*, London, Bodley Head, 1965; *The Bush Bandits*, Melbourne, Lansdowne, Press, 1969; *The Other Side of Sunset*, London, Mills & Boon, 1969; *No Ordinary Man*, London, Collins, 1974; *Beyond Capricorn*, London, Collins, 1976.
NON-FICTION *Lesbos, the Pagan Island*, Melbourne, F. W. Cheshire, 1963; *Sydney in Colour and Black and White*, Sydney, 1965; *Caviar for Breakfast*, Melbourne, Quartet Books, 1979; *The Eye of the Beholder*, Sydney, Hale & Iremonger, 1984.
OTHER Plays produced include: *The Gate of Bronze* (Geelong, 1925); *The Dark Soldier* (1932); *Are You Ready Comrade?* (Perth, Patch Theatre, 1938); *Daddy was Asleep* (Sydney radio, 1945); *The First Gentleman* (Melbourne radio 1945); *New Day* (radio adaptation of *Morning*, Melbourne, 1945); *Madame Bovary* (Sydney, Independent Theatre, 1946); *Granite Peak*, (BBC TV, 1952); *The White Cockade* (Lux Radio Theatre, n.d.) and *A Woman Scorned* (Lux Radio theatre, n.d.).
MANUSCRIPTS NL, Canberra: Betty Roland Papers (accessible upon request to the author).

SEE ALSO L. Rees in *The Making of Australian Drama* (Sydney, 1973) and J. Barbour in *Southerly*, Vol. 37, No. 1 (1977).

'Roland, Esther' *See:* **Crowley, Eena Marie**

Rose-Soley, Agnes, 'Rose De Boheme' (c. 1847–1938)
Journalist, poet. Born Agnes Rebecca Rose in Scotland and educated at Newnham College, Cambridge. Came to Australia for health reasons and spent over 50 years here in a career as a journalist. Wrote for the *Bulletin* and other magazines and papers. Founded the Lyceum Club, Sydney 1914 and was its secretary for some years. Married newspaper editor John Fisher Rose-Soley 1891 (they apparently combined their last names). Received a grant from the CLF at the age of 78 and died in Sydney at the age of 90.

POETRY *The Call of the Blood and Other War Verses*, Sydney, Lyceum Club, 1914; *Stray Chords*, Sydney, Tyrrell's, 1923.
OTHER Wrote for the *Bulletin, Electric Magazine*, the *Daily Telegraph* and the *Sydney Morning Herald*. Contributed to the *Bulletin Story Book* 1880–1901.

Rosman, Alice Grant (1887–1961)
Novelist, journalist. Born at Kapunda, SA, and educated at the Dominican Convent, Cabra. Early published stories, poems and articles in journals such as the *Bulletin* and the *Lone Hand*. As 'Rosna' was the Adelaide correspondent for the *Bulletin* 1908–11 until her departure for London. Here she worked as a journalist before devoting herself entirely to writing fiction from 1927. Became popular worldwide; at least four of her nvoels have connections with Australia.

FICTION *The Tower Wall*, London, Hodder & Stoughton, 1914; *Miss Bryde of England*, London, Melrose, 1915; *The Back Seat Driver*, London, Mills & Boon, 1928; *The Window*, London, Mills & Boon, 1928; *Visitors to Hugo*, New York, Balch, 1929; *Jock the Scot: The Adventures of the Dog of the House Who Gave Up Town Life to Run a Country Estate*, London, Cassell, 1930; *The Young and Secret*, London, Mills & Boon, 1930; *The Sixth Journey*, London, Mills & Boon, 1931; *Benefits Received*, London, Mills & Boon, 1932; *Protecting Margot*, London, Putnam, 1933; *Somebody Must*, London, Hodder & Stoughton, 1934; *The Sleeping Child*, London, Hodder & Stoughton, 1935; *Mother of the Bride*, London, Hodder & Stoughton, 1936; *Truth to Tell*, London, Hodder & Stoughton, 1937; *Unfamiliar Faces*, London, Hodder & Stoughton, 1938; *William's Room*, London, Hodder & Stoughton, 1939.

Russell, Frances Emily (1846–1899)
Novelist. Born Frances Emily Robey in Sydney. Married bank manager Henry Russell. Wrote two novels, the first a tragic story of a woman ruined by the jealousy of her first husband; the second a satirical social romance set in Sydney in the 1880s.

FICTION *Too Easily Jealous: An Australian Romance*, London, Remington, 1892; *Joyce Martindale*, London, Remington, 1894.
POETRY *The Federation of Australia: A Poem*, Sydney, Turner & Henderson, 1898.

'Russell, Lindsay' *See:* **Stonehouse, Patricia**

Ryan, Gig (1956–)
Poet. Born in Melbourne. Worked on the feminist journal *Luna* 1975–8 before moving to Sydney where she received a Literature Board grant 1979. Has read and performed poetry in various places, sometimes accompanying herself on the guitar.

POETRY *The Division of Anger*, Sydney, Transit Poetry, 1980; *Manners of an Astronaut*, Sydney, Hale & Iremonger, 1984; *The Lost Interior*, Melbourne, Scripsi, 1986.

Rydzynski, Liliana
Poet, short story writer, essayist. Born in Poland and studied at the University of Poland in the Faculty of Arts. Lived in Paris during the 1960s and arrived in Australia 1970. Obtained a BA from the University of Sydney. Continues to live in Sydney, writing both in Polish and English.

POETRY *Castle*, Sydney, Old Settlement Press, 1975; *Earthquake* (verse novelette), Sydney, the author, 1978; *Celebration*, Sydney, Saturday Centre Books, 1982.
OTHER Poems and a short story, *Greece in Winter*, have appeared in *Joseph's Coat* (Hale & Iremonger, 1985); essays on Henry Miller and Sylvia Plath have been published in *Aspect* (1980, 1982).

S

Salter, Elizabeth (1918–1981)
Novelist, biographer, academic. Born in Angaston, SA. Educated at the University of Adelaide and the Conservatorium of Adelaide. Worked as a record librarian and script writer for the ABC before joining the entertainment section of the WAAAF during WWII. Travelled overseas 1946, returning once to Adelaide before settling in England 1952. Here she worked for the BBC and wrote professsionally. Became secretary to Dame Edith Sitwell 1957 and held this position until Sitwell's death 1964. Lectured on Edith Sitwell and Patrick White at universities throughout England and Scotland. Travelled annually to Toronto University to conduct writers' workshops. Was a member of International PEN and the Crime Writers' Association. All her novels were mystery novels.

FICTION *Death in a Mist*, London, Geoffrey Bles, 1957; *Will to Survive*, London, Geoffrey Bles, 1958; *There was a Witness*, London, Geoffrey Bles, 1960; *The Voice of the Peacock*, London, Geoffrey Bles, 1962; *Once Upon a Tombstone*, London, Hutchinson, 1965; *Tails She Dies*, 1977.
NON-FICTION *Chaucer: The Knight's Tale and the Clerk's Tale*, London, Arnold, 1962; *Piers Plowman: An Introduction*, Oxford, Blackwell, 1962; *The Last Years of a Rebel: A Memoir of Edith Sitwell*, London, Bodley Head, 1967; *Daisy Bates, the Great White Queen of the Never Never*, Sydney, A & R, 1971; *Landscapes and Seasons of the Medieval World* (with D. Pearsall) London, Elek, 1973; *The Lost Impressionist, a Biography of John Peter Russell*, Sydney, A & R, 1976; *Edith Sitwell, Fire of the Mind*, (ed. with A. Harper), London, Michael Joseph, 1976; *Helpmann, the Authorised Biography of Sir Robert Helpmann*, Sydney, A & R, 1978; *Edith Sitwell, a Biography*, Sydney, A & R, 1978.
OTHER Also published an edition of William Langland's *Pier's Plowman* (with D. Pearsall, Arnold, 1967) and an edition of Geoffrey Chaucer's *Troilus and Cressida* (Brewer, 1978).
MANUSCRIPTS NL, Canberra: Elizabeth Salter MSS (lodged 1980).

Sanders, Dorothy Lucie, 'Lucy Walker' (1907–)
Novelist. Born in Kalgoorlie, WA, the daughter of an Irish clergyman. Began writing for newspapers and magazines and became a popular writer of romantic novels, published mainly under her pseudonym. Her books are particularly popular in the USA and Europe, their success due to realistic backgrounds and portrayal of aspects of Australian life, rather than the originality of storyline.

FICTION *Fairies on the Doorstep*, Sydney, Australasian Publishing Co., 1948; *The Randy, the Story of a Mystery Ship* (children's), Sydney, Australasian Publishing Co., 1948; *Six For Heaven*, London, Hodder & Stoughton, 1952; *Shining River*, London, Hodder & Stoughton, 1954; *Waterfall*, London, Hodder & Stoughton, 1956; *Ribbons in Her Hair*, London, Collins, 1957; *Pepper Tree Bay*, London, Hodder & Stoughton, 1959; *Heaven is Here*, London, Collins, 1960; *The Loving Heart*, London, Collins, 1960; *Love in a Cloud*, London, Collins, 1960; *Kingdom of the Heart*, London, Collins, 1961; *The Moonshine*, London, Collins, 1961; *Wife to Order*, London, Collins, 1961; *Monday in Summer*, London, Hodder & Stoughton, 1961; *Down in the Forest*, London, Collins, 1962; *The Distant Hills*, London, Collins, 1962; *Joyday for Jock*, London, Collins, 1962; *The Call of the Pines*, London, Collins, 1963; *Follow Your Star*, London, Collins, 1963; *The Man from Outback*, London, Collins, 1964; *A Man Called Masters*, London, Collins, 1965; *The Other Girl*, London, Collins, 1965; *The Ranger on the Hills*, London, Collins, 1966; *Reaching for the Stars*, London, Collins, 1966; *The River is Down*, London, Collins, 1967; *Home at Sundown*, London, Collins, 1968; *Come Home, Dear*, London, Collins, 1969; *The Gone-away Man*, London, Collins, 1969; *Girl Alone*, London, Collins, 1973; *The Runaway Girl*, London, Collins, 1975; *Gamma's Girl*, London, Collins, 1977.

Sandery, Effie, 'Elizabeth Powell' (c. 1898–?)
Juvenile author, journalist. Born in Adelaide and worked there as a journalist and illustrator. Edited the children's column of the Adelaide *Register* in which she wrote and illustrated a weekly fairy story. Also published in the *Observer*, sometimes writing under the name 'Kirckaldy' as well as under her real and assumed names. Illustrated Katharine Susannah Prichard's *The Wild Oats of Han*. From 1924 spent several years travelling in Australia, New Guinea and the Pacific Islands; was the first white woman to explore the remoter cannibal regions of New Guinea. Moved to Sydney c. 1926, worked for various papers and was on the staff of the *Daily Telegraph*. Later moved to Glenbrook in the Blue Mountains where from the 1930s she managed and edited a newspaper service, supplying syndicated articles to country newspapers.

FICTION *The Beehive* (for girls) Sydney, Cornstalk, 1928; *Mr Jigsaw* (children's), Sydney, Cornstalk, 1928; *Sunset Hill*, Sydney, Cornstalk, 1929; *The Need for Love*, Sydney, Midget Masterpiece Publ. Co., 1934; *The Old Brown House* (children's) Sydney, A & R, 1942.

Savage, Georgia
Novelist. Born in Tasmania but has lived mostly in Victoria. Met and married her husband in Melbourne and in 1980 after his death moved

to Queensland where she began to write full-time. Returned to Melbourne 1984. Has published short stories and also writes articles and reviews for journals and newspapers.

FICTION *The Tournament*, Sydney, Hale & Iremonger, 1983; *Slate and Me and Blanche McBride*, Melbourne, McPhee Gribble/Penguin, 1983.
SEE ALSO 'Self Portrait: Where is Home Anyway?' in *ABR* (May, 1980) and J. Ellison (interview) in *Rooms of their Own* (Penguin, 1986).

Schultz, Julianne (1956–)
Non-fiction writer. Born in New Zealand. Educated at Hamilton High School and later St Peter's Lutheran College, Brisbane, and the Universities of Brisbane and Sydney, graduating in arts and economics. Has worked as a journalist for ABC radio and television, for the *Australian Financial Review*, and contributed to the *National Times* and other papers. Her work is best described as literary journalism which deals with contemporary issues and debates. Was awarded a Social History grant 1983 from the NSW Premier's Department. Since 1982 has lectured in journalism at the NSW Institute of Technology, and lived at Scarborough, south of Sydney, with husband Ian Reinecke.

NON-FICTION *The Phone Book, Australia's Communication Future on the Line*, (with Ian Reinecke), Melbourne, Penguin, 1983; *Steel City Blues, the Human Cost of Industrial Crisis*, Melbourne, Penguin, 1985.
OTHER 'The Ingham Case', in *The Other Side of Rape* (UQP, 1978). Forthcoming: *The Future of Work.*

Scott, Margaret (1934–)
Poet, critic, academic. Born in Bristol, England; educated at Newnham College, Cambridge, graduating in Arts 1956. Married Michael Boddy, emigrated to Australia 1959 and worked for the Tasmanian Education Department as an itinerant research assistant in the 1960s. Joined the University of Tasmania as a teaching fellow 1966 and after completing a doctoral thesis was appointed lecturer 1981. Was divorced 1964, afterwards living with lawyer Michael Scott until his death 1984; has four children and three step-children. Began publishing poetry 1974 and was winner of the Borestone Mountain Poetry Awards 1974 and 1976. In the academic field, her two main areas of interest are seventeenth-century drama and modern Australian poetry.

POETRY *Tricks of Memory*, Sydney, A & R, 1980; *Visited*, Sydney, A & R, 1983.
OTHER Edited, with Vivian Smith, *Effects of Light: The Poetry of Tasmania* (Twelvetrees, 1985). Reviews and articles have appeared in various journals including *Quadrant*, *Island* and *English in Australia*. Poems have

appeared in newspapers such as the *Age* and magazines such as *Westerly, Island, Quadrant* and *Meanjin*.

Scott, Maria J., 'Mist'
Novelist. Born Maria Barney. Was married to David Charles Scott, a cousin of feminist Rose Scott and uncle of David Scott Mitchell, benefactor and founder of the Mitchell Library. Her novels were basically religio-moral romances.

FICTION *Annine*, by Mrs. M. J. S., London, Cantly Newby, 1871; *Pearl and Willie*, by Mist, London, Cantly Newby, 1893; *A Many Coloured Bubble*, A Tale by Mist, London, Cantly Newby, 1874; *Not So Ugly*, London, Morgan, 1874; *A Brother or a Lover? A Sister or a Bride?* and *The Lights and Shadows of Hazleglen*, by Mist, London, Cantly Newby, n.d.
MANUSCRIPTS ML, Sydney: Landscape sketches of Australia 1854–60.

Scott, Natalie
Novelist, journalist, children's author. Born in Australia. Has written for various newspapers and magazines. Prior to publishing her first novel also wrote short stories and books for children. Has lived in England and Europe and now in Sydney.

FICTION *Wherever We Step the Land is Mined*, London, Jonathan Cape, 1980; *The Glasshouse*, Adelaide, Rigby, 1985.
OTHER Short stories have also appeared in *Westerly* (1969) and *Southerly* (1970).

Scutt, Jocelynne (1947–)
Non-fiction writer, lawyer. Born in Perth. Educated at the universities of WA, Sydney, Michigan and Cambridge, attaining a large number of degrees and diplomas in various aspects of law. Has worked in the fields of law reform and the law as it relates to women, in particular rape law reform, female crime and family violence, and has also been on numerous related committees. Was lecturer and tutor in industrial, family and criminal law at the universities of Sydney, Michigan and ANU 1970–81. Is a member of the Labor Laywers, the Feminist Legal Action Group, WEL, and many other associations and societies. Also practises at the bar, but lately is mainly involved in research and writing and in the movement for legal reform.

NON-FICTION
The Female Offender: An Annotated Bibliography (with R. Sarri and others), Ann Arbor, University of Michigan, 1975; *The Fine as an Option for Sentencing*, Sydney, Australian Law Reform Commission, 1979;

Community Work Orders as an Option for Sentencing, Sydney, Australian Law Reform Commission, 1979; *Probation as an Option for Sentencing*, Sydney, Australian Law Reform Commission, 1979; *Domestic Violence in Australia*, Canberra, Australian Institute of Criminology, 1979; *Violence in the Family*, Canberra, Australian Institute of Criminology, 1980; *Rape Law Reform* (ed.), Canberra, Australian Institute of Criminology, 1980; *Restoring Victims of Crime*, Canberra, Australian Institute of Criminology, 1980; *Women and Crime* (ed. with S. Mukherjee), Sydney, Allen & Unwin, 1981; *Even in the Best of Homes – Violence in the Family*, Melbourne, Penguin, 1983; *For Richer, For Poorer – Men, Women and Marriage* (with D. Graham), Melbourne, Penguin, 1983; *Growing up Feminist*, Sydney, A & R, 1985; *Poor Nation of the Pacific – Australia's Future?* (ed.), Sydney, Allen & Unwin, 1985; *Different Lives – Reflections on the Women's Movement and Visions of its Future* (ed.), Melbourne, Penguin, 1987; *Lionel Murphy – A Radical Judge*, Melbourne, McCulloch Macmillan, 1987.
OTHER Has also contributed to various books including: *Women, Class and History* (Fontana, 1980), *Women, Social Welfare and the State* (Allen & Unwin, 1983) and *Women, Social Sciences and Public Policy* (Allen & Unwin, 1985). Has published many papers and book reviews and over 60 articles in numerous journals including the *Australian Law Journal, Family Law Review, Hecate* and *Australian Quarterly*. Edited *Women's Studies International Forum*, Vol. 9, No. 1 (1986) Special Issue: Women and the Law. Also contributes regularly to *Simply Living* magazine.

Seddon, Alexandra (1944–)
Poet. Born in London and came to Australia at the age of 2. Qualified as a teacher and taught creative writing, but has lived and worked on a farm for the last 10 years. After receiving a grant from the Literature Board 1977 went to Sydney for some months in order to write. Before moving to her farm taught drama and creative writing to Papua New Guinean teachers.

POETRY *Full Circle*, London, Workshop Press, 1970; *Sparrows*, Oxford, Carcanet Press, 1970; *Green Feet*, Sydney, Glandular Press, 1981.
OTHER Poems have appeared in *Meanjin, Aspect*, the *Bulletin, Post-Neo, New Poetry, Magic Sam, Makar*, the *Melbourne University Magazine*, and others including overseas publications.

Shaw, Winifred Maitland (1905–)
Poet. Born in Maitland, NSW and published her first book of poems when only 14. Her collections showed an extraordinary maturity and control over the ballad form she mainly employed. Was married to

R. M. Taplin, was in Singapore during WWII and suffered at the hands of the Japanese. Settled in England after the war.

POETRY *Poems*, Sydney, Carter's Printing Works, 1918; *The Aspen Tree and Other Verses*, Sydney, Tyrrell's, 1920; *The Yellow Cloak and Other Poems*, Sydney, A & R, 1922; *Babylon*, Illust. Hugh McCrae, Sydney, *Art in Australia, 1924.*

Shearer, Jill
Playwright. Born in Melbourne, but has lived mostly in Queensland. Was educated at the Brisbane Girls' Grammar School. Began to write 1971 and her first play won a competition in Brisbane; several others have since also received prizes including *The Foreman* at the Townsville Drama Festival 1973. Currently lives in Brisbane where she has worked for the Japanese Consul General in Queensland.

DRAMA *Catherine*, Melbourne, Arnold, 1977; *The Foreman*, Sydney, Currency Press, 1978; *The Boat*, in *Can't You Hear Me Talking to You* (ed. Alrene Sykes), St Lucia, UQP, 1978; *Echoes and Other Plays*, Brisbane, Playlab Press, 1980.
OTHER Plays produced (mainly in Brisbane) include: *But I Won't Wear White* (1972), *Ships that Pass* (1973), *The Trouble with Gillian* (1974), *The Job* (1974), *Release Lavinia Stannard* (1975), *The Expatriate* (1978) and *Shimada* (Melbourne Theatre Company, 1987).

Sheiner, Robin (1940–)
Novelist, short story writer. Born and educated in Perth, leaving school at 14 to work her way around Australia and later the world. Graduated as a nursing sister 1961 and later obtained a highly distinguished midwifery certificate from the King George V Hospital in Sydney. Has also worked as a housewife and mother, all experiences which have prompted her writing, which she began 1980. Is currently working upon a second novel.

FICTION *Smile, The War Is Over*, Melbourne, Macmillan, 1983.
OTHER Stories have appeared in journals and collections such as the *Bulletin Literary Supplement* (1981, 1983), *Tabloid Story* (1983), *Meanjin* (1985), *Australian Short Stories* (1985) and *Room To Move* (Redress/Unwin 1985).

Shepherd, Catherine (1912–1976)
Playwright. Born in Zimbabwe of English parents. Brought up in Wales and later studied at the University of London before coming to Australia in the 1920s where she settled in Tasmania. Had trained as a teacher but preferred to write for children. Also wrote stage plays and many radio plays (mostly for the ABC) including psychological studies, brief literary biographies, and adaptations of novels.

DRAMA *Daybreak, A Play in Three Acts*, Melbourne, MUP, 1942; *Delphiniums*, in *Six Australian One Act Plays*, Sydney, Mulga Publs, 1944.
FICTION *Tasmanian Adventure* (children's), London, Dent, 1964.
OTHER Plays produced for ABC radio (1930s–1940s) include: *Lethe Wharf, Seapiece, Exit Socrates, The Flying Swan, Three Mile Cross, A Citizen of the World, The Valiant Tinker, Balzac*, and *The Golden Cockerel*, and for stage: *Jane, My Love* (1951).
SEE ALSO A. Ashbolt in *Focus*, Vol. 1, No. 2 (1946– 47) and L. Rees in *The Making of Australian Drama* (A & R, 1973).

'Sidney, Neilma' *See:* **Gantner, Neilma**

Simpson, Helen (1897–1940)
Novelist, playwright, historian. Born Helen de Guerry Simpson in Sydney of a French family who settled in Goulburn, NSW in the mid nineteenth-century. Educated at Sacred Heart Convent, Rose Bay and Abbotsleigh, Wahroongah. Left Australia 1914 to study at Oxford but instead joined the WRNS during WWI and worked as a linguist. Married Denis Browne (a nephew of Rolf Boldrewood) 1927. Made a permanent home in England, but continued to visit Australia until her death 1940, and three of her books are Australian in content. She made a mark upon Australian literature with the wide-sweeping and original *Boomerang*, an extraordinary combination of history, fiction and romance. Several of her books were filmed or broadcast, including *Under Capricorn*, filmed 1949, directed by Alfred Hitchcock and starring Ingrid Bergman; it was also adapted for Australian television 1983.

FICTION *Acquittal*, London, Heinemann, 1925; *The Baseless Fabric*, London, Heinemann, 1925; *Cups, Wands and Swords*, London, Heinemann, 1927; *Mumbudgett* (children's), London, Heinemann, 1928; *Enter Sir John* (with Clemence Dane), New York, Cosmopolitan Books, 1928; *The Desolate House*, London, Heinemann, 1929; *Printer's Devil* (with Clemence Dane), London, Hodder & Stoughton, 1930; *'Vantage Striker*, London, Heinemann, 1931; *Boomerang*, London, Heinemann, 1932; *Re-enter Sir John* (with Clemence Dane), London, Hodder & Stoughton, 1932; *The Woman on the Beast*, London, Heinemann, 1933; *Saraband for Dead Lovers*, London, Heinmann, 1935; *The Female Felon*, London, Lovat, Dickson & Thompson, 1935; *Under Capricorn*, London, Heinemann, 1937; *A Woman Among Wild Men* (children's), London, Nelson, 1938; *Maid No More*, London, Heinemann, 1940.
DRAMA *Pan in Pimlico*, in *British Drama League: Four One-Act Plays*, London, OUP, 1923; *A Man of His Time: A Play in Four Acts*, Sydney, A & R, 1923; *The Woman's Comedy* (anon.) London, Pelican Press, 1926.
POETRY *Philosophies in Little*, Sydney, A & R, 1921.

NON-FICTION *The Waiting City: Paris 1782–1788* (trans. of *Le Tableu de Paris*, by L. S. Mercier), London, Harrap, 1933; *The Spanish Marriage*, London, Peter Davies, 1933; *Henry VIII*, London, Peter Davies, 1934; *The Happy Housewife*, London, Hodder & Stoughton, 1934; *The Cold Table*, London, Jonathan Cape, 1934; *Heartsease and Honesty* (trans.) London, Golden Cockerel Press, 1935.
OTHER Short stories appeared in various collections including *Nine O'Clock Stories* (Bell, 1934), *Great Unsolved Crimes* (Hutchinson, 1935), *Imaginary Biographies* (Allen & Unwin, 1936) and *Selected Modern Short Stories, Vol. 1* (Penguin, 1942). Stories, essays, reviews, etc also appeared in papers such as the *Listener*, the *Fortnightly*, etc. Made frequent broadcasts on the BBC, plus a series of talks for ABC radio (Aug/Sept. 1937). Plays produced included *Masks* (Sydney, 1921) and *Gooseberry Fool* (London, 1928).
SEE ALSO D. L. Sayers in the *Fortnightly*, Vol. 155 (1941), K. A. McKenzie in *ALS*, Vol. 10, No. 4 (1982) and, for a full bibliography, N. McNevin, 'Bibliography of Helen Simpson' (unpublished, ML QA823/S613.2/1A1).

Simpson, Mary, 'Weeroona' (1884–?)
Short story writer, playwright. Born Mary Williams at Stawell, Victoria, and lived on a selection there where her mother was a schoolteacher. Went to live in Melbourne following the death of her father and began contributing stories and sketches of a lively and humorous nature to the *Australian Journal*, the *Australian Woman's Mirror*, and the *Bulletin*. Was generally thought to be male since she always published under her pseudonym, and her style was likened to that of Henry Lawson.

FICTION *Tell-Tale Stories from the Bulletin*, Melbourne, Vidler, 1926.
DRAMA *Crossing Swords with Fate, Episodes in the Life of Adam Lindsay Gordon*, Melbourne, 1940.
OTHER Also included in Nettie Palmer's *An Australian Story Book* (A & R, 1928) and George Mackaness's *Australian Short Stories* (1928).

Skinner, Millie (1876–1955)
Novelist. Born Mary Louisa Skinner in Perth, WA, and was educated in England. On her return to Perth became a journalist, then trained as a nurse, later specialising in midwifery. Served in India during WWI, then worked as a Relief Matron in the WA government service before running a number of private hospitals. Her first literary publication, *The Letters of a VAD*, which draws upon her war experiences, was read by D. H. Lawrence when he stayed at her holiday house in Perth 1922. They subsequently collaborated over the novel *The Boy in the Bush;* this association has tended to eclipse her other writings, though she greatly valued

his friendship. Although blind as a child and plagued by minimal vision all her life she still managed a career as a writer and a nurse with some success; unfortunately much of her writing remains unpublished. *The Boy in the Bush* was adapted for ABC television in 1984.

FICTION *The Letters of a VAD*, by R. E. Leake, London, Andrew Melrose, 1918; *The Boy in the Bush* (with D. H. Lawrence) London, Secker & Warburg, 1924; *Black Swans*, London, Jonathan Cape, 1925; *Men Are We*, Perth, People's Publishing Co., 1927; *Tucker Sees India*, London, Secker & Warburg, 1937; *WX-Corporal Smith: A Romance of the AIF in Libya*, Perth, Sampson Printing Co., 1941; *Where Skies Are Blue, Stories of the 1880s*, rewritten by Mollie Skinner, Perth, Imperial Printing Co., 1946.

NON-FICTION *Midwifery Made Easy*, London, 1913; *The Fifth Sparrow, An Autobiography*, Sydney, SUP, 1972.

OTHER Short stories appeared in Nettle Palmer (ed.) *An Australian Story Book* (A & R, 1930) and Henrietta Drake-Brockman (ed.) *West Coast Stories* (A & R, 1959.

MANUSCRIPTS Battye Library, Perth: Mollie Skinner Manuscripts & Correspondence Acc/No. 1396A. A large collection (guide available) including seven unpublished novels.

SEE ALSO M. L. Skinner in *Meanjin*, Vol. 9, No. 4 (1950), M. Rees in *Westerly* (March 1964) and H. Croxford Simpson in *Women's Studies International Quarterly*, Vol. 2 (1979).

Spence, Catherine Helen (1825–1910)

Novelist, non-fiction writer, social reformer. Born in Scotland and came to Australia 1839 with her family, settling in Adelaide. Became a governess at 17, and took a great interest in public affairs. Was the first woman novelist to write in and about Australia although some of her fiction, such as *Handfasted*, was considered too advanced to be published in her lifetime. Was a social worker, journalist, electoral reformer, activist on behalf of destitute children and for proportional representation and women's suffrage. Lectured upon all these topics in Australia, England and the USA. Was also the first woman political candidate in Australia. Has become known as the 'grand old woman of Australia', a somewhat belittling acknowledgement of her extensive activities and achievements.

FICTION *Clara Morison: A Tale of South Australia During the Gold Fever* (anon.) London, Parker, 1854; *Tender and True: A Colonial Tale* (anon.), London, Smith & Elder, 1856; *Mr Hogarth's Will*, London, Bentley, 1865; *The Author's Daughter*, London, Bentley, 1868; *An Agnostic's Progress, From the Known to the Unknown*, London, Williams & Norgate, 1884; *A Week in the Future*, serialised in the *Centennial Magazine*, Sydney,

1889; *Gathered In*, Sydney, SUP, 1977; *Handfasted*, Melbourne, Penguin, 1984.

NON-FICTION *A Plea for Pure Democracy*, Adelaide, Rigby, 1861; *The Laws We Live Under*, Adelaide, Government Printing Office, 1880; *Effective Voting*, Adelaide, Shawyert & Co., 1898; *State Children in Australia*, Adelaide, Vardon & Sons, 1907; *Autobiography* (reprinted from the *Register*), Adelaide, W. K. Thomas, 1910.

OTHER Also published many other small pamphlets, plus articles, poems, lectures, etc in the South Australian *Register*, the *Observer Miscellany*, and other newspapers. Cf. *Catherine Helen Spence* (ed. H. Thomson, Portable Australian Authors, UQP, 1987).

MANUSCRIPTS SA Archives: Catherine Helen Spence Collection (main holding). ML, Sydney: Catherine Helen Spence Correspondence ML MSS 202 (uncatalogued). NL, Canberra: Catherine Helen Spence Papers MS 41 (microfilm copies of SA and ML holdings).

SEE ALSO J. F. Young, *Catherine Helen Spence, A Study and Appreciation* (Lothian, 1937), W. Birkett in *The Peaceful Army* (ed. F. Eldershaw, Sydney, 1938), H. Thomson in *Who Is She? Images of Woman in Australian Fiction* (ed. S. Walker, UQP, 1983) and S. Magarey, *Unbridling the Tongues of Women* (Hale & Iremonger, 1985). For a full bibliography see E. Gunton, *Bibliography of Catherine Helen Spence* (Libraries Board of SA, 1967).

Spence, Eleanor (1928–)

Children's author. Born in Sydney and educated at the University of Sydney. Worked as a children's librarian in England and as a teacher of autistic children in Australia. Won the Children's Book of the Year Award 1964 with *The Green Laurel* and again in 1977 for *The October Child*, and the NSW Premier's Literary Award 1981 for *The Seventh Pebble*.

FICTION *Patterson's Track*, Melbourne, OUP, 1958; *The Summer in Between*, London, OUP, 1959; *Lillypilly Hill*, London, OUP, 1960; *The Green Laurel*, London, OUP, 1963; *The Year of the Currawong*, London, OUP, 1965; *The Smitherby Pilgrims*, London, OUP, 1967; *Jamberoo Road*, London, OUP, 1969; *The Nothing-place*, London, OUP, 1972; *The Travels of Hermann*, Sydney, Collins, 1973; *The October Child*, London, OUP, 1976; *A Candle for St Anthony*, London, OUP, 1977; *The Seventh Pebble*, Melbourne, OUP, 1980; *The Left Overs*, Sydney, Methuen, 1982; *Me and Jeshua*, Melbourne, Dove, 1984; *Miranda Going Home*, Melbourne, Dove, 1985.

NON-FICTION *A Schoolmaster*, Melbourne, OUP, 1969; *A Cedar Cutter*, Melbourne, OUP, 1971.

Spender, Dale (1943–)

Feminist non-fiction writer, editor, lecturer. Born in Hamilton, NSW, and educated at the Universities of Sydney, NSW and New England. Taught secondary school for 8 years and lectured at James Cook University, Townsville. Departed for England 1975 to study for her doctorate in the philosophy of language at the University of London. Has lectured in education and women's studies at the University of London Institute of Education. Since 1982 has been a Visiting Professor at several North American and Canadian universities and a Visiting Fellow of the University of London. Is a consultant to several academic institutions and educational authorities on the subjects of language, education and women's studies in general. Was founding editor of *Women's Studies International Forum* and co-founder of Pandora Press, London. Currently divides her time between London and Sydney researching in the area of Australian women writers.

NON-FICTION *The Spitting Image: Reflections on Language, Education and Class* (with G. Boomer), Adelaide, Rigby, 1977; *Man Made Language*, London, Routledge & Kegan Paul, 1980, *Invisible Women, the Schooling Scandal*, London, Writers & Readers Publishing Co-operative, 1982; *Women of Ideas and What Men Have Done to Them, from Aphra Behn to Adrienne Rich*, London, Routledge & Kegan Paul, 1982; *There's Always been a Women's Movement this Century*, London, Pandora Press, 1983; *Scribbling Sisters* (with L. Spender), Sydney, Hale & Iremonger, 1984; *For the Record, the Making and Meaning of Feminist Knowledge*, London, The Women's Press, 1985; *Mothers of the Novel: 100 Good Women Novelists before Jane Austen*, London, Pandora Press, 1986; *The Women's Novel: A Graphic Guide*, London, Camden Press, 1986; *Reflecting Men* (with S. Cline), London, Andre Deutsch, 1987.

OTHER Also edited the following: *Learning to Lose: Sexism in Education* (with E. Sarah, The Women's Press, 1980), *Men's Studies Modified* (Pergamon Press, 1981), *Feminist Theorists* (The Women's Press, 1983), *Time and Tide Wait for No Man* (Pandora Press, 1984) and *How the Vote was Won* (Methuen, 1985). Has contributed chapters to a further ten books; articles and reviews have appeared in the *Times Literary Supplement, Spare Rib*, the *Listener*, the *Guardian* and the *Women's Review of Books*.

Spender, Jean Maud, Lady

Novelist. Born Jean Henderson, a third-generation Australian of Scots and English descent. Married 1923 young barrister Percy Spender, later politician, diplomat and knight. Her husband's career took her to Asia, Canada, the USA, Europe and the Pacific. Wrote thrillers and detective novels, some of which were originally serialised in the *Sydney Morning Herald*.

FICTION *The Charge is Murder*, Sydney, Dymocks, 1933; *Death Comes in the Night*, London, Eyre & Spottiswoode, 1938; *Full Moon for Murder*, London, Evans, 1948; *Seven Days for Hanging*, London, Robert Hale, 1958; *Death Renders Account*, London, Robert Hale, 1960; *Murder on the Prowl*, London, Robert Hale, 1960.
OTHER *Ambassador's Wife* (A & R, 1968).

Sperling, Leonie (1937–)
Novelist. Born in Sydney and educated at Sydney Girls' High and the University of Sydney, graduating in arts. Obtained a Diploma of Education through T.A.F.E. and since 1972 has taught full-time at North Sydney Technical College. Has published short fiction since 1978, been married and divorced and has four children. Her writing seeks to explore the darker side of human nature. Since December 1985 has been assisted by a writer's grant.

FICTION *Coins For the Ferryman*, Sydney, Pan, 1981; *Mother's Day*, Sydney, Redress Press/Wild & Woolley, 1984.
OTHER Short stories have appeared in *The White Chrysanthemum* (A & R, 1978); *Inprint* (1985) and *Room to Move* (Redress/Unwin, 1985).

Sproule, Mary Brodie
Essayist. Wrote for the *Age* and the *Spectator*, amongst other papers. *Gatherings of a Grandmother* is a collection of these demonstrating conservative views and espousing the virtues and happiness of the home and family for women.

NON-FICTION *Gatherings of a Grandmother During Seventy Years' Residence in Australia*, Melbourne, Arbuckle, Waddell, 1928; *In the Seventies and Eighties*, Melbourne, Arbuckle, Waddell, 1930.

Stead, Christina (1902–1983)
Novelist. Born in Sydney and spent her childhood in Sydney's Watson's Bay (later recreated in her fiction). Became a schoolteacher and also worked at the University of Sydney before leaving for London 1928. Lived in Paris where she worked in clerical positions with banking houses, and also travelled widely throughout Europe. Visited the USA 1935, returning 2 years later after marrying William Blech, who wrote under the name William Blake. Taught at New York University 1943–4 and was a senior writer for MGM in Hollywood. Achieved great fame and reputation as a writer particularly in America, but in Australia her books were hardly available until the mid–1960s. Returned to Europe

and settled again in England 1953, but in 1974 returned permanently to Australia where she died. Was created a Fellow of the Australian National University, Canberra in 1969 and received the Patrick White Award 1974. An intriguing and cosmopolitan novelist, her distinctive and brilliant qualities have often defied categorisation and have led (after years of critical neglect) to her being judged Australia's greatest novelist.

FICTION *The Salzburg Tales*, London, Peter Davies, 1934; *Seven Poor Men of Sydney*, London, Peter Davies, 1934; *The Beauties and the Furies*, London, Peter Davies, 1936; *House of All Nations*, London, Peter Davies, 1938; *The Man Who Loved Children*, New York, Simon & Schuster, 1940; *For Love Alone*, New York, Harcourt Brace, 1944; *Letty Fox: Her Luck*, New York, Harcourt Brace, 1946; *A Little Tea, a Little Chat*, New York, Harcourt Brace, 1948; *The People with the Dogs*, Boston, 1952; *Cotter's England*, London, Secker & Warburg, 1967; *The Puzzleheaded Girl*, New York, Holt, Rinehart & Winston, 1967; *The Little Hotel*, London, A & R, 1973; *Miss Herbert, the Suburban Housewife*, New York, Random House, 1976; *A Christina Stead Reader* (ed. J. B. Read), New York Random House, 1978; *Ocean of Story, the Uncollected Stories of Christina Stead*, Melbourne, Viking, 1985; *I'm Dying Laughing* (ed. R. G. Geering) London, Virago, 1987.
OTHER Also edited: *Modern Women in Love, 20thC Masterpieces of Fiction* (with W. Blake, Dryden Press, 1945) and *Great Stories of the South Sea Islands* (Muller, 1955).
MANUSCRIPTS NL, Canberra: Christina Stead Papers MS 4967. (NB. Professor R. G. Geering, Sydney, remains Christina Stead's literary executor).
SEE ALSO M. Barnard Eldershaw in *Essays in Australian Fiction* (MUP, 1938), *Southerly*, Christina Stead Issues (Vol. 22, No. 4, 1962, Vol. 38, No. 4, 1978 & Vol. 44, No. 4 1984), R. G. Geering, *Christina Stead* (OUP, 1969) and J. Lidoff, *Christina Stead* (Frederick Ungar, 1983).

Stellmach, Barbara (1930–)
Playwright. Born Barbara Lee in Warwick, Queensland. Educated at various schools and the University of Queensland. Won a scholarship to Trinity College, London 1948. Taught speech and drama 1953–69 and from 1959 has written over 20 plays for theatre, radio and television. Shared first prize in the Society of Women Writers Competition 1976 for *From the Fourteenth Floor You Can See the Harbour Bridge*.

DRAMA *Hang Your Clothes on Yonder Bush*, 1969; *Four Australian Plays*, St Lucia, UQP, 1973; *Not Even a Mouse*, Brisbane, Playlab Press, 1979; *From the Fourteenth Floor You Can See the Harbour Bridge*, Brisbane, Playlab Press, 1980.

Stonehouse, Patricia, 'Harlingham Quinn', 'Lindsay Russell'
Novelist. Born in Charlton, Victoria into a strict Irish-Catholic family. Began to write when still young and won prizes for her short stories, but was discouraged by her parents. Ran away from home and repudiated her religion when a teenager, moving to Melbourne and then to England, where her first book was an immediate success. Set her novels in many countries including India and the Middle East. Attracted attention because of her criticism of Catholicism in her early novels. Was married to Dr Ian Scott, and published under the above and other pseudonyms.

FICTION *Smouldering Fires*, Melbourne, Fraser & Jenkinson, 1912; *Love Letters of a Priest*, Melbourne, Australasian Authors' Agency, 1912; *Sands o' the Desert*, Melbourne, Speciality Press, 1913; *Souls in Pawn*, London, Ward Lock, 1913; *The Years of Forgetting*, Ward Lock, 1914; *Kathleen Mavourneen: An Australian Tale*, Melbourne, Speciality Press, 1915; *The Eternal Triangle*, London, Ward Lock, 1915; *Gates of Silence*, London, Ward Lock, 1915; *The Interior*, London, London, Ward Lock, 1916; *The Woman Who Lived Again*, London, Hurst & Blackett, 1916; *Son of Iscariot*, London, Ward Lock, 1916; *That Woman From Java*, London, Hurst & Blackett, 1916; *The Gates of Kut*, London, Cassell, 1917; *Land o' the Dawning*, London, Cassell, 1917; *Earthware*, London, Cassell, 1918.
POETRY *The Road of Yesterday*, London, Ward Lock, 1916; *The Caravan of Dreams and Other Verses of the Grampians Road*,, Terang, Vic., Express, 1923.
OTHER *America to Japan* (1915).

Strauss, Jennifer (1933–)
Poet, literary critic. Born Jennifer Wallace in Heywood, Victoria. Educated at boarding school and the University of Melbourne. Although began writing poetry in earlier years, ceased writing seriously until about 1964, meanwhile pursuing an academic career, marrying and having three children, and travelling. Lived in England, the USA and Germany, but mostly in Melbourne where she has taught at Melbourne and Monash Universities from 1964. Her poems have won two awards: second prize in the John Shaw Neilson Award of the FAW 1975 and first prize in the *Westerly* Sesquicentenary Competition 1979.

POETRY *Children and Other Strangers*, Melbourne, Nelson, 1975; *Winter Driving*, Melbourne, Sisters, 1981.
OTHER Poems have appeared in many journals and anthologies including most recently *Mrs Noah and the Minoan Queen* (Sisters, 1983) and *Clubbing of the Gunfire: 101 Australian War Poems* (MUP, 1984). Academic articles have been published in several journals including *Southern Review* (1972), *Luna* (1975), *Viewpoints* (1977– 84), *Meanjin* and *Kunapipi*.

Summers, Anne (1945–)
Journalist, historian, researcher. Born Anne Fairhurst in Deniliquin, NSW, and educated at the University of Adelaide. Later received a PhD from the University of Sydney for *Damned Whores and God's Police*, a feminist history of the stereotyping of Australian women. Has worked for the *National Times*, the *Australian Financial Review* and the *Far Eastern Economic Review*. Was co-founder of the women's studies journal *Refractory Girl*, and of the Elsie Women's Refuge in Sydney. Has served on many government committees and delegations. Received three international press fellowships during her career as a journalist, won the Walkley Award for journalism 1976 for reporting on prison conditions, and was the first woman president of the National Press Gallery 1982. Served as First Assistant Secretary of the Office of the Status of Women, Department of the Prime Minister and Cabinet 1983–6. Is currently the USA correspondent for the *Australian Financial Review*.

NON-FICTION *Damned Whores and God's Police, The Colonization of Women in Australia*, Melbourne, Allen Lane & Penguin, 1975; *Her Story, Australian Women in Print 1788–1975* (with Margaret Bettison), Sydney, Hale & Iremonger, 1979; *Gamble for Power: How Bob Hawke Beat Malcolm Fraser, the 1983 Election*, Melbourne, Thomas Nelson, 1983.
OTHER Has contributed many articles on a wide variety of topics to books and journals including: *Australia at the Polls, The National Elections of 1980 & 1983* (Allen & Unwin, 1983), *Women, Class and History* (Fontana, 1980), *Women & Crime* (Allen & Unwin, 1981), *Quadrant* (1983) and *Refractory Girl* (1972–4).

Sykes, Bobbi (1943–)
Poet, Aboriginal activist. Born in Townsville. Left school at 14 and has had many jobs, but mostly been active in Aboriginal affairs. Became first executive secretary of the famous Aboriginal Embassy on the lawns of Parliament House 1972. Has travelled overseas lecturing on the subject of race relations and has worked in Aboriginal legal and medical services. Worked with Mum Shirl (Colleen Shirl Perry) on her autobiography 1981. Received the Patricia Weickhardt Award 1981 and a doctorate in education from Harvard University 1984.

POETRY *Love Poems and Other Revolutionary Actions*, Sydney, Saturday Centre Books, 1979.
NON-FICTION *Black Power in Australia* (with Neville Bonner), Melbourne, Heinemann, 1975; *Mum Shirl: An Autobiography*, with the assistance of Bobbi Sykes, Melbourne, Heinemann, 1981; *Incentive, Achievement and Community*, Sydney, SUP, 1986.

T

'Tasma' *See:* **Couvreur, Jessie**

Taylor, Katherine, 'David Hamline' (1893–)
Children's author. Born Kay Glasson at Kywanna, Queensland. Studied medicine for 4 years at the University of Sydney before marrying and returning to station life in Queensland. Her first book was published under her psuedonym; *Wards of the Outer March* won a prize in the *Bulletin* novel competition 1930.

FICTION *Ginger for Pluck*, Sydney, Cornstalk, 1929; *Pick and the Duffers*, Sydney, A & R, 1930; *Many Years: A Story of Russia During the War and the Revolution*, New York, Appleton, 1931; *Wards of the Outer March*, Sydney, A & R, 1932; *Bim*, Sydney, Currawong, 1947.

Tennant, Kylie (1912–)
Novelist, historian, children's author. Born in Manly, NSW, and educated at the University of Sydney. Over the years worked in various jobs – in journalism, radio, as a barmaid, reviewer and lecturer – partly in an attempt to gain experience for her novels. Married schoolteacher Charles Rodd in 1932 and with his financial support began writing. Spent some years moving around NSW, partly to research her books and partly following her husband's teaching appointments. For several years was active in the CLF. Although never personally politically active, her fiction vividly documents the social effects of depression, unemployment and poverty. Her characters are the social outcasts, delinquents and dispossessed; her satire is directed towards the institutions which make them so. Won the S. H. Prior Memorial Prize 1935 for *Tiburon*, both the Prior prize and the Australian Literary Society's Gold Medal 1941 for *The Battlers*, and the Children's Book Award 1960 for *All the Proud Tribesmen*. Now lives in the Blue Mountains of NSW at an orchard. Was awarded the AO 1980.

FICTION *Tiburon*, Sydney, Bulletin Press, 1935; *Foveaux*, London, Gollancz, 1939; *The Battlers*, London, Gollancz, 1941; *Ride on Stranger*, Sydney, A & R, 1943; *Time Enough Later*, New York, Macmillan, 1943; *Lost Haven*, New York, Macmillan, 1946; *The Joyful Condemned*, London, Macmillan, 1953; *The Honey Flow*, London, Macmillan, 1956; *Ma Jones and the Little White Cannibals*, London, Macmillan, 1967; *Tell Morning This* (complete version of *The Joyful Condemned*), Sydney, A & R, 1968; *Tantavallon*, Melbourne, Macmillan, 1983.
DRAMA *John o' the Forest and Other Plays* (children's) London, Macmillan,

1950; *Tether a Dragon*, Sydney, Associated General Publishers, 1952; *The Bells of the City and Other Plays* (children's) London, Macmillan, 1955; *The Bushranger's Christmas Eve and Other Plays*, (children's) London, Macmillan, 1959.

NON-FICTION *Australia: Her Story*, London, Macmillan, 1953; *Long John Silver: The Story of the Film*, Sydney, Associated General Publishers, 1953; *The Development of the Australian Novel*, Canberra, CLF, 1958; *All the Proud Tribesmen* (children's), London, Macmillan, 1959; *Speak You So Gently*, London, Gollancz, 1959; *Trail Blazers of the Air*, Melbourne, Macmillan, 1965; *The Australian Essay* (with L. C. Rodd), Melbourne, Cheshire, 1968; *Evatt: Politics and Justice*, Sydney, A & R, 1970; *The Man on the Headland*, Sydney, A & R, 1971; *The Missing Heir* (autobiography), Melbourne, Macmillan, 1986.

OTHER Also edited *Great Stories of Australia 1–7* (Macmillan 1963–6) and *Summer's Tales I & II* (Macmillan, 1964–5). Short stories have appeared in the *Bulletin* (1935–45); *Coast to Coast* (1942); *Tales by Australians* (British Authors' Press n.d.); *Australian Writers* (Cheshire, 1953); *Australian Idiom* (Cheshire, 1963); *Australian Pavements* (Lansdowne, 1965) and *The Cool Man and Other Contemporary Stories by Australian Authors* (A & R, 1973). Articles and reviews have appeared in *Meanjin*, *20th Century*, *Overland*, *ALS*, etc.

SEE ALSO D. Auchterlonie in *Meanjin*, Vol. 12 (1953); T. Inglis Moore in *Southerly*, Vol. 1 (1957); M. Dick, *The Novels of Kylie Tennant* (Rigby, 1966) and X. Pons in *ALS*, Vol. 6 (1974). For a full bibliography see J. Rudd in *The Missing Heir* (Macmillan, 1986).

Thirkell, Angela, 'Leslie Parker' (1890–1961)

Novelist. Born Angela Mackail in England and educated privately. Married first to James McInnes but divorced 1917 after which she married Australian George Thirkell. Came to Australia 1920 finally settling in Melbourne where she made friends within literary and artistic circles. Began publishing in magazines and broadcasting on radio while in Melbourne but did not develop as a novelist until after her return to London 1929 following the collapse of her second marriage. Wrote 'middle-class novels for middle-brow tastes' (see Margot Strickland, below) but became one of England's most well-known and successful writers, almost all of her novels going into second and third editions.

FICTION *Three Houses*, London, OUP, 1931; *Ankle Deep*, London, Hamish Hamilton, 1933; *High Rising*, London, Hamish Hamilton, 1933; *Wild Strawberries*, London, Hamish Hamilton, 1933; *The Demon in the House*, London, Hamish Hamilton, 1934; *Trooper to the Southern Cross*, London, Hamish Hamilton, 1934; *O These Men, These Men*, London, Hamish Hamilton, 1935; *The Grateful Sparrow*, London, Hamish

Hamilton, 1935; *August Folly*, London, Hamish Hamilton, 1936; *Coronation Summer*, London, OUP, 1937; *Summer Half*, London, Hamish Hamilton, 1937; *Pomfret Towers*, London, Hamish Hamilton, 1938; *The Brandons*, London, Hamish Hamilton, 1939; *Before Lunch*, London, Hamish Hamilton, 1939; *Cheerfulness Breaks In*, London, Hamish Hamilton, 1940; *Marling Hall*, London, Hamish Hamilton, 1942; *The Headmistress*, London, Hamish Hamilton, 1944; *Northbridge Rectory*, London, Hamish Hamilton, 1944; *Miss Bunting*, London, Hamish Hamilton, 1945; *Peace Breaks Out*, London, Hamish Hamilton, 1947; *Private Enterprise*, London, Hamish Hamilton, 1947; *Love Among Ruins*, London, Hamish Hamilton, 1948; *The Old Bank House*, London, Hamish Hamilton, 1949; *County Chronicle*, London, Hamish Hamilton, 1950; *Ankle Deep*, London, British Publishing Guild, 1950; *The Duke's Daughter*, London, Hamish Hamilton, 1951; *Happy Returns*, London, Hamish Hamilton, 1952; *Jutland Cottage*, London, Hamish Hamilton, 1953; *What Did it Mean?* London, Hamish Hamilton, 1954; *Enter Sir Robert*, London, Hamish Hamilton, 1955; *Never Too Late*, London, Hamish Hamilton, 1956; *A Double Affair*, London, Hamish Hamilton, 1957; *Close Quarters*, London, Hamish Hamilton, 1958; *Love at All Ages*, London, Hamish Hamilton, 1959; *Three Score and Ten*, London, Hamish Hamilton, 1961.
OTHER *The Fortunes of Harriette: The Surprising Career of Harriette Wilson* (1936).
SEE ALSO G. McInnes, *The Road to Gundagai* (Hamish Hamilton, 1965); M. Roe in *Meanjin*, Vol. 28, No. 4 (1969) and M. Strickland, *Angela Thirkell, Portrait of a Lady Novelist* (Duckworth, 1977).

Thomas, Margaret (1843–1929)
Travel writer, sculptor, artist. Born in Surrey, England and came to Australia with her family 1852, settling in Melbourne. Studied sculpture and was the first Australian sculptor of any standing. First exhibited at the Victorian Society of Fine Arts 1857 and continued to exhibit regularly before leaving for England 1867. Continued studying in Rome, Paris, and London, where she returned 1870 and exhibited at the Royal Academy. Was particularly skilled as a portraitist and turned to travel and writing upon the financial success of this work. Also published poetry in English, US and Australian journals. Died in England.

NON-FICTION *A Scamper through Spain and Tangier*, London, Hutchinson, 1892; *Two Years in Palestine and Syria*, London, 1899; *Denmark Past and Present*, 1902; *From Denmark to Palmyra*, London, 1908.
POETRY *Friendship: Poems in Memoriam*, London, 1893; *A Painter's Pastime*, London, Greening, 1908.
OTHER Also published in London the following art books: *How to Judge Pictures* (1906); *How to Judge Sculpture* (1911); and a monograph on her

tutor, *A Hero of the Workshop* (1897). Contributed short stories to *Coo-ee: Tales of Australian Life by Australian Ladies* (1897) and *By Creek and Gully* (1899).

Tilton, May
Non-fiction writer. Was a nursing sister with the AIF during WWI 1915–18. Wrote a book based on war reminiscences contained in the diary she kept during that time.

NON-FICTION *The Grey Battalion: The Story of a Nursing Sister During the War*, Sydney, A & R, 1933.

Tomasetti, Glen (1929–)
Novelist, poet. Born Glenys Ann Tomasetti in Melbourne of mixed British and European ancestry. Educated at the Methodist Ladies' College and the University of Melbourne, graduating BA honours in 1950. Worked as a tutor and lecturer of Australian history, as a script-writer for the ABC and a reviewer for the *Age*. Has lived and travelled throughout Australia and overseas. Also plays the guitar and performs her own work which (especially in the 1960s and 1970s) reflects her ideological and political commitment. *Thoroughly Decent People* was praised for its realistic evocation of suburban Melbourne life in the 1930s. *Man of Letters* was adapted for ABC television by Alma de Groen (q.v.).

FICTION *Thoroughly Decent People*, Melbourne, McPhee Gribble, 1976; *The Kids' Own Book*, Melbourne, McPhee Gribble, 1978; *Man of Letters*, Melbourne, McPhee Gribble, 1981.
POETRY *Songs from a Seat in the Carriage*, West Heidelberg, Crosscurrents, 1970.
OTHER Work has also appeared in *LiNQ*, *Meanjin*, *Nation Review* and in the anthology, *Mother, I'm Rooted* (Outback, 1974).
MANUSCRIPTS La Trobe Library, Melbourne: *The Swiss at Blampied, the Irish at Eganstown* (local and ancestral history, 15 copies).
SEE ALSO M. Smith in *Gender, Politics and Fiction* (ed. C. Ferrier, UQP, 1985).

Townend, Christine (1944–)
Novelist, animal welfare activist. Born in Melbourne; educated at Macquarie University, Sydney, where she now lives. Is a member of several animal welfare organisations and is President of Animal Liberation in NSW. Was awarded two special-purpose grants by the Literature Board 1974 and 1975. Has had short stories, poetry and articles published in various literary magazines. Is currently working on her third novel.

FICTION *The Beginning of Everything and the End of Everything Else*, Melbourne, Macmillan, 1974; *Travels with Myself*, Sydney, Wild & Woolley, 1976.
NON-FICTION *In Defence of Living Things*, Sydney, Wentworth Press, 1980; *A Bill for the Animals*, Kenthurst, NSW, Kangaroo Press, 1981; *Pulling the Wool*, Sydney, Hale & Iremonger, 1985.
SEE ALSO S. Higgins in *Meanjin*, Vol. 34, No. 4 (1974).

Travers, Pamela Lyndon (1906–)
Children's author. Born in Queensland and worked as a journalist. Some of her poetry was published in Australia in the 1920s. Is best known for her children's books, in particular the *Mary Poppins* series, which brought recognition through the film of the same name starring Julie Andrews and Dick Van Dyke (1964).

FICTION *Mary Poppins*, London, Gerald Howe, 1934; *Mary Poppins Comes Back*, London, Lovat Dickson & Thompson, 1935; *I Go By Sea, I Go By Land*, London, P. Davies, 1941; *Mary Poppins Opens the Door*, London, P. Davies, 1944; *Mary Poppins from A to Z*, London, Collins, 1965; *Mary Poppins in the Park*, London, Collins, 1966; *About the Sleeping Beauty*, New York, McGraw Hill, 1975.

Trist, Margaret (1914–1986)
Novelist, short story writer. Born and brought up in Dalby, Queensland, and came to Sydney when aged 17 where she worked for the ABC. Wrote skilfully and humorously of the life of the small town, based on her own observations in Queensland and the Blue Moutains of NSW. Some short stories were originally published in the *Bulletin*.

FICTION *In the Sun*, Sydney, Australian Medical Publ. Co., 1943; *Now that We're Laughing*, Sydney, A & R, 1945; *What Else is There?*, Sydney, A & R, 1946; *Daddy*, Sydney, A & R, 1947; *Morning in Queensland*, London, W. H. Allen, 1958.
OTHER Is represented in E. M. Fry's *Tales by Australians* (1939) and *Coast to Coast* (A & R, 1941, 1942). Short stories also appeared in *Southerly* (1973) and the *Sydney Morning Herald* (1978).
SEE ALSO M. Franklin in *Laughter, Not for a Cage* (A & R, 1956).

Turner, Ethel (1872–1958)
Children's author, novelist. Born Ethel Burwell in Yorkshire, England. Took the last name of her mother's second husband. Was brought to Australia 1881 by her twice-widowed mother along with her two sisters. Attended Sydney Girls' High where with sister Lilian Turner (q.v.) edited the school magazine, *Iris*, and the *Parthenon*. Later became editor of the children's column of the *Illustrated Sydney News*. Married Herbert

Raine Curlewis (a NSW judge) 1896; her daughter Jean Curlewis (q.v.) also wrote for children. Became best known for her early book *Seven Little Australians*, a consistent favourite with readers. It has been translated into several languages and made into a television series.

FICTION *Seven Little Australians*, London, Ward Lock, 1894; *The Family at Misrule*, London, Ward Lock, 1895; *The Story of a Baby*, London, Ward Lock, 1895; *The Little Larrikin*, London, Ward Lock, 1896; *Miss Bobbie*, London, Ward Lock, 1897; *The Camp at Wandinong*, London, Ward Lock, 1898; *Three Little Maids*, London, Ward Lock, 1900; *The Wonder Child: An Australian Story*, London, Religious Tract Society, 1901; *Little Mother Meg*, London, Ward Lock, 1902; *Betty and Co*, London, Ward Lock, 1903; *Mother's Little Girl*, London, Ward Lock, 1904; *A White Roof-Tree*, London, Ward Lock, 1905; *In the Mist of the Mountains*, London, Ward Lock, 1906; *The Stolen Voyage*, London, Ward Lock, 1907; *Happy Hearts: A Picture Book for Boys and Girls*, London, Ward Lock, 1908; *That Girl*, London, Unwin, 1908; *Fugitives from Fortune*, London, Ward Lock, 1909; *Fair Ines*, London, Hodder & Stoughton, 1910; *The Raft in the Bush*, London, Ward Lock, 1910; *The Apple of Happiness*, London, Ward Lock, 1911; *The Secret of the Sea*, London, Hodder & Stoughton, 1913; *Flower o' the Pine*, London, Ward Lock, 1914; *The Cub, Six Months of his Life*, London, Ward Lock, 1915; *John of Daunt*, London, Ward Lock, 1916; *Captain Cub*, London, Ward Lock, 1917; *St Tom and the Dragon*, London, Ward Lock, 1918; *Brigid and the Cub*, London, Ward Lock, 1919; *Laughing Water*, London, Ward Lock, 1920; *King Anne*, London, Ward Lock, 1921; *Jennifer J*, London, Ward Lock, 1921; *The Sunshine Family* (with J. Curlewis), London, Ward Lock, 1923; *Nicola Silver*, London, Ward Lock, 1924; *The Ungardeners*, London, Ward Lock, 1925; *Judy and Punch*, London, Ward Lock, 1928.
POETRY *Gum Leaves by Ethel Turner*, Sydney, W. Brooks, 1900; *Ethel Turner's Birthday Book*, London, Ward Lock, 1909; *The Tiny House and Other Verse*, London, Ward Lock, 1911; *An Ogre Up-to-date*, London, Ward Lock, 1911; *Fifteen and Fair*, London, Hodder & Stoughton, 1913; *Oh! Boys in Brown*, Sydney, Australian Wounded Soldiers' Fund, 1914.
OTHER *Australian Soldiers' Gift Book* (ed. with B. Stevens, Sydney, 1918): *The Diaries of Ethel Turner* (ed. P. Poole, Ure Smith, 1979).
MANUSCRIPTS NL, Canberra: Ethel Turner Papers MS 749 & 2233.
SEE ALSO B. Niall, *Seven Little Billabongs* (MUP, 1979).

Turner, Lilian (1870–1956)
Children's novelist. Born in Yorkshire, England and came to Australia 1881 with her mother and sisters. With sister Ethel Turner (q.v.) she edited the juvenile magazine, the *Parthenon*. Won a prize for her first book from the publishers Cassell's. Less famous than her sister, she

nevertheless wrote many interesting stories directed mainly at teenage girls.

FICTION *The Lights of Sydney, or No Past is Dead*, London, Cassell, 1896; *An Australian Lassie*, London, Cassell, 1903; *Betty the Scribe*, London, Ward Lock, 1906; *Paradise and the Perrys*, London, Ward Lock, 1908; *The Perry Girls*, London, Ward Lock, 1909; *Three New Chum Girls*, London, Ward Lock, 1910; *April Girls*, London, Ward Lock, 1911; *Written Down*, London, Ward Lock, 1912; *Stairways to the Stars*, London, Ward Lock, 1913; *The Girls from the Back Blocks*, London, Ward Lock, 1914; *War's Heart Throbs*, London, Ward Lock, 1915; *The Noughts and Crosses*, London, Ward Lock, 1917; *Rachel*, Liverpool, Bookstall, 1920; *Peggy the Pilot*, London, Ward Lock, 1923; *Jill of Fourth Form*, London, Ward Lock, 1924; *The Happy Heriots*, London, Ward Lock, 1926; *Nina Comes Home*, London, Ward Lock, 1927; *Anne Chooses Glory*, London, Ward Lock, 1928; *Lady Billie*, London, Ward Lock, 1929; *There Came a Call*, London, Ward Lock, 1930.

U, V

Urquhart, Jessie
Novelist. Was an early secretary of the Society of Women Writers, Sydney. Wrote three novels and some of her work was serialised in the *Australian Woman's Mirror*. *Maryplace* examines the fates of four orphaned sisters still held by the spell of their strict parents and the old house, Maryplace, which represents traditions they find hard to challenge.

FICTION *Wayside*, Sydney, A & R, 1919; *Maryplace: The Story of Three Women and Three Men*, London, Nicholson and Watson, 1934; *Giving Amber her Chance*, Sydney, Endeavour Press, 1934.

Vassilieff, Elizabeth
Non-fiction writer, critic. Born Elizabeth Hamill and first published under that name. Met and married Russian-born artist Danila Vassilieff 1947; also published under the name Elizabeth Vassilieff-Wolf. Wrote articles and reviews on art (and specifically on her husband's work) and political pieces, mainly for *Meanjin* in the 1950s where she was Associate Editor 1951. Earlier edited its poetry *Broadsheet* for some years. Contributed regularly to the Contemporary Art Society Broadsheet in the 1950s; exhibited her own paintings along with those of her husband's. Taught on modern art for the Council of Adult Education 1948–9, and was tutor in modern literature for the University Extension Board. Politically active, was involved in the Peace Movement and greatly opposed to American involvement in the Korean War. Her house, Danila Vassilieff's largest sculpture, 'Stonygrad', in Victoria, was during the 1950s a focus for left-wing artists and writers such as Nettie and Vance Palmer.

NON-FICTION *These Modern Writers: An Introduction for Modern Readers*, Melbourne, Georgian House, 1946; *Peking Moscow Letters*, Melbourne, Australasian Book Society, 1953; *Alternative to War*, Melbourne, Australasian Peace Council, 1954.
OTHER Also contributed to *Meanjin* (1940s–1950s); *Voice* (Sept. 1952); *Ern Malley's Journal* (Oct. 1953) and *Overland* (Summer, 1958).

Vernon, Barbara (1916–1978)
Playwright, scriptwriter. Born in NSW and lived at Inverell, northern NSW. Served in the Air Force during WWII, later joining radio station 2NZ in Inverell. Went to Sydney 1959 and worked as a freelance writer before joining the ABC. During her time here wrote numerous plays and scripts for radio and television, as well as for the stage, but her reputation rests in particular with the famous *Bellbird* serial, which she

planned and originated 1967 and which ran for many years on ABC television.

DRAMA *The Passionate Pianist*, Hobart, Tasmanian Adult Education Board, 1958; *The Multi-Coloured Umbrella*, in *Theatregoer*, Feb.-April, 1961; *King Tide Running* (with Bruce Beaver) in *Australian One-Act Plays Book 3*, Adelaide, Rigby, 1967.
FICTION *Bellbird, The Story of a Country Town*, Sydney, Ure Smith, 1970; *A Big Day at Bellbird*, Sydney, Ure Smith, 1971.
OTHER Unpublished plays include: *Dusty Frangipani*, *Enough to Make a Pair of Sailor's Trousers*, *Hullaballoo Belay!*, *Launcelot and the Lady*, *The Loquat Trees*, *Naked Possum*, *No Picnic Tomorrow*, *The Questing Heart*, *Silver Bells and Cockle Shells*, *The Sleeping Planet*, *Swords to the Rescue* and *Theseus and the Minotaur.*
SEE ALSO M. Birch in *Australian Quarterly*, Vol. 29, No. 4 (1957) and R. Mathew in the *Australian Highway*, Vol. 39, No. 6 (1958).

Vidal, Mary Therese (1815–1869)
Novelist. Born in Devon, England, and was one of the first women writers of Australia. Married the Reverend Francis Vidal and came with him to Australia for 5 years in 1840. They lived at Penrith where she wrote *Tales for the Bush*, the only one of her books to be written and published in Australia. It was apparently intended chiefly as an instructive work for her servants, rather than, as the title suggests, giving an account of bush life. Descriptions of Australia came later, especially in *Bengala, or Some Time Ago*, 1860.

FICTION *Tales for the Bush*, Sydney, D. L. Welch, 1845; *Winterton: A Tale*, London, Rivington, 1846; *Esther Merle and Other Tales*, London, J. Hughes, 1847; *Cabramatta and Woodleigh Farm*, London, Rivington, 1850; *Home Trials*, London, Masters, 1858; *Ellen Raymond*, London, Smith, Elder, 1859; *Bengala, or Some Time Ago*, London, Parker, 1860; *Florence Templar*, London, Smith, Elder, 1862; *Lucy Helmore*, London, J. Morgan, 1863; *Trials of Rachel Charlcote*, London, J. Morgan, 1864; *Deb Clinton, The Smugglers Daughter*, London, MacIntosh, 1866.
SEE ALSO E. Morris Miller in *Australasian Book News and Library Journal*, Vol. 1, March (1947).

Viidikas, Vicki (1948–)
Poet, prose writer. Born in Sydney and educated at various schools until 15 when she left school and home. Had a series of jobs ranging from veterinary assistant, typist and bartender, to apple picker and research assistant. Began writing poetry when young and published her first poem at 19; received a $500 Promising Poet grant for under 25s in 1972. Travelled widely in India and other parts of Asia. Her consequent

involvement in Indian life and religion can be seen in two books of poems and her prose collection.

POETRY *Condition Red*, St Lucia, UQP, 1973; *Knabel*, Sydney, Wild & Woolley, 1978; *Indian Ink* (prose poems), Sydney, Hale & Iremonger, 1984.
FICTION *Wrappings*, Sydney, Wild & Woolley, 1974.
OTHER Poems have appeared in *Nation Review;* a short story appeared in *Cosmopolitan* (Dec. 1974).

Vivian, Edith (1881–1903)
Poet. Born in Sydney and lived there until a year before her death in Johannesburg, South Africa. Her posthumous volume of poems was reviewed sympathetically by A. G. Stephens. They were suggestive, delicate and rapturous lyrics, often of the natural world.

POETRY *The Pursuit of Poetry*, London, Truslove & Hanson, 1907.

W

'Waif Wander' *See:* **Fortune, Mrs Mary**

Walker, Kath (1920–)
Poet, story writer, artist. Born on Stradbroke Island, off the Queensland coast, of the Aboriginal Noonuccal Tribe. Received primary schooling before being sent out to domestic service aged 13. Has since become active in Aboriginal rights and education and became known as the first Australian writer of Aboriginal descent. Established and directed from 1972 the Noonuccal-Nughie Education and Cultural Centre on North Stradbroke Island, a centre for Aboriginal education for children and adults. Has lectured and tutored in various institutions including the University of the South Pacific and has assisted in numerous committees and organisations for the welfare of Aborigines. Her writings strive to draw attention to the worth of Aboriginal culture and the imminent danger of its loss. Has won a number of awards including the Jessie Litchfield Award 1975 and the Mary Gilmore Medal 1970; was created MBE 1970.

POETRY *We Are Going*, Brisbane, Jacaranda, 1964; *The Dawn is at Hand*, Brisbane, Jacaranda, 1966; *My People*, Brisbane, Jacaranda, 1970; *Father Sky and Mother Earth*, Brisbane, Jacaranda Wiley, 1985.
FICTION *Stradbroke Dreamtime*, Sydney, A & R, 1972.
SEE ALSO R. Doobov in *ALS*, Vol. 6 No. 1 (May, 1973), J. Wright in *The Australian Author*, Vol. 5, No. 4 (Oct. 1973), J. Beston in *Meanjin*, Vol. 36 (1977), U. Beier, *Quandamooka: The Art of Kath Walker* (1985) and C. Baker (interview) in *Yacker 2* (Pan/Picador, 1987).

'Walker, Lucy' *See:* **Sanders, Dorothy Lucie**

Wall, Dorothy (1894–)
Children's author and illustrator. Born in Wellington, New Zealand, and came to Australia as a young woman. Illustrated her own and other authors' fiction, early achieving a reputation that was enhanced by the well-known *Blinky Bill* series of stories, based on the adventures of a lovable koala who is still a popular children's character.

FICTION *The Story of Tommy Bear and the Zookies*, Sydney, Triumph Press, 1920; *Blinky Bill the Quaint Little Australian*, Sydney, A & R, 1933; *Blinky Bill Grows Up*, Sydney, A & R, 1934; *The Tale of Bridget and the Bees*, London, Methuen, 1934; *Brownie, the Story of a Naughty Little Rabbit*, Sydney, A & R, 1935; *Stout Fellows*, Sydney, A & R, 1936; *Blinky*

Bill and Nutsy, Two Little Little Australians, Sydney, A & R, 1937; *The Complete Adventures of Blinky Bill*, Sydney, A & R, 1939; *Blinky Bill Joins the Army*, Sydney, A & R, 1940; *Blinky Bill's ABC Book*, Sydney, Offsett Printing, 1947; *Fun With Blinky Bill*, Sydney, A & R, 1953.

Walwicz, Ania (1951–)
Prose and poetry writer, artist. Born in Swidnica, Poland. After coming to Australia took a diploma and post-graduate diploma at the Victorian College of Arts, Melbourne. Has held four one-woman exhibitions of her work as well as participating in group exhibitions. Is also involved in performance art and took part in 'Anzart' in New Zealand 1985. Since 1980 has worked in the field of community arts. Was artist/writer-in-residence at the Experimental Art Foundation in Adelaide 1986. Both her written and visual work is concerned with the notation and enactment of inner states of being; her poems have appeared in many literary magazines.

POETRY *Writing*, Melbourne, Rigmarole, 1982.
OTHER Work has appeared in the following anthologies: *Island in the Sun 2* (Sea Cruise Books, 1982), *Frictions* (Sybylla, 1982), *Network* (Fringe Network Anthology 1983), *The State of the Art* (Penguin 1983), *Soft Lounges* (Fringe Network, 1984), *Joseph's Coat* (Hale & Iremonger, 1985), *Difference* (Waterloo Press, 1985), *Off the Record* (Penguin, 1985) and *2 Plus 2* (Lausanne, Mylabris Press, 1985).
SEE ALSO S. Gunew in *Meanjin*, Vol. 42, No. 1 (1983).

Ward, Elizabeth (Biff) Russel (1942–)
Non-fiction writer. Born in Sydney. Educated in Sydney and Canberra and the University of New England, Armidale, qualifying as a teacher. Worked in secondary schools in NSW and the ACT 1965–78. Was Co-ordinator of the Canberra School Without Walls 1974–7 and of the Canberra Women's Refuge 1978–81, and has generally been active in the women's movement since the early 1970s. Has been publishing articles and poems in feminist journals since that time.

NON-FICTION *Father-Daughter Rape*, London, The Women's Press, 1984.
OTHER Also contributed to the *Women and Labour Conference Papers* (1978) and to *Different Lives* (Penguin, 1987).

Watson, Kathleen (1870–1926)
Novelist. Born in Wales; came to Australia as a young woman and married W. Dearden. Published fiction of a romantic and sentimental nature that concentrated upon the bleaker aspects of love and life.

Enjoyed some success particularly with her first book, a rather maudlin and religiose prose collection, which went into four editions.

FICTION *Litanies of Life*, London, Bowdon, 1897; *The Gaiety of Fatma*, London, Browns Langham, 1906; *The House of Broken Dreams: A Memory*, Melbourne, Lothian, 1908; *Later Litanies*, Melbourne, Lothian, 1913; *Henriette Says!*, Melbourne, A. McCubbin, 1921.

Weatherly, Marjorie
Novelist, poet. Published several collections of verse and prose and three novels. Her fiction demonstrates a familiarity with outback station life. *A False Balance* exposes the negative aspects of wealth and patronage within that world.

FICTION *The Keys of Heaven*, Melbourne, Australasian Authors' Agency, 1918; *Australia's Child: A Story of Station Life from a Child's Point of View*, Melbourne, F. W. Cheshire, 1951; *A False Balance*, Melbourne, F. W. Cheshire, 1955.
POETRY *Contrasts*, Melbourne, Robertson & Mullens, 1925; *Voices from My Garden*, Robertson & Mullens, 1928; *To My Sister*, Melbourne, the author, 1948; *Fragments*, Ballarat, Berry, Anderson & Co., 1950.

Webb, Elizabeth Catherine
Journalist, novelist. Born in Western Queensland where her father owned sheep and cattle stations. Began publishing stories at the age of 17 under the name 'Allan Morris'. Worked as a radio presenter for the ABC, Brisbane, where she had her own programme *Speaking Personally*; published articles, etc, in the Brisbane *Sunday Mail*. Moved to Sydney and became a newsreel commentator for Fox Movietone News. Later wrote a newspaper column and was a radio critic for 7 years. In the late 1950s had her own national radio half-hour, *Elizabeth Webb Calling*.

FICTION *Mine is the Kingdom*, Sydney, A & R, 1947; *Into the Morning*, London, Heinemann, 1958; *The Quondong Tree*, London, Chatto & Windus, 1963.
NON-FICTION *Do You Remember, a Selection of Broadcast Talks*, Sydney, A & R, 1942; *The Infinite Pursuit*, Hobart, Oldham, Beddow & Meredith, 1943; *Stet*, Brisbane, Smith & Paterson, 1950.

Welch, Sarah, 'Europa'
Novelist, poet. Wrote religious and moral fiction. *The Fernythorpe Choristers* is a boys' school adventure story with moral intentions.
FICTION *The Fernythorpe Choristers: A Tale for Boys*, by Europa, Melbourne, G. Robertson, 1876; *Mr Fumecrab's Breakfast-table Lectures*, Melbourne, McCarron Bird, 1881.

POETRY *The Dying Chorister and the Chorister's Funeral*, Melbourne, McCarron Bird, 1879.

Weston, Kate (1863–1929)
Novelist. Born in Victoria and lived in Sydney and Adelaide. Was widowed early after her marriage and eventually turned to writing to support herself and her children. Contributed to many Australian newspapers. Became Lady Superintendent of the Elder Conservatorium, Adelaide in the 1910s.

FICTION *The Partners: A Tale of the Nor-West Coast of Australia*, London, Hutchinson, 1911; *The Man Macdonald: A Story of Ceylon*, London, Holden & Hardingham, 1913; *The Prelude*, London, Holden & Hardingham, 1913; *A Vagabond Soul: A Sydney Girl's Bohemian Adventures in Australia and the East Indies*, London, Hutchinson, 1928.

Wheatley, Nadia (1949–)
Children's novelist, freelance writer. Born in Sydney and brought up as a foster child. Educated at the University of Sydney and Macquarie University, graduating MA 1975. Began writing when living in Greece 1976–7 and since returning to Australia has written film scripts, children's novels and journal articles. Three of her novels have won awards: *Five Times Dizzy* won the NSW Premier's Special Prize 1983; *Dancing in the Anzac Deli* won the Australian section of the International Board for Books for Young People 1986; *The House that was Eureka* won the Children's Book Award, NSW Premier's Prize 1985. All have been shortlisted and commended for other awards.

FICTION *Five Times Dizzy*, Melbourne, OUP, 1982; *Dancing in the Anzac Deli*, Melbourne, OUP, 1984; *The House that was Eureka*, Melbourne, Viking/Kestrel, 1985; *I is for One* (illus. Helen Leitch), Melbourne, OUP, 1985.
OTHER Short stories have appeared in: *Hard Feelings* (The Women's Press, 1979), *And So Say All Of Us* (Second Back Row Press, 1984) and *Room to Move* (Redress/Unwin, 1985). Historical articles have appeared in the following collections: *Social Policy in Australia* (Cassell 1976), *Twentieth Century Sydney* (Hale & Iremonger, 1980) and *The Wasted Years* (Allen & Unwin, 1981).

White, Myrtle Rose (1888–1961)
Prose writer. Born near Broken Hill, NSW and from the age of 16 lived in the outback where she remained most of her life. Her descriptive books were based on her experiences in the outback and achieved wide popularity. Is particularly remembered for *No Roads Go By* 1932 which describes her stay on Lake Elder station in north-west NSW; the book

influenced John Flynn to maintain and extend the Flying Doctor Service to remote regions. She died shortly after the publication of *From That Day to This* 1961.

NON FICTION *No Roads Go By*, Sydney, A & R, 1932; *Beyond the Western Rivers*, Sydney, A & R, 1955; *From That Day to This*, Adelaide, Rigby, 1961.
FICTION *For Those That Love It*, Sydney, A & R, 1933.
OTHER Also contributed to *The Book of South Australia* (ed. L. Brown, 1936).
SEE ALSO M. Bosworth in *JRAHS*, Vol. 70, Pt. 2 (Oct, 1984).

Whiting, Susan (1947–)
Poet. Born in Melbourne. Studied architecture at the University of Melbourne graduating 1970. Worked as an architect for several years before leaving the city to live on a farm. Began writing 1973 and has been writing and keeping a farm full-time ever since.

POETRY *Rites*, Sydney, A & R, 1979.
OTHER Poems have appeared in the anthologies: *Seven Poets* (Artlook, 1977), the *Age Anthology, Golden Apples of the Sun* (MUP), *Mother, I'm Rooted* (Outback Press, 1975), and have also been published in the *Age*, the *Melbourne Chronicle, Poetry Australia* and *Transatlantic Review*.

'Wickham, Anna' *See:* **Hepburn, Edith**

Wilcox, Dora (1873–1953)
Poet, playwright. Born Mary Theodora Joyce Wilcox in Christchurch, New Zealand. Became a teacher with the NSW Department of Education before travelling overseas to Europe where she met and married Jean Paul Hemelius, Professor of English at Liège University. Served as a VAD during WWI, during which her husband died. Returned to Australia and in 1923 married William Moore, writer, journalist and art historian. Wrote descriptive poetry mostly relating to her native country. Won a *Sydney Morning Herald* prize 1927 for a poem commemorating the opening of Parliament in Canberra.

POETRY *Verses from Maoriland*, London, Allen, 1905; *Rata and Mistletoe*, London, Allen, 1911; *Seven Poems*, Sydney, J. T. Kirtley, 1924.
DRAMA *Commander Capstan: A Comedy in One Act*, Sydney, the author, 1931; *The Fourposter*, in *Best Australian One-Act Plays*, Sydney, A & R, 1937.

Williams, Justina (Joan) (1916–)
Journalist, poet, historian. Born in Coolgardie, WA. Became a journalist with the *West Australian* and the *Daily News*, Perth, later resigning to

work full-time on left-wing papers. Turned to creative writing late in life and has since received a number of awards for her work. Is widely travelled and lived in Moscow 1977–8; her short stories have been published in Russian and German. Has been politically active and a member of various political organisations including the WEL and the Australian Peace Committee of WA.

POETRY *The Dreaming Vine*, Sydney, Realist Writers, 1970; *By All the Clocks*, Sydney, Saturday Centre Poets, 1975; *People and Peace, Selected Poems*, WA, Lone Hand Press, 1986.
FICTION *White River and Other Stories*, Fremantle, Fremantle Arts Centre Press, 1979; *The Bird Girl*, Kenthurst, NSW, Kangaroo Press, 1984.
NON-FICTION *The First Furrow*, WA, Lone Hand Press, 1976; *Trade Unionism*, Melbourne, Lothian, 1978.
OTHER *Which* (a play, Hayman Theatre, 1976).
MANUSCRIPTS Murdoch University Library, WA.
SEE ALSO E. Perkins in *Quadrant* (Dec. 1979) and E. Webby in *Meanjin:*, Vol, 40, No. 2 (1981).

Williams, Ruth (1897–)
Children's author. Born in London and came to Australia as a young girl with her parents. Met and married landscape artist Rhys Williams. Also an artist, has exhibited with the Royal Art Society of NSW and other galleries. Was winner of the Children's Book of the Year Award 1950 with *Verity of Sydney Town*.

FICTION *Our Friend Rodney*, Sydney, W. H. Honey, 1945; *Pirates' Gold*, Sydney, W. H. Honey, 1945; *The Adventures of Georgie Grub*, Sydney, Frank Johnson, 1946; *More Adventures of Georgie Grub*, Sydney, Frank Johnson, 1946; *Timothy Tatters*, Sydney, W. H. Honey, 1947; *Verity of Sydney Town*, Sydney, A & R, 1950; *The Aboriginal Story*, Sydney, Shakespeare Head, 1955.

Wilson, Helen Helga (1902–)
Novelist, short story writer, poet, historian. Born in Tasmania and brought up in the WA goldfields region where she developed an interest in the history of gold-mining in Australia. Educated at the University of WA graduating BA in history 1922. Over the years has contributed historical articles to a number of newspapers including the *West Australian*, the *Western Mail* and the *Australasian*, and to many Australian and British journals. Has been or is a member of many history organisations and associations. Her stories have won, and been commended in, 15 competitions. The perpetual H. H. Wilson Literary Prize was established in 1954 for the students of Wesley College, Perth. Received the AO 1980 for services to literature.

FICTION *Moonshine*, Hamilton, Paul's Book Arcade, 1956; *Quiet, Brat*, London, Robert Hale, 1958; *The Golden Age*, Sydney, Dymocks, 1959; *Where the Wind's Feet Shine*, London, Robert Hale, 1960; *If Golde Rust*, London, Robert Hale, 1961; *A Show of Colours*, Perth, London Publ. Co., 1970; *Island of Fire*, Sydney, A & R, 1973; *Bring Back the Hour*, Sydney, A & R, 1977; *The Skedule and Other Australian Short Stories* Sydney, A & R, 1979; *The Mulga Trees*, Melbourne, Macmillan, 1980; *The House at Hardy's Corner*, Adelaide, Rigby, 1984.
POETRY *Songs of Empire*, Perth, Paterson's Printing Press, 1941; *Occasional Verse 1942–43*, Perth, Paterson's Printing Press, 1944; *The Letters of Hueng Hu*, Perth, WA Newspapers Ltd, 1946.
NON-FICTION *Gateway to Gold*, Adelaide, Rigby, 1969; *Westward Gold!*, Adelaide, Rigby, 1973; *Albany Sketchbook*, Adelaide, Rigby, 1975; *Geraldton Sketchbook*, Adelaide, Rigby, 1976; *Avon Valley Sketchbook*, Adelaide, Rigby, 1977; *The Golden Miles*, Adelaide, Rigby, 1977; *Cyclone Coasts*, Adelaide, Rigby, 1980; *Bushman Born*, Adelaide, Rigby, 1982.

Winstanley, Eliza (Elizabeth), 'Ariele' (1818–1882)
Novelist, actor. Born in England and came to Sydney 1833 where she became a local stage favourite. Married H. C. O'Flaherty and returned with him to England 1846 where she continued to act and enjoyed great success, touring the USA shortly after and playing a number of important Shakespearean roles. Joined Charles Kean's company in London 1850. Towards the end of her acting career took up writing, giving up the stage entirely by 1864. Returned to Australia late in life and died 2 years afterwards in Sydney. Based some of her fiction upon her experiences in Australia, especially *Twenty Straws* 1864 which deals with women convicts around 1830.

FICTION *Lucy Cooper*, serialised in the *Illustrated Sydney News* (anon.) 1854; *Shifting Scenes in Theatrical Life*, 1859; *Margaret Falconer*, 1860; *Twenty Straws*, London, John Dicks, 1864; *What Is To Be Will Be*, London, John Dicks, 1867. The following novels serialised in *Bow Bells*, London: *The Mistress of Hawk's Crag*, Dec. 1864–Jan. 1865; *Voices from the Lumber Room*, Aug.-Dec. 1865; *The Humming Bird*, Dec. 1865–March 1866; *Desmond, or The Red Hand*, April-Sept. 1866; *The Cockletop*, Sept.-Nov. 1866; *Carynthia, a Legend of Black Rock*, Dec. 1866–Feb. 1867; *Who Did It?*, April-July 1867; *The Queen of Clithorly*, July-Oct. 1867; *Astrutha, an Irish Story*, Oct.-Dec. 1867; *Entrances and Exits*, Jan.-July 1868; *For Her Natural Life*, July-Dec. 1876; *Imogen Hubert*, July-Dec. 1876.
SEE ALSO E. Irvin in *Southerly*, Vol. 38, No. 2 (1978).

Wood, Susan Nugent
Poet, essayist. Published two volumes of poetry and a non-fiction work canvassing topics relating to women (marriage, education, occupation, etc) and offering conservative and strict opinions.

POETRY *Bush Flowers from Australia*, by a Daughter of the Soil, London, James Nisbet, 1867; *Waiting for the Mail and Other Sketches and Poems*, Melbourne, G. Robertson, 1875.
NON-FICTION *Women's Work in Australia*, by a Daughter of the Soil, Melbourne, Mullen, 1862.

Wright, Judith (1915–)
Poet, fiction writer, editor. Born in Armidale, NSW, into an old pioneering family. Studied arts at the University of Sydney 1936. Worked at the University of Queensland 1944–8 and 1967–8 and was awarded an honorary doctorate there 1962. Four other universities have awarded her honorary doctorates for her contribution to Australian literature. Apart from being a widely published poet, critic, essayist, short story writer and children's author, is also an active conservationist; a deep attachment to the Australian landscape is one of the abiding features of her poetry. Has been a member of several conservation societies, is patron of several others, and is currently ranger of the Half Moon Wildlife District, NSW. Began publishing poems early in 1940s in journals, but made a mark on the literary scene with the appearance of her first collection 1946 and established a reputation that has been consolidated in subsequent collections. Her poetry has attracted many awards including the Grace Leven Prize 1949 and 1972, the Encyclopaedia Britannica Prize 1964, the Robert Frost Memorial Award 1976 and the Asan World Prize for Poetry 1984.

POETRY *The Moving Image*, Melbourne, Meanjin Press, 1946; *Woman to Man*, Sydney, A & R, 1950; *The Gateway*, Sydney, A & R, 1953; *The Two Fires*, Sydney, A & R, 1955; *Birds*, Sydney, A & R, 1960; *Five Senses* Sydney, A & R, 1963; *Selected Poems* Sydney, A & R, 1963; *City Sunrise*, Sydney, A & R, 1964; *The Other Half*, Sydney, A & R, 1966; *Collected Poems 1942–1970*, Sydney, A & R, 1971; *Alive, Poems 1971–1972*, Sydney, A & R, 1972; *Fourth Quarter and Other Poems*, Sydney, A & R, 1976; *The Double Tree: Selected Poems 1942–1976*, Sydney, A & R, 1978; *Many Roads Meet Here: Judith Wright in Italian* (trans. Marina Pollizzer), Adelaide, Dezsery Publishers, 1985; *Phantom Dwelling*, Sydney, A & R, 1986.
FICTION *Kings of the Dingoes*, Melbourne, OUP, 1958; *The Day the Mountains Played*, Brisbane, Jacaranda, 1960; *Range the Mountains High*, Melbourne, Lansdowne Press, 1962; *Country Towns*, Melbourne, OUP,

1962; *The River and the Road*, Sydney, Lansdowne Press, 1963; *The Nature of Love*, Melbourne, Sun Books, 1966.

NON-FICTION *Australian Poetry 1948* (ed.), Sydney, A & R, 1949; *A Book of Australian Verse* (ed.), Melbourne, OUP, 1956; *New Land, New Language* (ed.), Melbourne, OUP, 1956; *The Generations of Men*, Melbourne, OUP, 1959; *Charles Harpur*, Melbourne, Lansdowne Press, 1963; *Shaw Neilson*, Sydney, A & R, 1963; *The Poet's Pen* (ed. with A. K. Thomson) Brisbane, Jacaranda, 1965; *Preoccupations in Australian Poetry*, Melbourne, OUP, 1965; *Henry Lawson*, Melbourne, OUP 1967; *Witnesses of Spring, Unpublished Poems of John Shaw Neilson* (ed.), Sydney, A & R, 1970; *Because I was Invited*, Melbourne, OUP, 1975; *The Coral Battleground*, Melbourne, Nelson, 1977; *The Cry for the Dead*, Melbourne, Lansdowne Press, 1981; *We Call for a Treaty*, Sydney, Collins-Fontana, 1985.

MANUSCRIPTS Baillieu Library, University of Melbourne, Meanjin Archive: Correspondence 1942–69. NL, Canberra: Correspondence 1947–75 (in various collections). Fryer Memorial Library, Brisbane: Correspondence 1959–75.

SEE ALSO A. K. Thomson (ed.), *Critical Essays on Judith Wright* (Jacaranda, 1968), B. Kiernan (ed.) *Considerations: New Essays on Kenneth Slessor, Judith Wright and Douglas Stewart* (A & R, 1971) and S. Walker, *The Poetry of Judith Wright: A Search for Unity* (Edward Arnold, 1980). For a full bibliography see S. Walker, *Judith Wright* (Australian Bibliographies, OUP, 1981).

Wrightson, Patricia (1921–)

Children's novelist. Born in Lismore, NSW; grew up in the country areas of the north coast of NSW. Had an isolated childhood and was educated at home where she developed a love of literature. Took up writing after her marriage and divorce when she began to invent stories for her two children. Since then has acquired a reputation as an outstanding and versatile author for children whose many awards include the Children's Book of the Year Award 1956, 1974, 1977 and 1984, the honours list for the Hans Christian Andersen award for four years and the NSW Premier's Award for ethnic literature 1979. Has also worked as a hospital administrator, and for 10 years was on the staff of *School Magazine*, five of them as editor. After giving up work in the city 1975, left Sydney to return to the north coast and to full-time writing.

FICTION *The Crooked Snake*, Sydney, A & R, 1955; *The Bunyip Hole*, Sydney, A & R, 1957; *The Rocks of Honey*, Sydney, A & R, 1960; *The Feather Star*, London, Hutchinson, 1962; *Down to Earth*, London, Hutchinson, 1965; *I Own the Racecourse*, London, Hutchinson, 1968; *An Older Kind of Magic*, London, Hutchinson, 1972; *Beneath the Sun* (ed.),

Sydney, Collins, 1972; *The Nargun and the Stars*, London, Hutchinson, 1973; *Emu Stew* (ed.), Melbourne, Kestrel Books, 1976; *The Ice is Coming*, London, Hutchinson, 1977; *The Dark Bright Water*, London, Hutchinson, 1978; *Night Outside*, Sydney, Rigby, 1979; *Behind the Wind*, London, Hutchinson, 1981; *A Little Fear*, London, Hutchinson, 1983.

Wylie, Ida Alexa Ross
Novelist. Born in Australia. After her mother's death she was taken at an early age to England and Europe by her father. Lived in Germany 8 years after leaving finishing school. Became active in the suffragist movement, worked in France during WWI and left for the USA 1917. Here she lived permanently, although regularly visited England, and became well-known amongst literary circles and especially women writers; was a friend of Radclyffe Hall, whose books she reviewed in America. Achieved a great reputation in America, particularly as a writer of short stories. *Towards Morning* was apparently her first successful novel. Some of her work refers to Australia.

FICTION *My German Year*, London, 1910; *The Red Mirage*, London, Mills & Boon, 1913; *Towards Morning*, New York, John Lane, 1918; *The Young in Heart*, London, Cassell, 1939; *Keeper of the Flame*, New York, Grosset & Dunlap, 1942; *Ho, the Fair Wind*, USA, 1945; *Candle for Therese*, Curtis Publ. Co., 1950; *The Undefeated*, London, Cassell, 1957. OTHER Publishing details not available in Australia for the following also listed as Ida Wylie's work: *The Rajah's People; The Daughter of Brahma; Where No Birds Sing; Flight to England; Strangers are Coming; My Life with George; Four Sons; Foreign Legion; Ancient Fires; Furious Young Man; The Shining Heights; Prelude to Richard; Some Other Beauty; Side Show* (short stories); *The Silver Virgin: To the Vanquished.*

Z

Zageris, Jane (1948–)
Poet, artist. Born in London, came to Australia 1966 and attended the National Gallery of Victoria Art School gaining a diploma 1970. Began writing poetry 1972 and, assisted by a grant from the Literature Board, was able to publish her first book of poetry 1974. Since then has continued to publish in journals and magazines as well as furthering her career as an artist. Completed a graduate diploma in art at the Swinburne Institute and participated in a number of exhibitions in Sydney and Melbourne. Also completed a diploma in education at the Hawthorn Institute 1984 and was writer in residence for the ASAL conference in Ballarat. Currently teaches in art, English and creative writing.

POETRY *Moon Buffers*, Melbourne, Nelson, 1974; *Australian Poets on Tape*, St Lucia, UQP, 1975.

Zwicky, Fay (1933–)
Poet, short story writer, critic. Born in Melbourne and educated at the University of Melbourne graduating MA 1956. Is currently a Senior Lecturer in English at the University of WA. Has been a member of the Literature Board and writer-in-residence at Macquarie Univerity, Sydney 1982, at Rollins College, Florida, USA 1984, and at La Trobe Unviersity, Melbourne 1985. Received the NSW Premier's Award for Poetry 1982.

POETRY *Isaac Babel's Fiddle*, SA, Maxims Press, 1975; *Kaddish and Other Poems*, St Lucia, UQP, 1982.
FICTION *Hostages and Other Stories*, Fremantle, Fremantle Arts Centre Press, 1983.
OTHER *The Lyre in the Pawnshop: Essays on Literature and Survival 1974–1984*, (University of W A Press, 1985). Edited: *Quarry: A Selection of WA Poetry* (Fremantle Arts Centre Press, 1981) and *Journeys: Poetry of Judith Wright, Rosemary Dobson, Gwen Harwood and Dorothy Hewett* (Sisters, 1982).